NAMING

Choosing a meaningful name

written by
Caroline Sherwood

edited by Matthew Barton

Hawthorn Press

Naming © 1999 Caroline Sherwood

Published by Hawthorn Press
Hawthorn House, 1 Lansdown Lane, Stroud, Gloucestershire, GL5 1BJ, UK
Tel 01453 757040 Fax 01453 751138

Cover illustration by Abigail Large
Cover photograph by Sean Williams
Cover design by Patrick Roe of Southgate Solutions Ltd
Typesetting by Frances Fineran at Hawthorn Press, Stroud
First edition, 1999
Printed by Redwood Books, Trowbridge, Wiltshire

Acknowledgments
Every effort has been made to trace the ownership of all copyrighted material. If any omission has been made, please bring this to the publisher's attention so that proper acknowledgment may be given in future editions.

Grateful acknowledgment to the publisher Macmillan for the photograph on page vii; permission applied for. Grateful acknowledgment to The Smithsonian Institution for the use of the Odinigun photograph on page 15. 'Please call me by my true names' by Thich Nhat Hanh on page 32 is reproduced by generous permission of Parallax Press, Berkeley, California. The elf illustration on page 83 is reproduced by kind permisssion of the Master and Fellows of Trinity College Cambridge. The illustration of the Horse Goddess on page 117 is reproduced with kind permission of the artist Chesca Potter. The illustration on page 265, naming of Tibetan babies, is reproduced by kind permission of Penguin Books Ltd. The Humanist naming ceremony passage on page 268 is quoted with kind permission of Jane Wynne Willson, author of the British Humanist Association's guide to non-religious naming ceremonies, *New Arrivals*. Illustrations on pages 11 and 64 are by Abigail Large and various illustrations of plants, saints, gods and goddesses in the Meanings Index are by Ant Fineran.

Sources of non copyright illustrations are: *Hart Picture Archives,* Hart Publishing Co. Inc, New York, 1976; *A Source Book of Advertising Art,* Bonanza Books, New York, 1964; *1900 Bewick Woodcuts,* Dover Publications.

CiP A catalogue record for this book is available from the British Library

ISBN 1 869 890 566

Contents

PART ONE
The Importancc of Naming

PART TWO
Meanings and Names

PART THREE
Naming Ceremonies

Acknowledgments

It is truly amazing to consider how many people it takes to produce a book. All one's influences since childhood have a hand in it, not to mention every other book one has ever read. There are so many people to thank and recognise: for instance, while researching this book I read (or skimmed through) well over a hundred books written by people from the 17th century to the 1990s. It was with a real sense of privilege that I sat in the beautiful circular Reading Room of the British Library (before the new one was built) and held in my hand the oldest book about personal names available in English.

So here are the people (and one dog) to whom I acknowledge my specific gratitude for the support, help or encouragement they have given me in the writing of this book:

My father, William Henry *(Will-helmet, Strong protector, Home-ruler)*, known to his friends as 'Sherry'. It was he who first kindled in me a love of and respect for language. He had first experienced the poetry and power of the English tongue through his reading of the Bible, and particularly Solomon's Song of Songs, so it was with a deep sense of privilege that I read a passage from that Song at his funeral in 1986.

My mother, Ann Rosemary *(Full-of-grace, Dew-of-the-Sea)*, known to her friends as 'Rosie' – for giving me a name to be proud of.

Mrs Evans, my refreshingly eccentric French teacher (in the context of a convent boarding school). On occasions I came into class, to encounter her standing by the blackboard adjusting her stockings, with suspenders in full view. One day, out of the blue, she suddenly began to explain the Latin root of the French verb *aimer,* to love. As she conjugated the verb amare: amo, amas, amat... on the blackboard, I felt a little leap inside me. She did it with such verve, such passion, and, in that moment I understood that language has *lineage.*

Joanna Gilpin – for fearless generosity, consistent support and encouragement, and for giving birth to my godson, Peter Francis, who inspired this book.

Kevin Redpath, my dear friend and 'unofficial agent' – for recognizing, supporting and promoting my whacky style of creativity.

Mr Abbas Mejbil Abbas and Dr Atef Mahmoud of the Bath Islamic Centre – for willingly and devotedly sharing their knowledge.

Philip Carr-Gomm – for being so enthusiastic and so generously allowing me to use the Naming Ceremony for his daughter.

Derek Chorley – for providing a rapid, over-the-phone Latin translation service!

Caitlín Matthews – for illuminating my ignorance of the Celtic tradition.

Martin Palmer – for putting me in touch with Alexander Belopopsky.

Alexander Belopopsky – for very generous advice, suggestions, contacts and information which helped me to embark on the Russian section.

Elena Averyanova – for taking the time to communicate with me from Moscow, and for providing additional Russian naming material.

Daphne West – for helping me to get to grips with Russian names, and Irina Kirillova and Dr Simon Franklin of Cambridge University for helping me to dot a few 'i's and cross a few 't's in the Russian section.

Phuntsog Wangyal of the Tibet foundation – for pointing me in the right direction; and Martin J Boord and Kyentse Norbu of the School of African and Oriental Studies, University of London – who devoted an afternoon to helping me with the Tibetan section.

Ilana Tahan, Curator of Hebrew books and Manuscripts at the Oriental and India Office of the British Library – for helping me track down a 16th century prayer book and a Hebrew Name-Changing ceremony, and for providing the English translation.

Dipali Ghosh, Curator of the South Asian section of the Oriental and India office collections at the British Library – for tracking down Sanskrit naming ceremonies at very short notice.

The patient, cheerful, long-suffering staff of the old Reading Room at the British Library (and especially the many-named Wung-Choi – for showing a particular interest) and also to the staff of my local Shepton Mallet and Glastonbury libraries for providing an excellent and speedy service.

John Bushel of Salisbury Cathedral and Canon Keith Walker, librarian of Winchester Cathedral – for information about Charlotte M. Yonge.

Arthur Bailey – for guiding me through the word-processing labyrinth and helping me to get over the first hiccups, and Richard Taylor – for detailed and professional computer advice.

Peter Matthews – my first word-processing guru – for skilful, humorous and empowering training, without which I would not have been able even to approach the indexes in this book – and for turning up again at exactly the right moment.

Gail Powell and George Milne – for expertly boosting my word-processing abilities at a critical moment, for some first class computer/printer ferreting to help me when I was at the hair-tearing stage and so helping me to steer the typescript through to completion.

Alison Monger – for dedicated and meticulous proof-reading, despite flu bugs and rainy January days.

All the people who responded to my requests for anecdotes about how they named their children, especially Fiona Carnie, John Firth, Ruth Heeks, Fiona Hingston, Martin Large, Alfredo J. Rosado, Ken Winter and Solveig Taylor.

Nick Campion of the Astrological Association – for assistance in shedding light on how astrological considerations can help with the naming process.

Colin and Denise Tavener and Tess (the excellent Giant Schnauzer, and my 'amusing Muse') and all the Kingwell team – for a spacious, luxurious and utterly supportive environment in which to write.

And, finally, all the men and women who have studied and written in this field before me, without whose centuries of effort I would not have known where to start – especially Elsdon C. Smith and Charlotte M. Yonge.

Caroline Sherwood

*Charlotte Mary Yonge, author of
'History of Christian Names'*

DEDICATION

*This book is dedicated
to all those who show us the
truth behind appearances
and to
all parents and the
children of the future.*

Foreword

In the past there have been many books and dictionaries of names. But Caroline Sherwood has produced a completely new and far more useful volume, in which the *meanings* of names are the prime focus. With a deep respect for language, its derivation, effect, symbolism, meaning and connotation, Caroline leads us across cultural and religious boundaries into a fresh and significant way for parents to set about finding the right name for their child. Her book offers a fascinating insight into the history of naming, but also brings the reader right up to date with examples of modern naming ceremonies.

A name is so important. It is the principle way in which people recognise each other, and can be a source of pride or embarrassment. Choosing a name for a new child is not easy – there are so many choices and pitfalls to consider. Much thought is given to naming, often before the child is even born, though readers will find that this book counsels against deciding on a name before you have come to know a little about the very individual nature of your own child.

Undoubtedly there are some circumstances which, with the best will in the world, one cannot foresee. Who was to know that my friend Barbara was going to marry an Italian with the surname Uggeri? She always makes sure that there is a large space between the B and the U when she signs her cheques!

As a child I always felt sorry for children whose names caused titters. Ann Onion and Pansy Root stand out in my memory. My brother once dated a girl with the surname Fitt, whom of course we referred to cruelly as 'Miss-Fitt'.

Then there is the very subtle influence of association. I like the name Susan and its diminutives and have two very dear friends with the name. But my perception of it has been somewhat tainted by an unpleasant girl at school who killed mice by swinging them by their tails and smacking their heads against the side of the bench!

Caroline Sherwood addresses many possible problems and offers common sense, practical advice in a book written with love, spiritual perception, integrity and humour. She offers a diversity to please all, and inspires confidence. This is a much-needed addition to the naming books already available, and will not disappoint anyone with an interest in names, or facing the awesome task of naming their child.

Rosie Styles
Director, the Baby Naming Society

Introduction

In the beginning was the Word,
and the Word was with God,
and the Word was God.

The Gospel According to John

This is a book about the power and significance of naming. In a world where expediency, fashion and commercialism widely govern the use of language, respect for the living power of the Word is being eroded. When language is corrupted, communication degenerates, and this has a disastrous effect on self-respect and on relationships, from the intimate to the international. As individuals we can put the life back into the language we use and nurture clarity of communication. A small step towards reclaiming our natural authority and responsibility for the quality of communication on this planet is to make it our business to find out what words really mean and to call things by their *true* names. Selecting authentic and supportive names for newborn children – names with which they can walk tall for life – is a worthwhile and important part of that step.

This book was inspired by the birth of my godson, Peter Francis Gilpin Spode. It was the first I had witnessed and filled me with deep gratitude and wonder. He arrived shortly after the glimmerings of dawn three days before the year's end – into a candlelit, lavender-fragranced bedroom (moist from the waterbath in one corner), surrounded by a gentle, silent team of six people. Each person had a specific commitment to the mother and baby and a function in the birthing room. Over the next few days, while Peter's parents were setting about choosing a suitable name for him, we discovered that, although there were several books listing a wide choice of names, there were none I knew of which were indexed the other way round – by meaning, quality or attribute. The challenge and implications of writing such a book appealed to me instantly.

This book is in three parts: the first talks about the power of language in our world and explains why naming is important and how it affects us, giving many examples of how ancient peoples respected the power of naming and used it not only to identify things but also to alter reality, change circumstances and heal themselves.

The second lists names under meanings, making it easy to choose a meaningful name. For instance, if you want to endow your child with the quality of a particular animal or flower, then all you have to do is look it up in the index – and you will find several names which bear that meaning. Names whose meanings are disputed or uncertain are discussed in a separate section; and I explain why I have chosen to include the names I have and to omit others.

Then follows a more conventional index of first names and their meanings. Although I do not take a scholarly or academic approach, I have tried to be as accurate as possible according to available, often conflicting information. Without the vast amounts of research of those on whose work I have drawn, this book would not have been possible.

Part Three explores naming ceremonies and the relevance of ceremony in our lives today, and gives examples of naming ceremonies from various traditions and cultures. There is also a step-by-step guide to creating your own naming ceremony if you do not want to stick to tradition.

Whenever we become aware of the origin, source and meaning of a word, we become more aware of ourselves. In truly naming a person or thing we connect with the reality of what we name, and with its origin. I hope that this book may help you, the reader, to touch into the power of names.

Caroline Sherwood

The author in christening dress, with her father

PART ONE

THE IMPORTANCE OF NAMING

And the whole earth was of one language and of one speech

Genesis XI 1

'Must a name mean something?'
Alice asked doubtfully.

'Of course it must,' Humpty
Dumpty said with a short laugh,
'my name means the shape I am –
and a good handsome shape it is,
too. With a name like yours, you
might be any shape, almost.'

Lewis Carroll:
Through the Looking Glass, 1871

(Author's note: *Alice* means 'noble')

The power, importance and history of naming

> The phenomenal world actually spells itself out in letters and even sentences that we read or experience. Through the mandala of speech, the world is seen as a world of syllables, a world of letters...

Chögyam Trungpa[1]

Words and names can tell us much about the origins in consciousness of our world. Our use of words both reflects and *affects* our reality. By tracing derivations of words we find the relationship with the world of the people who first coined them – which puts us in touch with the words' original source and meaning. The same is true of names. A name is a *vibrational symbol,* an embodiment of the person in language. This knowledge has been used for centuries in magical practices; and the same knowledge can be used to yield understanding – and for healing.[2] This is why a healer often only needs to hear the name of someone who is sick to 'tune into' his or her energy, no matter how great the physical distance which separates them.

What's in a name?

> *A good name is rather to be chosen than great riches*
> Old Testament Proverbs, c.350 BC

> *A good name menny folde*
> *ys more worthe than golde*
> Author unknown: 'Babees Book', c.1430

'To name is to acknowledge. It is to identify, single out, distinguish, separate and endow with meaning. It is also to empower and to bless. Shakespeare's Juliet asks *What's in a name?* declaring *...a rose by any other name would smell as sweet.* Juliet is referring to the level of absolute truth, where everything is in essence nameless, and is simply as it is. She is bemoaning the idiocy of being told to shun Romeo – whom she can't help loving – simply because he's got the wrong surname! On the other hand, at the level of day-to-day, relative truth, consider the confusion, distress and

3

rebellion that would ensue if from now on we were required by law, on pain of death, to refer to a rose as a 'skunk cabbage' and vice versa. Due to the weight of association that language now carries, the *name* of the rose is integral to our perception of it. The sounds of 'r' and 's' in rose resonate differently in consciousness from the 'k' and 'ge' in the other name. Sound carries meaning.

No tribe has ever been found that does not have a complete and thoroughly organised language. When you consider that there are at least 60 Aryan or Indo-European languages, 20 of the Hamito-Semitic family (which bear no relationship to the former), 168 of the Bantu family, and 35 of the Algonquin stock – to say nothing of all the ancient languages no longer in use and of all the regional variations and dialects, then you will have an idea of the wealth of names that man has produced to identify his world and distinguish his children.

Naming, naming everywhere

What's your name?

Ah…isn't he lovely! What's his name?
It's a girl. Her name's Jennifer.

May I say who's calling?

Sign here, please.

These are just a few of the many habitual phrases we use and hear every day. I'm sure you could write your own list. From birth to death, and including both, our *name* is requested as the first significant symbol of who we are: on certificates, licences, application forms, leases, deeds, registers, letters and documents of all kinds. *To make a name* for oneself or to become *a household name* is considered by many to be desirable; whereas to have one's *name taken in vain* or for someone's *name to be dirt* are thought unfortunate. At most important junctures in our life, we *put our name to something* and sometimes we change our name.

Naming and healing

I do beseech you
chiefly that I might set it in my prayers,
What is your name?'

William Shakespeare: *The Tempest*

The power of the word lies in its ability to harm or heal, to curse or bless, confuse or clarify, to bewilder or illumine. Causing sickness, or even death, by the mentioning of a name, as well as the healing of disease by the invocation of a name of power, are both traditional aspects of *onomancy* or naming magic. This is a large subject, about which a lot has been written, which would need a separate book to do it justice. My aim here is simply to sketch the broad picture and give a few examples.

In the ancient English and Scottish ballad of Earl Brand, the hero dies as a result of his lover calling out his name at a critical moment. Sounding the *name* is equivalent to making the *person* visible, vulnerable, available to attack.

Among Russian Jews it was considered bad luck to propose a name for a baby before birth and, as late as 1956, in Kentucky in America, it was believed that if a pregnant woman spoke the name of her unborn child, it would be stillborn. Some cultures believed that disease itself could be transmitted through a name.

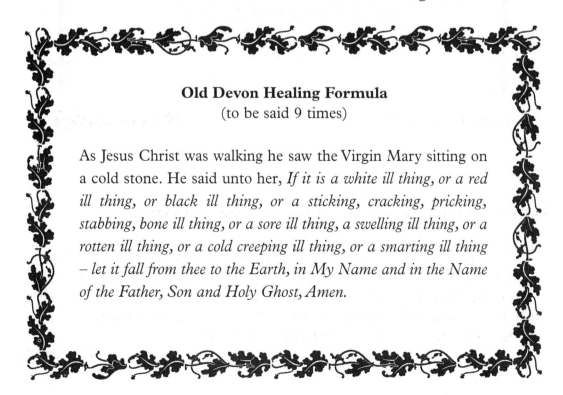

Old Devon Healing Formula
(to be said 9 times)

As Jesus Christ was walking he saw the Virgin Mary sitting on a cold stone. He said unto her, *If it is a white ill thing, or a red ill thing, or black ill thing, or a sticking, cracking, pricking, stabbing, bone ill thing, or a sore ill thing, a swelling ill thing, or a rotten ill thing, or a cold creeping ill thing, or a smarting ill thing – let it fall from thee to the Earth, in My Name and in the Name of the Father, Son and Holy Ghost, Amen.*

An Old Slovenian ritual cure advises: *For whooping cough, take a narrow white ribbon and while putting knots in it say, Jesus, Mary, Joseph.*

An Old Canadian and American cure for a nosebleed consisted of writing the person's name on his or her forehead. There are many such records of ancient charms and cures, in every culture, which rely on the invocation of a name, often of the Holy Trinity.

Other healing practices included writing names – either to invoke healing, or to trap disease so as to destroy it. These written names were placed on ailing parts, plugged into trees, transmitted to animals, swallowed, placed in the draught chamber of a fireplace for safe keeping or enclosed in an airtight receptacle. These names were often buried, burned, or floated away.

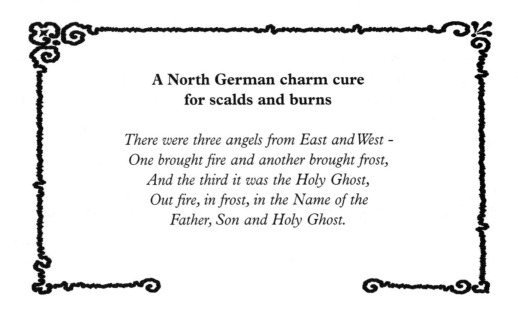

**A North German charm cure
for scalds and burns**

*There were three angels from East and West -
One brought fire and another brought frost,
And the third it was the Holy Ghost,
Out fire, in frost, in the Name of the
Father, Son and Holy Ghost.*

Naming through the ages – a brief survey

It is a natural instinct – from the hoary-headed Chaldean sages of old, who gave to each shining constellation, each twinkling star, separative and significative names, to the lisping little one in our nursery today, who, with her finger on her rosy lip, sits knitting her pretty brows, trying to think of some nice name for her kitten or her doll.

Sophy Moody[3]

What follows is far from exhaustive: I have not tried to be historically thorough, but to give a sense of the way various different cultures approached naming, and the great significance it had for many of them.

The civilization of **ancient Sumeria**, which grew up five thousand years ago between the Tigris and the Euphrates rivers, was the first to develop a system of writing – composed of 'cuneiform' symbols, drawn with the end of a sharpened reed or stick. The ancient Sumerians dedicated objects to divinities to ensure well-being, prosperity and long life. They did this by naming the objects, using a whole sentence of invocation to do so. They named statues, weapons, tables, bowls and instruments. The name given to one such bowl was *May-my-lady-goddess-watch-over-me* and a certain statue was called *Oh Ishtar! To-you-is-my-ear-turned.* Even canals, walls and gates were named in similar ways to provide protection from enemies.

Sumerian naming was performed to imbue objects with life since it was believed that living beings exist by the power of their name; thus the name was used to create a mediating bridge between the object or person and the god.

Babies were not usually named at birth. Names had religious significance and consisted of whole sentences.

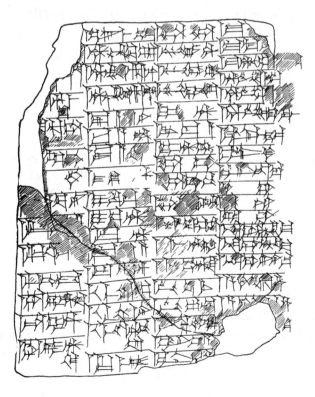

Example of cuneiform

7

The idea of a child being a gift from god was contained in many **Assyrian and Babylonian** names[4] and the custom continued later among the Hebrews. Thus the Hebrew name El-Nathan is found in Babylonia and Assyria as *Ilu-Nadin*. The name *Matthew* existed in Hebrew as *Mattan-El* or *Gift of God*.

Female names often included the name of a deity. For example, *Tabni-Istar* or *Ishtar has given*. Ishtar was the fertility mother-goddess, the embodiment of the planet we know as Venus. She was worshipped (as the daughter of Anu), as the goddess of gentleness, love and desire and, (as the daughter of Sin), in her warlike aspect.

The **Egyptians** made greater use, perhaps, of the art of naming than any other ancient civilisation. The name was considered as much a part of the being as the soul or 'double' *(ka)* of the body.[5]

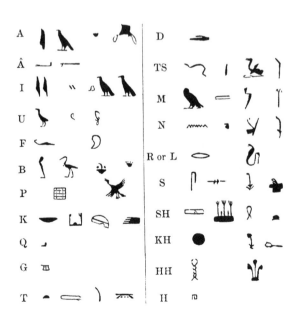

Egyptian hieroglyphic writing

The early Egyptians recognised the human being as possessing a number of non-physical 'vehicles' which were essential for successful navigation of the subtle planes and after death. One of these was the *Ren* or name. This carried the meaning of the personal 'sonic', i.e. the very specific sound or vibrational pattern which denoted a particular individual.[6]

The remains of the native religious literature of ancient Egypt reveals that a belief in the power of magical names and invocations formed a significant part of Egyptian spiritual life. It was understood, for instance, that if a man knew the name of a god or devil, and addressed him by it, he was bound to answer him and to do whatever he wished.

The Egyptians also employed the power of naming to heal the sick, cast out demons which were causing disease, restore life to the dead, bestow the gift of incorruptibility to a corpse, enable humans to assume other forms, project themselves into animals or creatures, animate or inanimate objects, and control the weather. As in the creation myths of many cultures, it was through *the utterance of a word* by Thoth that the Earth itself came into being.

Naming was also of great significance to the ancient **Hebrews**:

> There are three crowns: the crown of Torah, the crown of priesthood, and the crown of kingship; but the crown of a good name exceeds them all.
>
> Rabbi Simeon (Ben Jochai), c. 150 AD

Like the Egyptians, the Hebrews equated the name with the person:

> In that hour there was a great earthquake, and the tenth part of the city fell; and there were killed in the earthquake names of men seven thousand.
>
> Revelations XI:13

The name carried the essence of its bearer.[7]

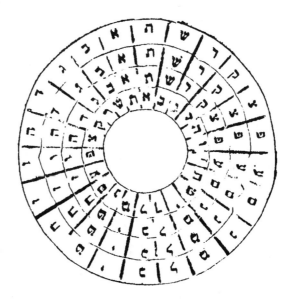

Hebrew Wheel of Letters

Above all, the name of God was considered holy. So holy that it was known as the 'Ineffable Name' and never pronounced, except once a year on the Day of Atonement, by the High Priest in the Holy of Holies in the Temple. The Third Commandment which said ... *for Yahweh will not hold him guiltless that taketh his name in vain* was intended to prevent blasphemy, and this is certainly the sense in which it has been inherited by us. It had another meaning and purpose, however; originally it forbade the use of the name for magical purposes, which was a reaction against Egyptian practices.

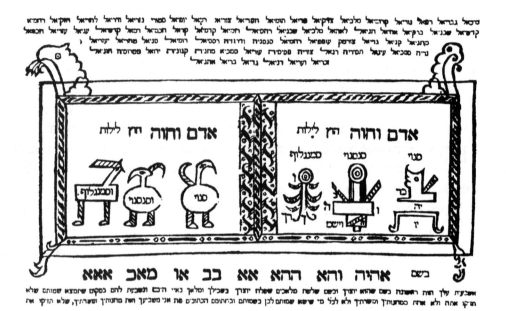

This is an amulet to protect a mother during childbirth, from the Book of Raziel, a collection of mystical, cosmological and magical Hebrew works, published in Amsterdam in 1701. This book was reprinted many times, as it was believed it protected the owner's house from fire and other dangers. The amulet illustrates the three angels: Sanvai, Sansanvai and Semanglof who were charged with the task of warding off Lilith at childbirth.

See also BIRDS - Screech Owl (Lilith)

In the Satapatha-Brahmana of **ancient India** there is the earliest reference to a Hindu naming ceremony; in Book III of the Third Brahmana it says:

> Prajapati said to him, 'My boy, why criest thou, when thou art born out of labour and trouble?' He said, 'Nay, but I am not freed from evil; I have no name given me: give me a name!' Hence one should give a name to the boy that is born, for thereby one frees him from evil; even a second, even a third, for thereby one frees him from evil time after time.

Sacred Books of the East[8]

The *Namadheya* (The Naming Rite) is laid down in the list of sacraments which must be performed by the father or a priest as soon as the 'term of impurity' from the birth is over. There are several rituals which were used at birth and for naming.

In the nineteenth century, an Indian trading class called the Banians were recorded as performing an unusual naming ceremony, in which the baby was placed on top of some rice which had been scattered on a large cloth in the centre of the floor. Several young children were invited to surround the cloth, to raise it and shake the baby and the rice for fifteen minutes or so. Then the baby's sister conferred the name.

Banian naming ceremony

In **ancient Greece**, the *Onomasteria* or 'Festival of Naming' took place. One week after birth, sacrifices were offered and banquets held for relatives and friends. At this ceremony the midwife ran round the fire carrying the child in her arms, to place it under the protection of the household gods. During these naming-day ceremonies an olive garland, for a boy (symbolizing agricultural work) and a woollen fleece for a girl (signifying spinning) were hung from the door.

Names containing elements of aesthetic taste or fine qualities were considered to be lucky, such as *kleos* – fame or glory, *phil* – lover of, and *aristo* – best. Name elements connected with public institutions were also considered favourable; such as *agora* – assembly, *demos* – the people, *dike* – justice. These elements continue in words we use today, such as 'philosophy' (the love of wisdom), 'aristocrat' and 'democracy'; and of course many of our common personal names derive from Greek.

The **Roman** *Nominalia* or Naming Festival – took place eight days (for a girl) and nine days (for a boy) after birth. This was accompanied by a ritual washing.

A Roman received four names – but not all at once. He received a *praenomen* or personal name which was indicated by an initial, as for many years there were only about 16 of these in common use; a *nomen* or clan name, indicating the tribe or *gens* to which the person belonged, placed before the personal name, of which there were about a thousand in use; he also received a *cognomen*, which distinguished him by family – rather equivalent to our surname; and the last name was known as the *agnomen*, which was a nickname, such as *Faustus* – long life, *Felix* – happy and fortunate, or *Vitalis* – strength or an honorific title, gained later in life for a particular accomplishment. The nomen and praenomen described personal characteristics and the last two often indicated honourable distinctions:

Example of a Roman name:

Publius	**Cornelius**	**Scipio**	**Africanus**
praenomen	*nomen (gens)*	*cognomen*	*agnomen*
'One honoured by the people'	From *cornu* – 'horn', 'trumpet', i.e. 'far-sounding'	Scipio – 'staff', because he supported and guided a blind father	He received this name for victory over the Carthaginians in Africa

The term 'Christian name' derives from the days of the **early Christians**, who, when they welcomed a new friend into their company through baptism, gave him or her a 'Christ-ened' name.[9]

Formerly Christians showed indifference to choosing special names and would simply adopt names from the culture in which they lived. Sometimes they created names from festivals, such as *Epiphania* and *Paschalis* (Epiphany and Easter); or from qualities or virtues, such as *Aeternalis, Anastasia, Refugenus, Sanctus;* or from divine names (some used formerly by non-Christians), such as *Dorotheus* and *Theodorus* (the root *theo* meaning divine). They adopted and adapted names such as love, hope and joy from the Greek and Latin – *Agape, Spesina* and *Exillaratus*. Records survive of Christians called Albanus – white, and *Margarita* – pearl. This adaptation was often necessary in order to disguise their Christianity from the surrounding hostile culture, until persecution ceased in the fourth century.

In 1560 the first Bible ever to be printed in English was published in Geneva. It listed a thousand personal names and meanings and in its introduction said:

> Whereas the wickednesse of time, and the blindenesse of the former age
> hath bene such, that all thinges altogether haue bene abused and corrupted,
> so that the very right names of diuers of the holy men named in the
> Scriptures haue bene forgotten, and nowe seeme straunge vnto vs....we haue
> nowe set forth this table of the names that be most vsed in the olde
> Testament with their interpretations, as the Hebrewe importeth, partly to call
> backe the godly from that abuse... but chiefly to restore the names to their
> integritie, whereby many places of the Scriptures and secret mysteries of the
> Holy Ghost shall better be vnderstood...

In 1915 Leone Caetani and Giuseppe Gabrieli published their famous *Onomasticon Arabicum* in which they outlined the name-giving criteria which were generally in use in **pre-Islamic Arab** culture. Omens often dictated the giving of names, namegivers were consulted and dreams had an influence in the choice of names.

In **Islamic** culture, selecting a good name is one of the three obligations of a father towards his son (the others are to teach him to write and to marry him off when he comes of age). The importance that Muhammad placed on naming is demonstrated in this saying:

> You must not name your slaves *Yasar* (abundance), *Rabah* (gain), *Najih* (prosperous), *Aflah* (felicitous), because if you ask after one of these your domestic servants, and he be not present, the negative reply will express that abundance, or gain or prosperity, or felicity are not in your dwelling.
>
> *The Koran*[10]

Most Arabs know what their name means, and almost every vocabulary word has appeared as a proper name. Names are considered to carry *baraka* – blessing or grace, and the names of great people and women should not be mentioned.

In **Arabic, Persian** and **Turkish** love songs the poet always refuses to tell his lady's name. Naming customs abounded in Arabic culture. Sometimes children were named after famous people, most popularly the Prophet and his relatives. Babies were also named according to the day of their birthday, and each weekday had certain famous names associated with it.

All **Native American** tribes placed great store in the importance of names and naming. There are many stories in Native American tradition of how different names came to be given. One Dakota woman allowed her baby to lie with its face outside the tepee in the rain. It appeared dead, but another woman noticed that it was alive, so the child came to be called *Rain-in-the-face*. Such names as *Seeing Afar Off* and *Three Suns* indicate abilities or qualities of the person concerned.

The Karok of North West California did not name their children until they were eight or nine years old. Certain names ran in families and the childhood name would be discarded at marriage and never used again. At that time the person would be known by the name of the house, by his marital status or by a nickname based on a body trait. Examples of Karok nicknames are *Slughunter,* after a childhood pastime and *Little Flash,* the name of a sorcerer who gave off flashes of light in the dark.

Among the Delaware, whoever had visions qualified as a Namegiver (Way-huh-wee-huh-lahs) – 'One who gives names over and over'. He would sing the words given to him by his spirit visitor. The following is the account [11] of the dream of a Chippewa namegiver, Odinigun, which gave him his authority and power:

> *In my dream I saw a wigwam with the door toward the north. Three men were there, one from the sky, one from the north, and one whose body was half under the ground.*
>
> *The man whose body was half under the ground was beside the door, outside the wigwam...I stood in front of him wondering why he had sent for me.*
>
> *At last he spoke and told me to enter the wigwam, and to sit next the door on the same side as he was sitting...I sat down and after a while a woman came in with a baby in her arms. She came towards me and handed me the baby. After I took the child she asked me to name it.*

Then the man whose body was half under the ground spoke, and I could hear voices in the air, as of many people answering him.

After I had returned the child to its mother, another woman came with a child which she asked me to name. The first mother kept her place next me, and as others came they stood in order one after another.

Others brought children who were a little older, and then a little older. They came until the wigwam was full, and I named them all...

Odinigun – a Chippewa name-giver

If a person had not received a vision he was not even allowed to name his own children (except to give them nicknames), and such a person was described as 'empty', but no shame was attached to this. The Delaware child-naming ceremony was performed after the Namegiver (who never revealed the whole of his or her vision) had pondered the right name. First the name was revealed to the Creator, then a holy fire was kindled. Tobacco was sprinkled on this and a 'smudging' was performed with cedar to ensure fresh, new and pure influences for the one to be named. Tobacco was sacred to the native peoples. It was used as an offering to the Earth Mother and to the beings of the spirit world, as well as being used in the smoking of the sacred Pipe. Tobacco is the traditional gift which was exchanged between medicine people. The 'smudging' ceremony is a purification and blessing by smoke, which is still performed today by Native Americans and those who follow the 'medicine path'. Often sage and sweetgrass are burned – to expel negative influences and to call in beneficial ones. The Delaware namegiver would use an eagle feather to waft the smoke from the smudge around the gathering. This smoke would be drawn towards the heart and up over the head and down the body to cleanse and harmonise. The Namegiver would then give the child the name and repeat it several times. Then the child would be given a string of wampum beads which symbolised sincerity and purity and the Namegiver would also be given one by the child's family. New clothing and moccasins would be presented to the guests and the parents would present the Namegiver with skins and tobacco. A feast followed.

The Kwakiutl Indians would sometimes pawn their names for a year (as security for a loan), using another or being anonymous during that time. If a man had borrowed, say, thirty blankets, sometimes he might need as many as one hundred to redeem the loan (and the use of his name!). Kwakiutl elders had different names during the winter and summer.

In 1903, Roosevelt commissioned a full-blooded Sioux, Dr. Charles Alexander-Eastman to give Indians new names. He visited every agency and tribe throughout the country and three main ways of renaming the Indians emerged from his efforts: sometimes they adopted native names, sometimes they changed their native name to its English equivalent and sometimes the native name would be translated and adapted to an English version; for example *She who has a beautiful home* was rendered as 'Goodhouse'. There is a record of a man named *Bob-tailed Coyote* being renamed as 'Robert T. Wolf'!

The kinds of confusion which reigned during this process of awkwardly trying to fit the tribal inhabitants of Turtle Island into the new 'civilisation' of the United States of America is illustrated in the following story: it is the account of a ticket reservation which was made for a Native American to travel between Denver and Los Angeles. The first telegram arrived, worded:

'Need reservation: No-Name L.A. to S.F – Denver'

'Reservation made: No-Name L.A. to S.F – L.A.'

'Re your No-Name reservation must have name for same – L.A.'

'Re your message: 'No-Name' is name. Passenger an Indian – Denver'

The term **Celtic**, which refers more to languages than to nations, is given to the people who appeared in Central Europe between 1000 and 500 BC and settled the whole region between Hungary and the western seaboard. Some say that they were in the British Isles as far back as the early Bronze Age, around 1180 BC, or even as long ago as 3000 BC. Celtic naming traditions are very old and entirely interwoven with folklore and legend; the Welsh *Mabinogion* and the Arthurian tales are rich sources of ancient names.

In Celtic tradition, a child was given a 'cradle name' as soon as it was born, to hide it from the faeries, who often tried to steal children for their enviable human qualities; and this was often reinforced with protective spells and rituals to disguise their potential virtues and prevent them from straying into the Otherworld.

The second naming of a Celtic child was its proper name, which was inherited; and later a third name would be given as a title to denote status or personal qualities. For instance Merlin's title was *Vortigern*, meaning 'the High Lordly One'.

The naming of the hero was of utmost importance in Celtic culture. It was a magical act because the one who chose the name had either to be a druid or be witness to a brave deed in the hero's childhood. Deirdrú (Deirdre) for instance, was named by the divinatory powers of Cathbadh, who foretold her sex, name and deeds by placing his hands on her mother's belly before the baby's birth.

To the Celts, who understood the capacity of the Word, poetry was a spiritual path. A poet had to pass through seven grades, and the training lasted at least twelve years. It included philosophy, practical work and memorizing many stories. Poets would often spend long hours in complete darkness, lying with a stone on the body to maintain attention. Poets were skilled in invocation, and the Irish Celts developed a particular form of prayer called a *lorica* or breastplate – in other words a protective spell.

HI, tha comhnadh nan ard, [12]
Tiur do bheannachd 'na thrath,
Cuimhnich-s' leanabh mo chri,
An Ainm Athar na sith;
Trath chuireas sagart an Righ
Air uisge na brigh,
Builich da beannachd nan Tri
    Ta lionadh nan ard.
    Beannachd nan Tri
      Ta lionadh nan ard.

Crath nuas air do ghras,
Tabh dha feart agus fas,
Tabh dha trein agus treoir,
Tabh dha seilbh agus coir,
Rian agus ciall gun gho,
Gliocas aingeal r'a lo,
Chum's gun seas e gun sgeo
    'Na d' lathair.
    Gun seas e gun sgeo
      'Na d' lathair.

Most **Anglo-Saxon** names are derived from Old German roots, and were compounds composed of two naming elements. *Aethelraed*, for instance, was formed from *aethel* meaning noble, and *raed* meaning counsel or wisdom. The following are a few common Anglo-Saxon naming elements: *aelf* – elf; *beorht* – bright (as in modern Albert); *beorn* – warrior (and in German and Norse – bear); *eald* – old; and *ric* – powerful or noble (as in the modern bishopric).

AGAINST WITCHES AND ELVISH TRICKS [13]

Against every evil witch and against elvish tricks write
this writing in Greek letters.
++A++O+°y+iFByM+++++BeppNNIKNETTANI
Then another powder and a drink against witches. Take a blackberry and lupine
and pennyroyal, pound them together, sift them, then put them
in a bag, lay them under the altar, sing nine Masses over them.
Put the powder in milk and drip some holy water into it.
Give to drink at three times of the day: at nine a.m., at midday, at three p.m.
If animals have the disease, pour the same powder into their mouth
together with the holy water.

Anglo-Saxon names often combined elements of parents' and relatives' names. For example, the parents of *Wulfstan*, the tenth century bishop of Worcester, were *aethelSTAN* and *WULFgifu*.

Another common naming practice was the 'alliterative principle' where names in a family line all started with the same letter. The list of West Saxon kings from 519-688 runs: Cerdic, Cynne, Ceawlin, Ceol, Ceolwulf, Cunegalis, Cenwalh, Centwine etc.

Puritan naming customs stand in a category of their own, as they employed three characteristic groups of names: unusual biblical names, such as *Jehoida, Jachin, Barzillai, Benaiaah* and *Shadrach;* names of abstract virtues, such as *Honour, Humanity, Steadfast,* and *Clemency;* and invented (often critical or encouraging) names, such as *Safe-on-High, Faith-my-joy, Be-thankful, Abuse-not, Love-God, Fight-the-good-fight-of-faith, Humiliation, Faint-not, Sin-denie,* and *Much-mercy.* In 1644 in Baltonsborough in Somerset an illegitimate girl was named *Misericordia-adulterina. Lament* and *Trial* were also commonly given to illegitimate girls.

With the rejection of the Roman Catholic Church by the Puritans there was also a turning away from non-scriptural Christian names. At the same time, the **Royalists** were going to the opposite extreme of giving their children increasingly outlandish pagan names, such as *Venus* and *Cassandra.*

The Old Testament became the prime source of first names for Puritan families; sometimes the parents would open the Bible and bestow upon the baby the first name their eyes fell upon.

The publication of the Geneva Bible led to the adoption of many more scriptural names by ordinary people. Simple people were sometimes tricked into giving inappropriate or foolish names to their children, as a result of asking for the advice of people who knew the Bible better or were more literate. The longest name in the Bible – *Maher-shalal-hash-baz* – was freely used by the Puritans. Even during their lives some poor Puritans suffered teasing as a result of their outrageous names.

In **Russia**, naming spans the pre-Christian pagan days, ten centuries of Christianity, and the Soviet years. With the demise of Communism, many Russians are welcoming a reburgeoning of interest in their country's mythical and pagan past, as well as an open rekindling and reaffirmation of the Christian Orthodox flame.

Little or nothing has been written about naming rites in pre-Christian Russia, as written records only came into existence with Christianity. To trace Russia's pagan roots means going back to the Scandinavian, Finnish and Slavonic peoples who gave birth to them. The belief in spirits lingered well into Christian times and customs and taboos of folk tradition became interwoven with Christian practices. This grafting of Christian elements onto pagan beliefs later became known as *dvoeverie* – 'double faith'.

As well as naming children after saints, it was also popular to give them the names of angels, naming them after the 'Angel Day' nearest to that of the birth. Often this would be celebrated instead of a person's birthday. In Finland, and probably other countries too, 'namedays' are still celebrated, as well as birthdays.

In Russian Orthodoxy the name of Jesus Christ is considered to carry special power and the repetition of the sacred name occupies a very specific place in the spiritual practices of both priests and laity alike:

> Rather than gazing downwards into our turbulent imagination and concentrating on how to oppose our thoughts, we should look upwards to the Lord Jesus and entrust ourselves into his hands by invoking his Name; and the grace that acts through his Name will overcome the thoughts which we cannot obliterate by our own strength.

Kay Ware[14]

So central is this practice to Russian spirituality, that whole books have been written on the subject and holy men *(starets)* of the past have devoted their whole lives to the repetition of the Name. At the clothing of a Russian monk, as the prayer rope *(komvoschoinion)* is handed over, the abbot says:

> *Take, brother, the sword of the Spirit, which is the Word of God, for continual prayer to Jesus; for you must always have the Name of the Lord Jesus in mind, in heart and on your lips, ever saying: Lord Jesus Christ, Son of God, have mercy on me a sinner.*

Quite specific guidelines are laid down for the practice of the Jesus Prayer – and for those who want to pursue it deeply, it offers an esoteric path to union with the Name invoked.

Before the Revolution of 1917, you could tell from a person's name if he was noble or a peasant, if he came from the country or the town. *Ivan* and *Vasiliij* were typical country names, and *Aleksandr* and *Nikolai* indicated more urban, 'tsarist' influence. Equally a countrywoman could be picked out by her name of *Avdotya* or *Anna*, whereas, a Russian would instinctively know that *Olga* and *Elena* were townswomen.

Today every Russian still has three names – a Christian name, a patronymic (a name which indicates parentage or ancestry, from Gk. pator – father + onoma – name), and a surname – for example: *Ivan Ivanovich Ivanov* – John, son of John, Johnson. Often only the Christian and surname are used in a signature. Affectionate diminutives continue to be popular among Russians, such as *Katushienka* which is a diminutive of *Ekaterina* – Katherine.

The Union of Soviet Socialist Republics (USSR) was formally organised on 30 December 1922. Just as Christianity swept away most of the Old Slavonic names, so did Communism in its turn sweep away many of the Greek-based Christian names in favour of a new wave of totally different names; wrenching the Russians firmly into the materialism of the 20th century.

Since 1917 many 'new names', which are not in the traditional Calendar of Saints, were adopted by fanatical supporters of the new regime. Though it must be said that this craze only lasted for the first few years after the Revolution and went completely out of fashion in the 1930s, when people no longer wanted to be associated with the excesses of the Stalinist purges. *Svetlana* was the most popular non-Calendar name, which was not recorded prior to the Revolution. It was the name of Stalin's daughter. Invented names were rarer and included names connected with Lenin, such as *Vladimir* (his own name); *Leniana* or *Ninel* (Lenin spelt back-

wards!), *Volja* – will, *Svoboda* – freedom, *Isdra* – spark (the name of a revolutionary newspaper), *Barrikada* – barricade, and *Revoljucija* – Revolution. Even such words as *Kombayu* – combine harvester, *Raketa* – rocket, and *Elektrostancija* – electric power station, were adopted as personal names!

A survey conducted in 1979 showed a general return to the use of traditional Christian names in Russia. Nowadays names from the Soviet era are not to be found in anyone under 45 years of age. It remains to be seen what new developments in naming practices the vast changes which are occurring in Russia and the lands which surround her will bring.

I have dwelt at some length on naming in Russia because its history so clearly incorporates many diverse approaches to naming, and shows how names are intimately connected with prevalent culture and belief.

So what of our own times? What can names mean for us now, in a world increasingly divorced from old, sustaining traditions? It is my aim to show that names can still mean something, and that in conferring a name on a child – whatever one's religion or lack of it – one can still touch into an archetypal realm from which all names derive. In the act of naming we can try to connect with the true being of an individual child.

Yet shall thy name, conspicuous and sublime,
Stand in the spacious firmament of time,
Fixed as a star.

William Wordsworth, c. 1820

What to take into account when choosing a name

> One little word has to epitomise all the wishes and hopes of the parents and express their ideals and traditions.
>
> *Harrap Book of Boys' and Girls' Names*

In naming a child, or anything else, we can either reflect a quality we perceive as already present, or we can choose to imbue the one to be named with the blessing of a quality or attribute.

Sometimes one of the children of the family intuitively knows the name of the baby-to-be. One child pointed to his mother's large tummy, announcing **Daniel** – and Daniel he was named.

Usually, though, it may be ill-considered to choose a name for a baby before birth. If I had been a boy, I was to have been called **Charles** (but my parents had the feminine form ready in waiting for a girl).[15]

How much more appropriate to choose a name for the baby once you know the sex and have had a chance to observe and sense his/her qualities. A newborn baby is not a blank page. Babies are born with distinct physical, emotional and psychological characteristics.

One woman wrote to say: 'We chose the name **Joel** from several Hebrew names that came to mind at the time he was born. I feel it was a strong past life in need of expression, and we liked the sound of the name (he can be a bit of a prophet at times!)'

A child named **Elinor** (after one of her father's favourite characters, from the Morte d'Arthur) declared at the age of one: 'I Ella', and from that day on that has been her name.

A mother during pregnancy is often able to communicate directly with the foetus and through this, and her dreams, can already have a clear idea of the child's characteristics by the time of birth. When the mother of Prince Siddhartha Gautama conceived her son, she dreamed of a white elephant, which foretold his future destiny as Sakyamuni Buddha. In our own times, in 1984, on the night that Maria Torres conceived little Ösel, who was to become Lama Ösel (having been recognised, according to Tibetan tradition, as the rebirth of Maria's former spiritual teacher, Lama Thubten Yeshe), she dreamed that Lama Yeshe placed his hand upon her head.[16]

My friend, the late Sun Bear (Gheezis Mokwa in his own Ojibwa tongue) was so named because of his early visions which predicted his future role as leader, medicine man and teacher.[17] There are many such accounts in recent days, as well as in the traditions of ancient peoples. These characteristics can soon be observed by a sensitive and open observer and can be confirmed and expanded upon by other means, such as the natal astrological chart.[18]

> One couple combined the father's requirements for 'something short, strong and clear' with the mother's wish to choose a name with particular meanings and associations. They knew their son would be a Taurean, so chose the name **Peter** with its associations of earth and rock. Also, while carrying him, his mother kept hearing the name Peter everywhere, and liked the sound of it. This same mother called her daughter **Tara** because of her fondness for the Tibetan goddess of that name.

You might also consider taking the place of birth into account.

> One man, whose son was conceived in William Wordsworth's house in Cockermouth called the child **Adam Charles Derwent.** From the windows of the room where he was conceived, across the lawns, you could see the river Derwent.

Or perhaps the time of day might even be significant.

> In a remote house in Maine, amongst woods and mountains, a woman was having a home delivery. The doctor was called and came, but the labour went on intermittently all night. Everyone there stayed up partying, and finally at first light the child was born – and was given the name **Dawn.**

A name is usually for life of course, and not just for childhood, so it is worth taking time and care in its choosing.

Here are some questions which may be helpful:

- WHO is this child?
- WHAT are this child's CHARACTERISTICS?
- What is this child's PURPOSE?
- With what do I/we want to ENDOW this child?
- What GIFT OF SPIRIT do I want to offer him or her?

> One man I spoke to remarked that 'every baby kicks in a different way', implying that this could perhaps give clues about the right name to choose! The same man told me that he and his wife had named one of their daughters **Bronwen** (white breast or wave) as she was conceived in a Welsh clifftop field overlooking the sea.

As well as a convenient means of describing, identifying and attracting someone's attention, a name is also a blessing (or a curse!), a dedication, and an invocation (lit. an in-calling of power).

> Keep in mind that a name is more than a verbal badge of identification. It is a token of parental affection; and will become part of the owner as a perfume becomes part of a flower.[19]

> One father told me how he had chosen the names **Matthew** and **Meredith** for his children because he liked the sound resonances between the two names, and also because of his love of the sea, echoed in MERedith.

So the circumstances of the birth, the time of day, the season of the year and the phase of the moon may all have a bearing on the naming of a child. The natal astrological chart, which can be drawn up immediately after birth, reflects a wealth of information about the child's character and temperament: strengths, weaknesses, potential and likely destiny. I would strongly recommend that you do have the child's chart drawn up (this can save a lot of time-wasting and red-herring-chasing later in life), even if astrology is unfamiliar to you. As well as getting a clearer picture of the new being's characteristics, it can also provide you with information about the quality of your growing relationship to the child – both the easy facets and the more challenging.[20]

Calling children after famous or inspiring people is a route chosen by many parents.

> A woman wrote to tell me that she decided to call her daughter *Jessie* after an older woman who struck her as strong, honest, 'knowing' about why people act as they do. Jessie senior came from a hard, working class country background, but had the gift of mixing with anyone.

Giving a name, indeed, is a poetic art; all poetry...is but a giving of names

Carlyle in his journal. 18 May 1832

Brainstorming for the right name

- You may want to make a list of your favourite names, cultures, most respected people of the past and present etc.
- Do you want your chosen name to be ancient or modern; from another tradition, language, culture, religion?
- You could, for example, scour the sacred books of the world for inspiration.
- Or perhaps you would like a name from one of the great mythologies of the past? [21]
- As well as taking the child's astrological chart into account, you might also find out what animal and element govern the child's birth in the Chinese astrological system.
- You could also consult an astrologer.
- Some people like to choose diminutives. I have included very few of them in this book, but other books list them at length.
- How will others react to the name?
- How does it sound?
- All letters have numerological value which carries significance.[22]

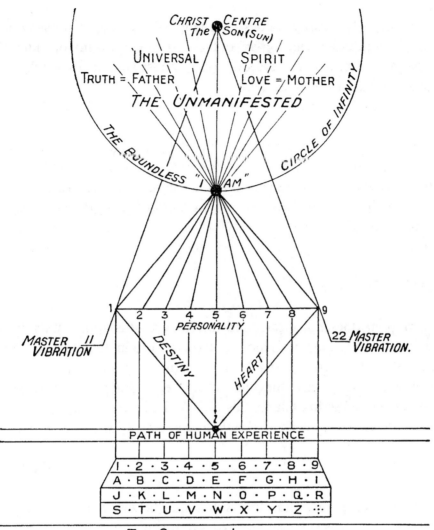

Vibramentology chart [23]

Is it appropriate?

> We instinctively classify names as being fashionable or unfashionable, having a youthful image or an old one, being pleasant or ridiculous. Gladys, for instance, arouses one kind of response in us, while Susan evokes a different image entirely.
>
> Leslie Alan Dunkling[24]

Some people consider family tradition in their choosing of a name, but is this really relevant for this child? And what about the nationality of the child and the name? **Isaac McGillicuddy,** for example, is not a harmonious name! **Jesus** is considered a fine choice of name in Spanish, South American and Portuguese speaking countries, but not usually elsewhere.

Naming pitfalls

> A name that does not clearly indicate its pronunciation by its spelling may prove a life-long nuisance. I know a certain Gerald who spends precious hours expostulating that his name does not begin with a 'j'; Americans usually omit the final 'e' in Irene, though it is sounded in England; and Miss Ina Claire tells me that half her acquaintances called her *Eenah* and the other half *Eynah*. She answers docilely to either.
>
> Winthrop Ames[25]

If you want the name to serve the child well, it may be wise to consider how the name will weather. Will it be as suitable for a 20, 40, 60 year-old as for a small child? Is it a faddish name which will tarnish with passing fashion? Will it be appropriate in a wide variety of situations, places and circumstances; or might it make the child feel awkward, foolish or too different? Is it a *flexible* name, adaptable to the many roles the person may have to fulfil as an adult? Does the name indicate the sex of the child? Is it easy to spell and pronounce? Might it lend itself to unfortunate nicknames or short forms? How will it partner the surname? Calling your daughter **Rose,** if your surname is Bush, might not be to her advantage. I knew a couple whose respective surnames were **Green** and **Freke.** When they married they amalgamated them into a double-barrelled surname. My heart bled for their children! It is also wise to check how the child's initials blend with the surname. There was an old English belief that a child would become wealthy if the initials of his or her full name spelt a word. More recently, there are recorded instances of examples of combining certain initials and surnames, with unfortunate results – W.C. Bowles and W.C. Drane. Sometimes initials alone can spell another name or word, such as L.N. – *Ellen* or A.B. – *Abie*.

A Newsweek article reported that schoolchildren with funny or unusual names were often picked on by their classmates and even discriminated against by their teachers. Professor Hubert Harari conducted an experiment in several elementary schools which showed that children with 'loser' names, such as *Elmer* or *Hubert* tended to receive consistently lower grades than those with names like *Michael* or *David*. When his research was published, he was inundated with questions from anxious parents. His basic advice was: 'I don't think it necessary for every parent to give his child an ordinary name. Just stay away from the really strange ones. For instance Sonny and Cher named their daughter *Chastity*.[26] Can you imagine what that child is going to have to face?'

Giving the 'wrong' name

It is possible to give a child the wrong name; a name which is disharmonious with his or her inner nature and purpose. To name is to recognise and to empower. Ancient cultures understood this: the purpose of a person's life, his or her inner task and striving was instantly recognizable on hearing his name. We still have faint echoes of this today, in a degenerate form, in surnames which indicate occupation.

It is possible to change one's experience and the circumstances of one's life by changing one's name. Sometimes it is practical or advantageous to have a public name, a private name and even a 'secret' one.

> Ged sighed sometimes, but he did not complain. He saw that in this dusty and fathomless matter of learning the true name of each place, thing and being, the power he wanted lay like a jewel at the bottom of a dry well. For magic consists in this, the true naming of a thing.
>
> U.K. Le Guin[27]

Unfortunate associations

Some names are inadvisable because of association, such as **Adolph** or **Judas**. **Ajax** means 'eagle' and was the name of the Greek hero of Homer's Iliad. It implies strength and bravery, but, at least to people of my generation, has become inextricably linked to a certain household scouring powder! It probably doesn't even need mentioning, but names with excellent meanings and which formerly carried dignity and nobility, such as **Marmaduke** ('servant of St Maedoc') or **Clarence** (from a surname from the Latin *clarus* – bright, clear) may seem ridiculous today and are now considered pretentious or too effeminate to give to boys.

> In Tennessee, a Mr. Damm was granted a change [of name] when he complained that a publisher of souvenir postcards was selling a family portrait entitled 'The Whole Damm Family'...
>
> In England, a Mr. Bedbug was allowed to take a new name on the grounds that he didn't want his children to be known as 'little Bedbugs'.
>
> *The Coronet*[28]

Names and jobs

> The theory has been advanced that given names influence the character of children upon whom they are conferred, and that a short one-syllable name is likely to shape an extroverted character which will dominate in the world of sports and outdoor life. A polysyllabic multi-rhythmed name may contribute to an introverted personality likely to be listed in learned societies and college catalogues. Plural patterns of decorative names often appear in the art galleries of the world. Furthermore, names might produce negative vibrations as well as positive, causing protest in a child and contributing to crime and delinquency.
>
> T. M. Pearce[29]

Wilbur G. Gaffney began his research into how first names affect a person's future career when he was doing a monotonous army job which involved checking through long lists of personnel.[30] He observed that most high-ranking officers had short, sharp, to-the-point, one-syllable names, such as **Tom, Bob, Dick** etc. He became so convinced that there was something in this that he went on to check names against professions in widely differing fields. He recounted the story of a boy who was christened **Ricardo Sebastian Taylor**. He was given the middle name after Johann Sebastian Bach, because his mother was a music devotee and had high ambitions in that direction for her son. On his twenty-first birthday, after twelve years of violin lessons, Ricardo Sebastian went with his uncle to the courthouse and legally changed his name to **Dick Taylor**. Returning home, he called his mother into the parlour, smashed the violin across his knee and went off to become an engineer!

So a great deal depends on the choice of a name. Our name is something which grows with us and which we also grow into, and which becomes an intimate part of our experience of ourselves. It is kind of cloak or garment which both protects and reveals our true identity.

Please Call Me By My True Names

Do not say that I'll depart tomorrow
because even today I still arrive

Look deeply; I arrive in every second
to be a bud on a spring branch,
to be a tiny bird, with wings still fragile learning to sing in my new nest,
to be a caterpillar in the heart of flower,
to be a jewel hiding itself in a stone.

I still arrive, in order to laugh and to cry,
in order to fear and to hope,
the rhythm of my heart is the birth and death
of all that are alive.

I am the mayfly metamorphosing on the surface of the river,
and I am the bird which, when spring comes,
arrives in time to eat the mayfly.

I am a frog swimming happily in the clear water of a pond,
and I am the grass-snake, who, approaching in silence,
feeds itself on the frog.
I am the child in Uganda, all skin and bones,
my legs as thin as bamboo sticks,
and I am the arms merchant, selling deadly weapons to Uganda.

I am the twelve year old girl, refugee on a small boat,
who throws herself into the ocean
after being raped by a sea pirate,
and I am the pirate, my heart not yet capable of seeing and loving.

I am a member of the Politburo with plenty of power in my hands,
and I am the man who has to pay his debt of blood to my people
dying slowly in a forced labour camp.

My joy is like spring, so warm it makes flowers bloom in all walks of life.
My pain is like a river of tears, so full it fills all four oceans.

Please call me by my true names,
so I can hear all my cries and laughs at once,
so I can see that my joy and pain are one.

Please call me by my true names,
so I can wake up and so the door of my heart can be left open,
the door of compassion.

Thich Nhat Hanh[31]

PART TWO

MEANINGS AND NAMES

By the name one may know the man

J. Merlot: *Proverbes*

Which names have been chosen, and which left out, and why

I have not included names which sound melodious but with which you probably would not want to endow your children because they carry unfortunate meanings, such as **Desdemona** which means 'misery'.

Sometimes a name which sounds lovely and has an excellent meaning has fallen out of use and come to have negative associations. **Uriah** means 'light of God', but is now linked to the cringing Dickensian character, Uriah Heep. **Ananias**, which is actually a worthy name, has come to be a byword for a liar.

Many of the early names in Genesis are actually not Hebrew, but were borrowed from an unknown language, although they have come to be associated with a particular meaning.[1] An example of this is **Ruth** which has, because of her story, come to be associated with compassion. The name, however, is not Hebrew. Ruth was a Moabitess (see Disputed Meanings section). **Jacob** is often given as 'supplanter' or 'heel', but other authors say that it was borrowed from an older unknown language.

I would have liked to be able to include a number of Native American names in the index, as these are peoples for whom I have the deepest respect and from whom I have learned much. They also had a complex and profound system of naming practices, some of which are mentioned in the historical section of this book. However, without the necessary linguistic and etymological knowledge of these languages, I felt it was disrespectful to use such names. If you are interested in adopting Native American names for your children, you may feel inspired to go to authentic sources in search of them.[2]

I have omitted pet names, nicknames, family names and most diminutives and variations. There are many of these which can be found in other books. Formerly, surnames denoted occupation, such as **Cooper** (barrel maker), **Fletcher** (arrow maker), **Lister** (dyer) and **Wayne** (wagon maker or driver).

I have included some rather ostentatious-sounding names because of their meaning, such as **Jupiter** (Gk. Zeus), which means 'Father Sky'. But beware of burdening your child with a pretentious name!

Where the etymology of a name is unknown or is disputed, I have discussed it in the Disputed Names section. Where origins or meanings are very doubtful or vigorously disputed, I have left the names out. Some books make outrageous approximations which make nonsense of the authenticity of some names. I have seen **Gareth** interpreted both as 'one who ravages' and as 'gentle' or 'benign'! Where possible, I have tried to go back to the root meaning of the word, for example **Gerard** – lit: gaini (spear) and hardu (hard); translated as 'brave-with-a-spear' or 'spear hard'.

It is interesting to see how root words re-occur in names, such as **bert** (beorht) – 'bright, famous'; as in **Albert(ina)** and **Robert**. The Old English root ed means 'rich' or 'happy', as in **Edmund** and **Edwina**.

I have included most names in current usage and have added several from the Tibetan language, for which I have a personal affection, and also because they offer a range of qualities not available through English naming. Many have been omitted – from such ancient cultures as the Chinese and Japanese and from many countries in Europe, as well as the wealth of the African languages. This was beyond the scope of my research for this book. I trust you will be inspired to seek out names in the languages and belonging to the countries and cultures with which you have an affinity – or to create your own.

Sometimes I have passed on the meanings which have come to be generally accepted for usual names, such as **Helen** from the Greek, meaning 'light' or 'bright', though more meticulous etymologists explain that it is more likely pre-Greek and actually of unknown meaning.

Several names in common usage were actually invented by writers and therefore have no meaning. **Pamela** was coined in 1590 by Sir Philip Sidney for his poem, *Arcadia*. Some eager compilers of dictionaries say it means 'honey' (from Latin) or that it means 'gift of the elf' (German) and therefore suggests intellectual ability. **Leslie** (m) is translated as 'one who leases' and **Lesley** (f) as 'one who dwells by a garden pool' or related to 'gladness' (from Latin, laetitia.) Take your pick!

Lorna could mean 'lost' from the Anglo-Saxon, but was in fact made up by R. D. Blackmore in 1869 for the heroine of his book, *Lorna Doone*. Luther is rendered as both 'illustrious warrior' and 'lute player'. **Mary,** sometimes translated as 'bitter' (marah is the Hebrew word for bitter, but who would call their child that?), or 'wished-for child', actually derives from the Hebrew Miriam, which is itself uncertain in meaning and origin, and probably not Hebrew, but more likely Egyptian. **Nancy** may derive from **Ann** – 'grace' or **Agnes** – 'pure'.

Birth – *Natalie (f)*

KEY

Arab.	Arabic
AS/OE	Anglo-Saxon/Old English★
Cel.	Celtic
Cor.	Cornish
Fr.	French
Gael.	Gaelic
Gk.	Greek
Heb.	Hebrew
Ir.	Irish
Lat.	Latin
ON	Old Norse
Pers.	Persian
Russ.	Russian
Scot.	Scottish
Slav.	Slavic
Tib.	Tibetan
Wel.	Welsh

★Anglo-Saxon = Germanic tribes which invaded Britain around 500 AD. This period came to an end in 1066 with the Norman Conquest.

Meanings index from *Admirable* to *Youth*

ADMIRABLE

MIRABELLE (f)
Lat. – very common in the Middle Ages.

MIRANDA (f)
Lat. miranda – 'worthy to be admired', from mirari – to wonder at /admire. The name was coined by Shakespeare for his heroine of *The Tempest*.

Of the ADRIATIC

ADRIAN (m), ADRIANA (f), ADRIENNE (f)
(Fr. but used in England)
Lat. Hadrianus – of the Adriatic. Hadria was a North Italian town which gave its name to the Adriatic sea, originally derived from the Latin ater – black, because of the black sand on its beaches. The Roman clan Hadrianus was named after this town. It was during the reign of the famous Emperor Publius Aelius Hadrianus (117-38 AD) that Hadrian's Wall was built across Northern England. It was also the name of six Popes, and the only English Pope, Nicholas Breakspeare, took the name of Adrian IV. There was a Christian convert from the Emperor's praetorian guard named Adrian who was martyred in 303 AD. His limbs were struck off on an anvil and then he was beheaded. St Adrian is considered the patron saint of soldiers in Germany and Northern France and his feast day is September 8th (see **SEA**).

ALDER (see TREES)

ALIVE AND WELL

AISHA (f)
Arab. asha – to live. One of the most popular Islamic names, as Aisha was Muhammad's third and favourite wife. She is said to have been only nine when she married and to have had a very strong personality.

ALL

ELLA (f)
Norman French from OG. alja – all/entirely

PAN (m)
Gk. god of woodlands and nature. Pan means 'all' in Greek, as in the modern word 'pantheism' (see **WOODS**).

ALL-GIVING

PANDORA (f)
Gk. literally 'every gift', from pan – all + doron – gift. A name of mixed blessings! In classical myth, the name of the first woman, created by Hephaistos, the god of fire, as a scourge for men –

in revenge for Prometheus having stolen fire from the gods. She was given in marriage to Prometheus' brother and given a box which she was forbidden to open. Curiosity overcame her and, opening it, she unleashed all types of suffering on the world. Hence the term 'Pandora's Box'. However, Hope remained inside the box… It is a pity that a such a beautifully sounding name with such a beneficent meaning should have been so besmirched with anti-female associations.

ALWAYS

AINA (f)
This is a Scandinavian name which is especially popular in Finland and is sometimes used in English speaking countries. It means 'always' or 'until the end'.

AMBER (see JEWELS)

AMBITIOUS

ALMETA (f) Lat.

AMIABLE

MUNGO (m)
Scot. This was the nickname of the 6th century missionary, St. Kentigern. His biographer described him as a carissimus amicus – dearest friend, and so his name came to be interpreted as 'amiable', though it has no meaning in Gaelic (also see **LOVEABLE** and **LOVED**).

ANCESTOR RELICS

AULAY (m)
A form of Gael. Amhlaibh.

AULIFFE (m)
This name replaced the native Irish Amalgith.

HAVELOCK (m) Wel.

OLAF (m)
From Norse a(n)leifr – ancestor relics.

OLIVER (m)
This name is possibly an altered form of a Germanic name and not Latin in origin (also see **TREES** – olive).

ANCHOR

ANCHOR (m)
One of the more unusual names which have been given to children born at sea or to the off-spring of seafaring folk (see also **SEA, OCEAN**).

ANCIENT

ETHAN (m)
Heb. 'firmness' or 'long-lived'. The name of a biblical sage.

PRISCILLA (f)
Lat. from old Roman family name Priscus – former. It was the name of an active supporter of St Paul in the New Testament, whose feast day is July 8th.

ANGEL

ANGEL (m/f), ANGELA (f)
Gk. angelos – messenger (see **MESSENGER**)

ELEN (f)
Wel. <u>elen</u> – angel/nymph

FIRISHTA (m/f)
Arab. (see also **FIRE, BURNING ONE**)

ANGELIC

ANGELICA (f)
English from Church Latin (see **MESSENGER**)

Bright ANGEL

ENGELBERT (m) Ger. (see **ANGEL**)

Sweet ANGEL

MELANGEL (f)
Wel. <u>mel</u> – sweet + <u>angel</u> – angel.

ANIMALS (and Insects)

Much of the spirit of the nation is to be traced
in the animals whence their names are derived.
C. M. Yonge[3]

BEAR
Older cultures, living in more conscious relationship with nature, and the creatures on whom they
relied directly for food and shelter, developed
deep respect for, and even taboos surrounding,
those creatures. Though no longer indigenous to
the British Isles, it formerly roamed freely in
most of Europe. It features in manuscripts
illustrated by Celtic monks and was valued for
its strength, stamina and hibernatory habits,
making it a helpful guide into the realms of sleep
and dreaming. Some northern cultures would
placate the bear (both needed and feared) by
the use of euphemistic names. The Lapps and
Swedes would call the bear 'Old Man', or 'Broad-
Footed' or 'Grandfather', which was also the
name that certain Native American tribes gave
to the buffalo, upon whom they depended in
exactly the same way as the more northern
dwellers relied on the bear. In Native American
tradition the bear is associated with strong
healing power, being an animal which digs up
medicinal herbs. It was customary to beg the
bear's pardon, to worship him and hang up his
skull as a charm. Among the Finnish people, the
46th Rune of Kalevala was the capture and
killing of the 'sacred Otso' whose name was
taboo and who was addressed as 'Honey-Eater',
'Fur-Robed', 'Forest apple' or the one who gives
his life as 'a sacrifice to Northland'. It is hard
for us to intuit the depth and power of these
early cultures' relationship to the creatures with
whom they shared the earth, but something of it
survives in names such as <u>Arthur</u> and <u>Ursula</u>
(bear) and <u>Ingram</u> (raven). The intention behind
naming a child after the bear was not only to
endow him with some of the bear's power, but
also to give him power in hunting the bear
when necessary.

BEAR BRAVE

BERNARD (m)
Ger. <u>ber(n)</u> – <u>bear</u> + <u>hard</u> – hardy/brave. St.
Bernard of Menthon (923-1008), after whom

ANIMALS (and Insects)

the dogs are named, founded hospices (resting places for travellers) on the Alpine passes named after him. He is the patron saint of mountaineers and skiers and his feast day is May 28th. The famous reformer St Bernard of Clairvaux (1090-1153) founded the monastic order of the Cistercians. His feast day is August 20th.

BERNADETTE (f)
Fr. Bernadette Soubirous, whose saint's day is May 20th, had visions as a little girl of the Blessed Virgin Mary, and uncovered a healing spring near Lourdes in France where healings (considered miraculous) still take place today. 'Our Lady of Lourdes' is prayed to in the Catholic Church in time of illness.

BEAR FRIEND

BERWYN (m)
OE. ber – bear + wine – friend.

BEAR HERO

ARTHUR (m)
Probably originally from the Roman clan name Artorius. Cel. from arth, Celtic artos – bear + gwr – hero. It is also possible that this name derives from the word arth which meant 'high' in other Celtic tongues. The earliest record of this name in English was in Adamnan's *Life of St Columba,* where it appeared as Arturius. This name has also been associated with the Anglo-Saxon name Arnthor or Earnthor which means 'Eagle of Thor' (see **THOR**).

ARTHEK (m) Corn.
ARTHENE (f) Fr.

BEAR POWER

BERNAL (m) Ger.

Fortunate BEARCUB

EDEN (m)
Eng. from a surname, derived from a medieval given name, Edun; from OE. ead – prosperity, fortune, riches + hun – bearcub. In modern times the name has been associated with the biblical Garden of Eden, which actually means 'place of pleasure' in Hebrew (see **PLEASURE, DELIGHT**).

Little BEAR (bearcub)

ORSON (m)
From an old Norman French nickname, from Lat. ursus – bear.

URSULA (f)
Lat. A popular saint in the Middle Ages. Her feast day is October 21st. Legend tells that she was a 4th century British princess, fleeing from an unwanted marriage, when, with 11,000 virgin companions (probably a misreading from an early manuscript which actually said eleven!), she was martyred in Cologne by the Huns on her way back from a pilgrimage in Rome.

Noble BEAR

ADELBERN (m) Ger.

Noble BEARLIKE

AUBERON (m)

Ger. <u>adal</u> – noble + <u>ber</u>(n) – bear. The Old German name was <u>Adalbero</u> and it occurs in Shakespeare's *A Midsummer Night's Dream* as Oberon, the king of the Fairies.

Son of the BEAR

ARTHGEN (m)

Wel. <u>arth</u> – bear + <u>geni</u> – to be born.

ARTHYEN (m) Corn.

BEAVER STREAM

BEVERLEY (m/f)

OE. <u>beofor</u> – beaver + <u>leac</u> – stream. This name is spelt 'Beverly' exclusively for boys.

BEE

DEBORAH (f)

Heb. from a verb meaning 'to hum or buzz'. The name of an Old Testament prophetess. Her name day is September 1st. Also the name of Rebekah's faithful nurse who was so well-loved that the tree under which she was buried was known as the 'oak of weeping'. This name was revived by the Puritans in the 17th century as a symbol of industriousness.

MELISSA (f)

Gk. from <u>melisso</u> – to sweeten or soothe, or possibly the word for 'honey bee'. She was the Greek nymph who first taught mankind the use of honey. She may derive from a more ancient Earth goddess, as important goddesses associated with bees are found in Minoan Crete and in earlier cultures. It has been suggested (in an interesting article dealing exclusively with the name <u>Melissa</u>, by Demetrius Georgacas) that the name combines the meanings of both <u>melissa</u> – honey bee and <u>mylitta</u> – sacred temple prostitute. Originally it meant an industrious woman and implied living a sweet and pleasant life and then came to mean 'companion, courtesan, concubine'. Earlier the name had been applied to priestesses of Apollo, Demeter, Artemis and Cybele. The term <u>Hierai Melissai</u> was applied to priestesses of the cult of Demeter and Persephone and referred to temple prostitutes. The Assyrian goddess, <u>Mylitta</u> is the same as the Greek goddess Aphrodite. Like Ishtar, she was concerned with caring for women in childbirth. Every Babylonian woman, once in her life, sat in the precinct of the goddess' temple and was chosen by a stranger to have sexual intercourse. The fee was a sacred silver coin and, as it was thrown into the lap of the woman, the stranger would say: 'I summon you in the name of the goddess Mylitta'. A similar custom was practised in parts of Cyprus (see **HONEY**).

BOAR BATTLE

AVERIL (f)

OE. <u>eofor</u> – boar + <u>hild</u> – battle. The boar's head was considered sacred to offer to a Saxon deity (see **BEAR**). St Everild was a 7th century saint. The boar was a totemic creature of great strength and power in Celtic literature.

ANIMALS (and Insects)

ANIMALS (and Insects)

BUTTERFLY

EILIR (m) Wel.

CHIEF KID (goat)

CYNFYN (m) Wel. cyn – chief + myn – kid.

CUB

CENEU (m) Wel. cenau – cub or whelp.

DEER

AYALA (f)
Modern Jewish name, meaning 'hind' or 'doe'.

EWIG (f) Wel. ewig – deer/roe.

DOLPHIN

DOLPHIN (m)
DELFINE (f) Fr
DELFINIA (f)
These names are associated with the ancient Greek site of the oracle at Delphi, which derived from delphis – dolphin. Delphi was believed to be the centre (womb) of the earth, as Jerusalem was to the Medieval Christians. The name Delphinia was applied to Artemis, who had a shrine at Delphi. The most important healing centre in mainland Greece was the shrine of Asklepios near Epidaurus. There Apollo was worshipped as the god of medicine and sometimes took the form of Delphinius – the dolphin. In Celtic culture, the dolphin, with the salmon and the whale, was considered one of the three sacred fishes. The poet Taliesin ('radiant brow') was related to the Greek god, Apollo, who shared the temple of Artemis at Delphi. In Celtic culture the dolphin was therefore invoked for poetic inspiration (see **FLOWERS, GODS & GODDESSES, HEALER, MOON**).

EWE

RACHEL (f)
Heb. The beloved wife of Jacob and mother of Joseph, described in the Bible as 'beautiful and well favoured'. As a child, she tended her father's sheep (hence her name, which means 'lamb' or 'ewe'). This was a characteristically Jewish name in the Middle Ages and is still popular today with Jews and Gentiles alike.

FAWN

ELAIN (f) Wel. elain – fawn/young hind.

GAZELLE

DORCAS (f)
Gk. dorkas – gazelle or doe. Not actually used as a personal name by the Greeks, but popular among the early Christians, and much used by the 16th century Puritans. Dorcas societies were formed by women who would meet to make clothes for the poor, in imitation of the biblical Dorcas who was described as being 'full of good works and almsdeeds'. The feast of St Dorcas is October 25th.

TABITHA (f)
Aramaic. In the bible Dorcas is given as the Greek equivalent of this name. The name of a woman whom St Peter brought back from the dead.

Young GOAT

GILES (m), EGIDIA (f)

Gk. Aigidios – a kid or young goat. There was a late Latin name – Aegidius which derived from the Greek. This name may refer to the kid leather used in the making of shields. The shield (aegis) of Pallas Athene was made of goatskin. A popular name in the Middle Ages. St Giles was an 8th century Athenian who fled to Provence to escape the fame he was receiving for his miracles. He is the patron saint of cripples, and his feast day is September 1st. In Catholic tradition he is invoked against sterility and is prayed to for the grace of a good confession. St Giles is the patron of the High Kirk of Scotland and his feast is celebrated on September 1st.

JAEL (f)

Heb. and popular Jewish name YAEL comes from the word which means a 'female wild goat'.

HORSE

Lover of HORSES

PHILIP (m), PHILIPPA (f)

Gk. philein – to love + hippos – horse. The name of the father of Alexander the Great, and of one of Jesus' apostles and several early saints. In England women were also called Philip, but the name was spelled in the feminine form above in written records. The feminine form did not come into regular use until the 19th century. Philippina was a common name in the Middle Ages and was then interpreted as being composed of Gk philein – to love + poine – pain or punishment, referring to the Christian practice of self-flagellation and mortification. The joint feast day is May 1st.

HORSE-PROTECTION

ROSAMUND (f)

Ger. (h)ros – horse + mund – protection. Hrosmund was the name of a 5th century chieftainess of the Gepidae. She was compelled by her husband to drink his health from the skullcup of her slaughtered father, after which he murdered her. Perhaps this is one reason why the name came to be re-analysed as 'rose of the world'. Many of the seemingly 'rose' names actually originally derived from Old English, not Latin and trace their meaning back to 'horse' (see **DISPUTED NAMES**).

HORSE-TAMER

DAMASPIA (f)

Pers. equivalent of Hippodameia, which is the feminine of Greek Hippodamus.

HORSE-FREER

HIPPOLYTUS (m), HIPPOLYTA (f)

Gk. from Hippolytos; hippos – horse + lyein – to loose, set free. The name of several early saints and a 3rd century writer of the early Church. Also the name of a Greek legendary figure. Hippolyta was the Queen of the Amazons, a tribe of female warriors who amputated one breast in order to facilitate the carriage of their arrow sheaths. St Hippolytus is said to have been martyred by being torn apart by horses and thus is the patron saint of horses and horsemen.

ANIMALS (and Insects)

Yellow HORSE

XANTHIPPE (f)

Gk. xanthos – yellow + hippos – horse. Probably meant 'light-coloured horse'. The name of the reputedly shrewish wife of the philosopher Socrates (469-399 BC). (See **COLOURS**)

Lover of HOUNDS

CONNOR (m)

Ir. anglicised form of Gael. Conchobhar, a very ancient Irish name, which has also been interpreted as meaning 'high will' or 'desire'. Conchobhar was a semi-legendary Irish king who lived around the 1st century. The surname, O'Connor derives from this name.

Small HOUND

CONAN (m)

Ir. diminutive of cu – hound. The name of at least six Irish saints. St Conan's day is March 8th.

LAMB

AGNES (f) Lat. agnus – lamb – (see **PURE**)

UNA (f)

Ir. probably from the word uan – lamb, though it is identical with the vocabulary word for 'hunger'. Sometimes anglicised as Winifred. The name Juno, made famous by Sean O'Casey in his play *Juno and the Paycock*, is sometimes also used as an anglicization of this name (see **MONTHS OF THE YEAR, PURE** and **UNITY**).

LION

The lion, as symbol of might, dignity and kingship features in the names of many nations; even those to whose country the animal is not indigenous. The lion names probably derive from the early Indo-European races.

LEO (m), LEONIE (f)

Lat. leo, Gk. leon – lion. This was the name of 13 popes and often occurs among Christians in the Roman Empire. The saint's day is April 11th.

LEON (m) LEONA (f)

Eng. form of LEO. Popular Jewish name – Jacob's dying words were 'Judah is a lion's whelp'.

LION OF GOD

ARIEL (m)

Heb. Jewish name from biblical place name, meaning 'lion of God' (see **GOD**). Also the name of a Cabbalistic water sprite and an air spirit of medieval fable, from which Shakespeare drew the name for the attendant of the magician, Prospero, in his last play, *The Tempest*.

LION-LIKENESS

LLEWELLYN (m)

Wel. llew – lion + eilun – likeness. There is an old Celtic name, Lugobelinos which probably derives from the god, Lugh, also spelt Llew. These were the gods of light and warmth –

relating both to the physical sun and to spiritual inspiration. The British warrior god, <u>Llew</u>, was known as 'skilful hand'. This name may also derive from <u>llyw</u> – leader. It was the name of two particularly famous Welsh princes who united the inhabitants of North Wales against the Normans. The feast of St Llewellyn is April 7th.

LION MAN

LEANDER (m)
Gk. <u>leon</u> – lion + <u>andros</u> – man.

LION WOMAN

LEANDA (f)
Gk. feminine of <u>Leander</u>.

Little LION

LIONEL (m)
Diminutive of the OF. name LEON.

Strong as a LION

LEONARD (m)
OG. <u>leon</u> – lion + <u>hard</u> – strong/hardy/courageous. Introduced into Britain by the Normans. The name of a 5th century Frankish saint, who is the patron of peasants and horses and whose feast day is November 26th.

PANTHER

FAHD (m)
Arab. The name indicates courage and fierceness.

ROEBUCK LEAP

SACHEVERELL (m)
This is a surname, sometimes used as a first name. It is said to derive from the Norman castle of <u>Saute de Chevreuil</u> – 'the leap of the roebuck'!

SEAL

MARUNA (m) Manx. <u>raun</u> – a seal.

RONAN (m)
Ir. 'little seal' (from <u>ron</u> – seal) – an important animal in Celtic mythology. The name of the legendary king of Leinster. The name of several early Irish saints, including a bishop consecrated by St Patrick himself who worked as a missionary in Cornwall and Brittany. The feast of St Ronan is June 1st. RHONA is sometimes given as the feminine form (see **Rough ISLAND**).

Beautiful SERPENT

BELINDA (f)
ON. <u>lindi</u> – serpent + a first syllable of uncertain meaning. The snake was a symbol of wisdom and immortality. Nowadays the name is sometimes considered to be a combination of <u>belle</u> Fr., or <u>bella</u> Lat. – beautiful and <u>linda</u> Sp., which also means beautiful. The name was introduced into England by Alexander Pope in the 18th century.

LINDA (f)
Eng. First appeared in the 19th century and of uncertain origin, but probably a short form of <u>Belinda</u>. Now a name in its own right. Some have linked it to a Germanic word <u>lind</u>, meaning weak, tender, soft.

ANIMALS (and Insects)

ANIMALS (and Insects)

SERPENT-BORN

IPHIGENIA (f)
Gk. <u>iphis</u> – serpent. Symbol of wisdom and immortality (because it sheds its skin). A serpent was in the royal diadem of Egypt, in the shield of the Greek goddess of wisdom, Athena, and wrapped around the <u>caduceus</u> (the healing wand) of Apollo.

WOLF

BLEDIG (m)
Wel. – 'wolflike'.

ZEEV (m)
Heb. a Jewish name sometimes used to translate European names which mean 'wolf'.

Famous WOLF

ROLF (m), RUDOLF (m)
OG. <u>hrothi</u> – fame + <u>vulf</u> – wolf. RUDOLF is the anglicised version of Lat. <u>Rudolphus</u>, from the Germanic name <u>Hrodwulf</u> (also see **FAME**).

Little WOLF

BLEDDYN (m)
Wel. <u>blaidd</u> – wolf + diminutive suffix. This could have been a symbolic name, indicating a tribe under the protection of a certain god who manifested in animal form.

Noble WOLF

ADOLF (m) OG. <u>Adolphus</u>
from <u>athal</u> – noble + <u>wolf</u> – wolf. The Old English name was <u>Aethelwulf</u> (see **NOBLE**).

WOLF COUNSEL

RALPH (m), RALPHINA (f), RANULF (m) Scot.
ON. <u>regin</u> – advice/decision/counsel and also means 'the gods' + <u>ulfr</u> – wolf.

WOLF LAND

BLEIDDUD (m)
Wel. <u>blaidd</u> – wolf + <u>tud</u> – tribe/tribal territory.

WOLF POWER

ULRIC (m), ULRICA (f)
OE. WULFRIC, from <u>wulf</u> – wolf + <u>ric</u> – power. The name of a 12th century saint who ended his days as a hermit in the village of Haselbury Plucknett in Somerset! The feast of St Ulric is July 4th.

WOLF RULER

BLEDRI (m)
Wel. <u>blaidd</u> – wolf + <u>rhi</u> – ruler (also see **RULER**).

WOLF SHIELD

RANDAL (m), RANDOLPH (m)
OE. <u>rand</u> – rim/edge (of a shield) + <u>wulf</u> – wolf. This was a common name before the Norman Conquest and more so afterwards, as the Normans had a similar name derived from Norse.

ANIMATED

ALVITA (f)
Lat. – animated/vivacious

VIVIAN (m. occasionally f.)
VIVIEN (f. formerly m.)
Lat. vivianus from vivus – alive.

VYVYAN (m)
Wel. (see **ALIVE, LIFE, LIVELY**)

ANVIL

EINION (m)
Wel. einion – anvil; denoting stability and forti-
tude. Some say the name derives from the word
for 'upright' or 'just'. They were probably separate names which have become mixed.
Various spellings.

APOLLO (see **SUN**)

APPLE

POMONA (f)
Lat. the Roman goddess of fruit (see
FLOWERS, TREES)

APRIL
(see **MONTHS OF THE YEAR**)

AQUILINE (see **BIRDS** – eagle)

ARCADIA

ARKADI (m)
Russ. Refers to a region of Greece which, in the
later classical period, became the conventional
setting for pastoral idylls. St Arkadios was a 4th
century missionary bishop revered in the Eastern
Church.

ARDENT

RHYS (m)
Wel. rhys – ardour/a rush. The name implies
'fiery warrior' and was the name of two 12th
century Welsh warriors who fought the English.
Anglicised as REES, REECE, RICE.

ARDENT LORD

IDRIS (m)
Wel iud – lord + ris – ardent/impulsive.
An ancient name with a long history. Idris the
Giant, who was killed in 632, was a legendary
astronomer-magician who used Cader Idris
('Idris Chair' – one of the highest Welsh moun-
tains) as his observatory.

ARDENT METAL

MAELRYS (m)
Wel. mael – metal/iron + rhys – ardent/rushing.

ARDOROUS FAIR ONE

SELWYN (m)
Wel. sel – ardour/zeal + (g)wyn – fair(see also
DISPUTED NAMES).

ARMOUR

SERLE (m)
OE. from OG. Sarlo, from sarva – armour. This
was a favourite Norman name. It died out in
the 14th century, but continues in surnames.

ARMY BRIGHT

HERBERT (m)
OG. harja – army + berhta – bright. St Herbert's day is March 20th.

ARMY DEFENCE

HEREWARD (m)
OE. here – army + weard – guard/protection. Hereward the Wake was the last Saxon leader against the Normans.

ARMY MAN

HERMAN (m)
OG. harja – army + mana – man. There are many names deriving from Old German words associated with battle and army.

ARMY POWER

HAROLD (m)
OG. harja – army + weald – ruler/power. N.B. modern word 'wield'. The source of the modern name is probably Norse, from Haraldr. The name of the last king of England before the Norman Conquest, who died at the Battle of Hastings in 1066 (see also **BATTLE, POWER, RULER**).

AROMATIC (see FRAGRANCE)

ARTFUL (see SKILFUL)

ASTRAL (see STAR)

ATTRACTIVE

DEINIOL (m)
Wel. deiniol – attractive/charming (see also **GOD is my judge**)

AUGUST (see MAJESTY and MONTHS OF THE YEAR)

AWARENESS

RIGDZIN (m)
Tib. lit. 'holder of awareness', from rig – awareness + dzin – holder. The Tibetan language has many words which describe the mind and its attributes. Rig-pa relates to the innate, alert, clear, natural awareness of mind.

AWESOME / AWFUL

RHUN (m) Wel. rhun – awful/grand.

Armour – Serle (m) OE. from OG.

BALD

CALVIN (m)
Norman. calve – little bald one + (Norman form of French) chauve – bald. This is a surname used as a first name which became popular because of the French Protestant theologian Jean Calvin (1509-64).

BAPTIST

BAPTIST (m), BAPTISTE (f)
Gk. baptein – to dip, means one who baptises. St John the Baptist's Feast Day is June 24th.

BATTLE

Although a name meaning 'battle' or in some way associated with battle may seem a strange choice for a new born baby, remember that formerly such a name would be chosen to endow the child with courage and strength. As you will see, some familiar as well as some less common names include ideas of battle or war in them.

HILDA (f)
Ger. hild – battle. A very respected Northumbrian princess, who founded a monastery at Whitby. Caedmon, a cowherd, is supposed to have composed the first religious poetry in England there. St Hilda's feast day is September 17th.

BATTLE GLORY

BORIS (m)
Russ. Originally from a Tartar nickname, Bogoris – small, but later used as a short form of Borislav, from bor – battle + slav – glory. This was the name of a 10th century Russian saint, whose feast day is July 24th, and is one of the few non-classical names that the Orthodox Church allows to be given at baptism.

BATTLE READY

ALPHONSO (m)
English spelling of Sp. Alfonso. Probably from Old German Hildefuns – battle ready.

BATTLE STONE

WYSTAN (m)
OE. wig – battle + stan – stone. The name of a 9th century Mercian saint.

BATTLE STRONGHOLD

HILDEGARDE (f)
Ger. hild – battle + gard – enclosure/fortress. This was the name of Charlemagne's second wife and of the famous 12th century mystic and writer Hildegard of Bingen, whose feast day is September 17th.

BATTLE WORTHY

HARVEY (m)
Transferred use of a surname, from the Breton name Haerveu – worthy of battle (haer – battle + vy – worthy). Introduced to Britain through East Anglia by the Breton settlers. This name implied a mature, strong and well-trained man

and therefore was a very auspicious name to give a son. St Herve was a 6th century Breton itinerant monk and minstrel who was blind. A cradle, reputed to have been the saint's, was held in veneration and kept in a church in Brittany until the French Revolution in 1789. His feast day is February 17th.

Famous BATTLE

CLOTILDA (f)
Ger. hlod – famous + hild – battle ie.'renowned in battle'. This was the name of the daughter of the king of Burgundy who married Clovis the king of the Franks and converted him to Christianity (see also **FAME**, and **ARMY, SOLDIER, WAR**).

Fortunate BATTLE

EDITH (f)
OE. Although this name seems to make no sense, at least as a feminine name, it is composed of the elements ead – riches, happiness, prosperity + gyth – strife/battle, and is, in fact, the only surviving feminine name which contains the element ead, so common in Old English masculine names. St Eadgyth, the 10th century nun, (daughter of 'Edgar the Peaceful') made the name popular. The feast of St Edith is September 16th.

BEANGROWER

FABIAN (m)
Lat. from Roman family name Fabianus – of Fabius, possibly originally from faba -bean (because the family were bean-growers). The name of a 3rd century Pope and martyr, whose feast day is January 20th.

BEARER

AMOS (m)
Heb. Biblical prophet of 8th century B.C. whose sayings are collected in his book of the Bible. May be from amos – to carry; sometimes interpreted as 'borne by God'. This was a popular Puritan name.

BEAUTIFUL

EAVAN (f)
Ir. Aoibheann – 'fair form'. An ancient Irish name which has been revived in the anglicised form of Eavan.

JAMAL (m/f). JAMIL (m), JAMILA (f)
Arab. jamala – to be handsome or comely. Not a traditional Islamic name, but popular in Arab countries.

TEGAN (f)
Wel. teg – beautiful + diminutive suffix. The name of a legendary heroine whose mantle would fit only a virtuous woman.

TEGID (m)

BEAUTIFUL and BLESSED

CEINWEN (f)
Wel. cain – fair/lovely + (g)wen – white/blessed/holy. The Welsh root gwyn (m) and gwen (f) means 'white' and also blonde, light in colour or beautiful. It carries the secondary meaning of 'blessed', eg. Croeswen – 'Blessed Cross'. Ceinwen was a 5th century saint.

BEAUTIFUL and FAIR

TEGWEN (f) Wel. teg – beautiful + (g)wen – fair.

Divinely BEAUTIFUL

ASTRID (f)

From the Old Norse ass – god + fri r – fair /
beautiful. A long standing Norwegian royal name
(see **GOD**).

Very BEAUTIFUL

ANWEN (f)

Wel. (g)wen – fair, white, blessed + an – 'very'
or much. The Welsh prefix an is here used to
intensify the other syllable of the word. Sometimes it is used as a diminutive.

BEAUTY

AOIFE (f) Old Irish name, anglicised as Eve.

BEGINNING

ALPHA (f/m)

Gk. first letter of alphabet. This name was given
as a reference to God as the beginning (and end
– omega) of all things, or to the firstborn and
also as a symbol of excellence or primacy.

BEHOLD! A SON

REUBEN (m)

Heb. the name of the first son of Jacob and Leah.

BELL

GERSHOM (m) Heb.

BELOVED

'AZIZ (m), 'AZIZA (f)

Arab. from azza – to be powerful or cherished,
and so it combines the meanings of beloved and
invincible. Its use to denote endearment is more
common today.

DAVID (m)

Heb. The second King of Israel. The name is said
to come from a Hebrew nursery word for 'darling', a shortened form of Dodayahu, from the
Hebrew root 'to love', meaning 'the man after
God's own heart' (beloved of Ya). He was the
famous boy who slew the giant, Goliath, and went
on to become King of Judah and the greatest of all
kings of Israel. He was a poet and the Psalms are
attributed to him. He is the patron saint of poets.

DAFYDD (m)

Wel. Under the name of Dewi he is the patron
saint of Wales and his feast day in the Catholic
Church is celebrated on December 29th. St
David's Day is celebrated in Wales on 1st March,
the anniversary of the death (in 588) of the
ascetic bishop of Menevia, who was not canonised until the 12th century. According to legend
a victory was won by the Welsh over the Saxons
on the saint's birthday in 540. On that occasion
the Welsh wore leeks to distinguish them from
the invaders. This is also a very popular name in
Russia, and occurs in several variations.

DAVINA (f) Scot.

ERASMUS (m)

Gk. eran – to love (N.B. Eros – the god of Love;
note our modern word 'erotic'). This was the
name of a 4th century martyr who became the
patron saint of sailors in southern Italy where he
was killed. In the Roman Catholic Church he is
invoked against intestinal disorders, and his feast
day is June 2nd. The great Dutch humanist scholar

and reformer, Gerhard Geerts (1466-1536) adopted the name <u>Desiderius Erasmus</u>, believing it to be the Greek translation of his name.

HABIB (m), HABIBA (f)
Arab. <u>habba</u> – to love.

MYRNA (f)
Anglicised version of Gael. <u>Muirne</u>.

PHILOMENA (f)
Gk. <u>Philomenes</u>; <u>philein</u> – to love + <u>menos</u> – strength. The name of a 3rd century saint. In 1527 bones were discovered under the altar in a church near Ancona in Italy, with an inscription which declared them to be the remains of St Filomena. In 1802 another set of relics of another St Philomena was discovered in the catacombs in Rome. Outside the tomb they found pictures of an anchor, an olive branch (symbols of hope and peace), a scourge (symbol of suffering and penance) and 2 arrows and a javelin (perhaps depicting how the occupant of the tomb had died). The inscription read 'lumena pax te cum fi' which was interpreted as referring to <u>Filumena</u> but which actually simply meant 'Peace be with you, beloved'. In 1961 the Sacred Congregation of Rites demoted Philomena from saintly status and decreed that no babies were to be called after her and that churches bearing her name were to be renamed (see **LOVE**).

BENEFICENT

MUHSIN (m), MUHSINA (f)
Arab. <u>ahsana</u> – to do right/be charitable.

BERRY

AERON (m)
Wel. from name of river in Cardiganshire. (see **FLOWERS** and **TREES**)

BIRDS

BIRD

ADERYN (f) Wel.
AVIS (f) Lat.
ENDA (m) Ir.

BLACKBIRD

MERLE (f) Fr.
This bird is associated, in Celtic mythology, with magic and the ability to pass easily in the Otherworld. Its twilight song is credited with the power to put the listener to sleep or enchant him into an out-of-time state. The Gaelic name of the blackbird – <u>Druid-dhubh</u> indicates its associations with the Druids.

BOLD BIRD

EDNYFED (m)
Wel. <u>edn</u> – bird + <u>nyf</u> – bold. This might indicate an eagle or a hawk, or it could derive from <u>ednyfedog</u> – spirited, vigorous.

DOVE
The carriage of <u>Astarte</u>, the Syrian Goddess, equivalent to the Greek Aphrodite and the Roman Venus, was drawn by doves. In Syriac the word for dove was <u>Semiramis</u> and this was the name of an Assyrian queen. The Syrian town of Askelon

worshipped the goddess <u>Astarte</u>, and flocks of pigeons and doves lived freely there as they were not allowed to be killed. The nearby village of Hamami also meant dove and this was the birthplace of Semiramis.

COLM (m) Gael

COLMAN (m)

Anglicised form of Irish name borne by nearly a hundred Irish saints. From Late Lat. <u>Columbanus</u>. Sometimes a transferred use of the surname. Feast day November 24th.

COLUMBA (Columcille) (m)

Ir. Famous Irish saint (where he was sometimes known as St <u>Columkill</u> or <u>Columba of the Cell</u>) and founder of Iona Monastery, off the west coast of Scotland. His name referred to the fact that he was the dove that brought the peace of the Gospel to the wild Hebrides. His birth was heralded by this prophecy:

A manchild shall be born of his family,
He will be a sage, a prophet, a poet,
A lovable lamp, pure and clear.

Who will not utter falsehood.
He will be a sage, he will be pious,
He will be King of the royal graces,
He will be lasting, and will be ever good,
He will be in the eternal Kingdom for his
consolation. [4]

After Columba's birth his mother had a vision in which an angel handed her a mantle which spread over all the land. He was given the name of <u>Crimthan</u> – Fox, at first, and later was called <u>Columba</u> when he received the tonsure (shaven

head) of a monk. He was of royal birth and was learned in both pagan and Christian tradition, promoting the oral tradition and the dissemination of knowledge. He once copied a whole book of Psalms and for this reason it has been suggested by Caitlín Matthews that he might be considered to be the patron saint of photocopiers! Thursday, the 'day between the fasts' was dedicated to St Columba. It was considered lucky for warping thread and for beginning a pilgrimage. On Wednesday night the mother of the family would make barley, rye or oatcake and put a silver coin in it. The cake would be toasted before a fire of rowan, yew, oak or another sacred wood. The father would then cut the cake on Thursday morning into sections for all the children of the family. All the pieces were then put into a <u>ciosan</u>, a beehive basket, and each child would draw a piece out – in the Name of the Father, the Son and of the Holy Ghost. The child who got the coin got the crop of lambs for the year. This was called the '<u>sealbh uan</u>' – lamb luck (see **DAYS of the Week**).

The feast of St Colum is September 22nd, and that of St Columbanus is on November 21st.

JEMIMA (f)

Heb. although usually interpreted as 'dove', the name may well mean 'as fair as the day'. This was the name of the first daughter of Job (the sister of <u>Kezia</u> and <u>Kerenhappuch</u>): 'And in all the land were no women found so fair as the daughters of Job.'

JONAH (m)

Heb. the biblical character who was swallowed by a whale and suffered many misfortunes. A popular Puritan name.

BIRDS

BIRDS

EAGLE

AQUILA (m) Lat.

HAYTHAM (m) Arab. 'young eagle'.

EAGLE POWER

ARNOLD (m)
This name was introduced by the Normans, from the Old German name Arnwalt.

HAWK

In Celtic tradition, the hawk is a symbol of far-reaching memory and shamanic breadth of knowledge.

GALAHAD (m)
Wel. gwalch – hawk/falcon/crested one/hero + cad – battle. The famous pure knight and hero of Arthurian legend.

GAWAIN (m)
Wel. gwalch – hawk/falcon + diminutive suffix (i.e. little falcon) or gwalch + (g)wyn – white (i.e. white falcon).

GAVIN (m)
Cel. sometimes translated as 'hawk of the plain', though meaning and origin uncertain. First appeared as French Gauvain. This is the same name as Gawain, the Arthurian Knight of the Round Table.

GWALCHMAI (m)
Wel. gwalch – hawk/falcon + mai – plain or open country.

JACKDAW

GALINA (f)
Russ. Galya is the short form.

LINNET

LLINOS (f)
Wel. llinos – linnet; implying a pretty woman.

NIGHTINGALES

ANADIL (f) Arab.

SCREECH OWL

LILITH (f)
Heb. vocabulary word for 'screech owl' or 'night monster'. Has also been translated as 'of the night', 'serpent' and 'vampire'. This name deserves a book to itself and indeed has been the subject of an excellent one by Barbara Black Kultov.[5] Lilith is the much maligned, misunderstood, rejected and forgotten dark side of the feminine (the insulted moon, who was originally equal to the sun until God intervened) – the shadow-side of Eve, the acceptable wifely, motherly feminine. Lilith has become associated with an unshapely swift-flying nocturnal malevolent creature. All manner of evil has been projected onto her; she has been blamed for infant deaths of all kinds, for destroying marriages and even for epilepsy. The Lilith figure featured in Sumerian, Babylonian, Assyrian, Canaanite, Persian, Arabic and Teutonic mythology, as well as in the Hebrew. In 8th

able name of God. Three angels – Sanvai, Sansanvai and Semangelof were sent after her. She was given the charge of all newborn children, and swore that wherever she saw the names of these three angels she would not harm the child. This accounts for the custom of making amulets to protect against Lilith, inscribed with the angels' names. These would be tied to the baby, attached to the cradle or painted on the floor.

Cooing of PIGEONS

HADIL (f)
Arab. hadala – to coo; denotes soft sound. The traditional name of a bird that existed with Noah. It was eaten by a bird of prey and mourned by the other pigeons and doves.

RAVEN

Two ravens perched on the shoulders of the Norse god, Odin, who gave his name to our Wednesday. They served him as mind and memory. The bird was painted on the shields of Thor's warriors and was the symbol of battle. In Germanic mythology the raven is a symbol of wisdom. The raven is also a powerful symbol in Native American culture; the messenger from the Great Spirit.

FIACHRA (m)
Ir. fiach – raven. In the 7th century a St Fiachra settled at Meaux in France and was regarded as the patron saint of gardeners. He gave his name to the Hotel de Saint Fiacre in Paris, outside which certain carriages (fiacres) were available for hire. Hence he has become the modern patron saint of cab drivers! His feast day is August 30th.

century B.C. Syria she became linked to a child-killing witch, and from the 6th century B.C. she was suppressed and denied. Lilith personifies the wildness in woman. She represents the instinctive, earthy feminine who refuses to be bound or possessed. She carries the qualities not represented by the conventionally acceptable feminine, the part of the Great Goddess rejected and cast out in post-biblical times. She is concerned with lunar consciousness (the cycles of life, death, re-birth and the female wisdom stages of maiden, mother and crone); she represents the body – instinct, sexuality and the Earth; she presides over prophetic *inner* knowledge and experience, as opposed to logic and law; she is God the Mother – the feminine creatrix. In Jewish tradition, as Lilith fled from Adam she pronounced the ineff-

INGRAM (m)

Ger. <u>engel</u> – 'Angle' + <u>hramn</u> – raven. <u>Engelram</u> was a Norman name. The name may also relate to the old Norse fertility god, <u>Ing</u>; meaning 'Ing's raven'. Ing was another name for Frey, the god of peace and fertility. The Angles regarded Ing as their ancestor and the name was popular throughout the Middle Ages.

Bright RAVEN

BERTRAM (m)

Ger. <u>beorht</u> – bright, shining + <u>hramn</u> – raven. The name BERTRAND means 'bright shield' but has come to be interchangeable with BERTRAM. The feast of St Bertram is on June 6th and is shared with Bertrand (see **BRIGHT** and **WISDOM**).

Chief RAVEN

CYNFRAN (m)

Wel. <u>cyn</u> – chief + <u>bran</u> – raven. The raven was considered by the Native Americans to be a spiritual messenger. In Celtic mythology it was an oracular bird and bringer of omens, though it had a rather dark and dubious power. Among the Tibetans the raven was also considered to be a bird of oracular power. A lama once told me how a raven which landed on his horse's ear, combined with a dream he had had the previous night, indicated a safe path for his party through the Chinese encampments. During his escape from Tibet in the late 1950s a mysterious mist descended, allowing the party to pass unseen.

SEAGULL

LARA (f)

Russ.

SONGTHRUSH

MAVIS (f)

This is an old dialect Old French (probably originally Breton) word which was not used as a name before the 19th century.

Like the STORK/HERON

CRANOG (m)

Wel. <u>garan</u> – stork/heron + adjectival suffix. St Cranog was a Welsh saint whose altar was said to have floated on the Severn.

SWALLOW

GWENNOL (f)

Wel. <u>gwennol</u> – swallow or martin.

BIRTH

NATALIE (f)
Lat. natalis dies – day of birth, often referring to and given to children born on Christmas Day.

NATALYA, NATASHA (f)
Russ. St Natalia was a 4th century Christian martyr, whose feast day is July 27th (see **FESTIVALS**).

BLESSED

AYMAN (m)
Arab. yamana – to be fortunate. Name of Muhammad's nanny – 'Um-Ayman' – the mother of Ayman. She was with the Prophet when his mother died at the age of six ,and Muhammad called her his 'second Mother'.

BARUCH (m)
Heb. from word meaning 'blessed'.

BEATA (f) Lat. beatus (m) – blessed

BEATRICE (f)
Italian and French form of Beatrix – bringer of joy and blessing (see **She who Makes HAPPY**).

BENEDICT (m)
Lat. benedictus – blessed. St Benedict (c. 480-550) founded the famous Benedictine Order of monks and established his simple, practical Rule. His feast day is March 21st. VENEDIKT is the Russian form of this name.

GWEN (f)
Wel. gwen – blessed. WYN was originally a byname for this name but is now an extremely popular Welsh name in its own right (see **WHITE** and **BEAUTIFUL**).

GWENDA (f)
Wel. from (g)wen – blessed etc. + da – good.

MUBARAK (m)
Arab. baraka – to bless, this also carries the idea of being showered with grace.

BLESSED LOVE

CARWYN (m)
Wel. A modern coinage, from car – love + (g)wyn – blessed, white, fair (see **LOVE, BELOVED**).

BLESSED MARY

GWENFAIR (f)
Wel. gwen – blessed + Mair – Mary.

BLESSED PEACE

HEDDWEN (m), HEDDWYN (f)
Wel. hedd – peace/tranquillity + (g)wyn – blessed.

BLESSED RECONCILIATION

GWENFREWI (f)
Wel. (g)wen – blessed + ffrew – reconciliation.

WINIFRED (f)

Anglicised form of Gwenfrewi; probably from OE. wynn – joy + frith – peace. Winifrid was a 7th century Welsh princess who was decapitated by Prince Caradoc for rejecting his advances. When her head was replaced on her body she miraculously returned to life and became a nun. The name developed an English form as her relics were moved to Shrewsbury in 1138. The well which is dedicated to her is associated with healings. Her feast day is November 3rd.

BLESSED RING

GWENDOLEN (f)

Wel. gwen – blessed (fair or white) + dolen – ring/bow. This is an ancient name and probably that of a moon goddess (see **WHITE**).

BLIND

CECIL (m), CECILY (f)

Lat. and Wel. This is the Medieval English form of the Roman family name, Caecilius, from caecus – blind. Also, more recently, it is the Welsh surname, Seissyllt, used as a first name, from the old Welsh form of the Latin name Sextilius – the sixth. St Cecil was a 3rd century saint and his feast day is February 1st. After the Reformation CICELY was a name used to indicate a milkmaid.

CECILIA (f)

'Caecilia' was the Latin name for a slow-worm, which is considered to be blind. Others of the Roman clan Caecilius said that they were descended from Caecas, the companion of Aeneas, and others that they were descended from the son of Vulcan, Caeculus, who was said to have derived his name from caleo – heat

(Vulcan was the blacksmith of the gods who had his forge in a volcano) – because they did not want to foster the slow-worm association! Saint Cecilia is the patron saint of music and musicians, who sang hymns as she was being martyred. Two hundred years after her death her body was exhumed and found to be incorrupt. Her body was placed in a church built over the site of her own house. In 1599 the tomb was opened again and a statue was made imitating the lovely, easy, graceful position in which her limbs still remained. She is credited with inventing the organ. Her feast day is November 22nd.

SHEILA (f)

Anglicised form of Ir. Gael. Sile (original Irish form of Cecilia) or Shelagh.

BLISS

HANA (f)

Arab. bliss/happiness/well-being, from hani'a – to take pleasure in/be delighted.

GWYNETH (f)

Wel. bliss or happiness (see **HAPPY**)

Great BLISS

ENDDWYN (f)

Wel. intensifying prefix en + dwyn – bliss / pleasantness.

BLONDE

ELVIRA (f) Lat.

BLOOD STRENGTH

GWAEDNERTH (m)
Wel. gwaed – blood + nerth – strength.

Truly BOLD

ARCHIBALD (m)
Scottish name, from Norman French, originally Old German name Erkenbald, meaning excellent or very bold: ercan – genuine + bald – bold/brave. The name arrived in Britain with the Normans in the 12th century. It was used in the East Anglian royal family and was the name of a 7th century bishop of London. It now appears rather old-fashioned, aristocratic and even slightly ridiculous. When James VI of Scotland became James I of England, he brought a jester by the name of Archie Armstrong with him to London. The name has been a consistent favourite in Scotland. It was used to anglicise the Gaelic name Gilleasbuig (Gillespie), as bald was taken to mean 'hairless', or with shaven head, indicating a tonsured monk. The name Gilleasbuig means 'the shaven devotee of the bishop'. Gille – shaven was translated by bald and Arch was taken to mean archbishop! It was first adopted by the Campbell chiefs.

BOLD FRIEND

BALDWIN (m)
Norman name from Ger. bald – bold/brave + wine – friend. A common name in the Middle Ages, which gave rise to the surname. The saint's day is July 15th. (also see **FRIEND**)

BOUNTY PATTERN

CEDRYCH (m)
Wel: ced – bounty/boon + drych – spectacle/pattern.

BRAVE

CONRAD (m)
Ger. kuon – bold/brave + rad – counsel. St Conrad's feast day is February 19th.

BREATH

ABEL (m)
Heb. hevel – breath/vapour; originally implying worthlessness or transitoriness, presumably because Abel, in the Old Testament, was murdered when young by his jealous brother, Cain. This name may also derive from the Assyrian word aplu – son. Abel is considered a pre-Christian saint and is invoked in the Litany for the Dying. His feast day is December 2nd.

BREEZE

AWEL (f) Wel.

Mistress of the BRIDLE

CYRENE (f)
Gk. (see **ANIMALS** – Horse)

❋ BRIGHT ❋

The Old English word beorht meant 'bright' and also conveyed the idea of fame; it carries over today in several names containing the syllable bert, such as Bertha, Albert, and Robert (see **FAMOUS**).

BELI (m)
Wel. belos – bright. Belenos was a Celtic Sun-god.

BERTHA (f)
Ger. berhta – bright/illustrious. St Bertha's day is July 4th. She was the Germanic equivalent of the Roman goddess of grain – Ceres, and it was said that the wind and the clouds were under her direction (see **GODS & GODDESSES**).

CLARA (f), CLAIRE (f) Fr.
Lat. clarus – clear/bright/famous. St Clare (c. 1194-1253) was the companion of St Francis of Assisi and foundress of the Order of nuns called the Poor Clares. Her feast day is August 12th.

CLARENCE (m), CLARISSA (f)
(see **ILLUSTRIOUS**)

CUTHBERT (m)
OE. cuth – known + beorht – bright/famous. The name of two early English saints, one of whom was the 7th century bishop of Lindisfarne. This Cuthbert was a very saintly and kindly man who taught throughout northern England and showed equal love of people and nature. He was very popular and 72 churches were named after him. He was buried on Lindisfarne, but his grave had to be moved to Durham due to Viking raids. St Cuthbert's day is March 20th.

HELEN (f)
Gk. helios – the sun + elenos – 'the bright one'. This was the name of the famously beautiful wife of Menelaus who was seized by the Trojan prince, Paris, which started the Trojan Wars. Also the name of a famous saint, the mother of the Emperor Constantine, who is said to have found the true Cross in Jerusalem. Her feast day is August 18th.

EILIDH (f) Scot. Gael.

EIBHLIN (f) Ir.

EILEEN (f) Eng.

ELAINE (f)
Fr. (see **DISPUTED NAMES**).

YELENA (f) Russ. (see **LIGHT**)

NIAMH (f)
Ir. A princess of the otherworld Land of Promise.

PHOEBE (f)
Gk. from phoibos – pure/bright. This name means 'shining one' and was one of the names of the goddess Artemis, the sister of Phoebus Apollo. Of this name Sophy Moody wrote in the 19th century: 'As a Bible name PHOEBE is often heard in the cottages of our English poor, separated long since from all connection of ideas with the great goddess Diana of the Ephesians; its lovely meaning of *the light of life*, radiant and pure, may well be remembered by Christians, and laid to heart'[6] (see **MOON** and **SUN**).

BRIGHT CIRCLE

ELGAN (m) Wel.

BRIGHT GOD

OSBERT (m)
OE. (see **GOD** and **GODS & GODDESSES**).

BRIGHT LAND

LAMBERT (m)
OG. (see **LAND – BRIGHT**)

BRIGHT MIND

HUBERT (m)
Ger. hug – heart/mind/ spirit + berht – bright /
famous. This name was introduced to England by
the Normans among whom it was popular. St
Hubert was an 8th century bishop of Maastricht
and is the patron saint of hunters, because he is
supposed to have seen a vision of Christ crucified
between the antlers of a stag. In paintings he is
represented with a stag as his emblem. His feast
day is November 3rd.

BRIGHTNESS

AEGLE (f)
Gk. aigle – brightness/splendour. The name of
various Greek mythological characters, for example a daughter of Jupiter, the 'king' of the
gods.

AGLAIA (f) Gk. (see **GRACES**)

AINE (f)
Ir. Traditional name of the Queen of the Fairies,

meaning brightness or radiance. Now it is also
interpreted as joy/praise (see **ALWAYS**).

DIYA (m)
Arab. da – to gleam, shine or glow.

SORCHA (f)
Ir. and Scot. Gael. from Old Celtic word
meaning 'brightness'.

BRIGHT POWER

BERTHOLD (m)
Ger. berht – bright/famous + wald – ruler.

BRIGHT SHIELD

BERTRAND (m) Ger.

BRIGHT SWORD

EGBERT (m)
OE. ecg – (edge of a) sword + beorht – bright.
This was the name of the first Wessex King of
all England who died in 839 and also the name
of two 8th century saints, including the famous
hermit Northumbrian saint. St Egbert's day is
April 24th.

BRIGHT WARRIOR

HUMBERT (m)
Ger. hun – warrior (or bearcub) + berht –
bright /famous. This name came to Britain with
the Normans (see **BEAR**).

✳ ✳ ✳ ✳ ✳

BUDDHA

SAN-GYE (m)

Tib. <u>sang</u> – purity + <u>gye</u> – vast/expanded. It is important to realise that the term 'Buddha' is not a name, but a *title*. Thus someone is a Buddha, from the Sanskrit root <u>budh</u> which means 'awake', in the sense of 'awakened', 'enlightened' or arrived at the state of the fullness of consciousness. The Sanskrit term <u>Buddha</u> is translated by the Tibetans as a being who has achieved a 'vast and expanded purity'. It may seem strange to us to name a child 'Buddha', but to the Tibetans this is to endow the child with the *qualities* of a Buddha – the greatest of blessings.

The BURNING ONE

SERAPHINA (f)

Lat. from Heb. <u>seraphim</u> – 'burning ones' or 'noble'. This was the name of an order of angels seen by Isaiah in a vision. They had six wings – two to cover the face, two covering the feet and two with which they flew. Ezekiel struggled to express the quality of the <u>Seraphim</u> by comparing them to amber, glowing embers and the intense fervour of their love (see **ANGEL** and **FIRE**). It was also the name of a 5th century saint whose feast day is July 29th.

SERAFIMA (f) Russ.

CALM

ALCYONE (f)
Gk. The daughter of Aeolus, who was changed into a kingfisher.

GALEN (m)
Gk. – galene – calm/serene. Claudius Galenus (c 130-200) was a Graeco-Roman medical writer. Jalinus az-zaman was a nickname, meaning 'the Galen of the Age', given by a ruler to a great physician (see **HEALER**).

SERENA (f)
Lat. serenus – calm, serene. The name of an early Christian saint whose feast day is August 16th.

CAREFREE

NAIM (m), NAIMA (f)
Arab. na'ima – to live in comfort/be carefree. Implies contentedness and tranquillity.

CAREFULNESS

PRYDERI (m)
Wel. pryderi – care/carefulness.

CELTIC

WALLACE (m)
A name used by the Normans, meaning 'foreign' (from 'of Waleis') and indicating members of the minority Celtic races. It was originally a surname which has become a personal name.

CHAMPION

NOLAN (m)
From the Irish surname O' Nuallain – descendant of Nuallan. This is an old Gaelic personal name which may be a diminutive nickname form from nuall – chariot-fighter or champion.

CHARIOTEER

CARBRY (m)
Manx name, from Old Irish cairbre – charioteer.

CHARITY

CHARITY (f)
Lat. from caritas, from Gk. – Charis – the name of one of the Three Graces. Their original names – Bloom, Mirth, and Brightness became translated into the Christian 'virtues' of Faith, Hope and Charity! (see **GRACES**)

CHERRY (f)
A contraction of Charity, which occurred after the Reformation, or anglicised spelling of cherie (Fr.) – darling. The feast day is August 1st. This name has been said to indicate the bearer has a good education.

CHERYL (f)
Eng. coined in 1920s (from a cross between
<u>Cherry</u> and <u>Beryl</u>?) and common in 1940s.

CHARMING

FATIN (f)
Arab. <u>fatana</u> – to enamour or enchant. This name
is a modern coinage.

CHARMS

MAHASIN (f)
Arab. charms and good qualities, from <u>hasuna</u> –
to be good and beautiful.

CHEERFUL

HILARY (f)
Lat. <u>hilaris</u> – cheerful (N.B. modern words
'hilarity/hilarious'). Formerly, this was exclusively a man's name. St Hilarius of Poitiers, who
died in 368, was an opponent of Arianism, a
'heresy' which was condemned at the Council
of Nicaea, and he became known as Athanasius
of the West. His feast day is January 14th and,
in the Catholic Church, he is sometimes invoked against snake bites! He lends his name to
the <u>Hilary</u> Term (winter/spring) of the Law
Courts and some universities.

SEIRIOL (f/m)
Wel. <u>siriol</u> – cheerful/bright (see **HAPPY** and
BRIGHT).

CHEERFULNESS

EUPHROSYNE (f)
Gk. cheerfulness, mirth, festivity. The name of one
of the Three Graces. In 1884 Charlotte M. Yonge
wrote in her *History of Christian Names* [7] that
she had seen this name embroidered on a Greek
child's school sampler, and that a common short
form of this name was <u>Phroso</u> (see **GRACES**).

✳ CHIEF ✳

(Having the quality of a) **CHIEF-HERO**

CYNWRIG (m)
Wel. <u>cyn</u> – chief + <u>(g)wr</u> – man/hero + suffix of
quality.

CYNYR (m) Wel. <u>cyn</u> – chief + <u>(g)wr</u> – hero

CHIEF-LIKE

CYNHAFAL (m)
Wel. <u>cyn</u> – chief + <u>hafal</u> – like or equal to. There is
a holy well dedicated to a 7th century St Cynhafal.

CYNOG (m)
Wel. <u>cyn</u> – chief + adjectival suffix.

CHIEF MONARCH

CYNDEYRN (m)
Wel. <u>cyn</u> – chief + <u>teyrn</u> – monarch/ kingdom.
St Cyndeyrn founded the Welsh episcopal see of
Llandwy and then returned to become the
patron saint of his own see of Glasgow, where
he is known as <u>Kentigern</u> or <u>Mungo</u>.

CHIEF SEA

CYNFOR (m)
Wel. <u>cyn</u> – chief + <u>mor</u> – sea (or, possibly, <u>mawr</u>
– great) (see **SEA**).

CHIEF SNAKE

CYNIDR (m)
Wel. <u>cyn</u> – chief + <u>neidr</u> – snake/serpent (see **ANIMALS**).

Horse CHIEF

CYNFARCH (m)
Wel. <u>cyn</u> – chief + <u>march</u> – horse (see **ANIMALS**).

Iron CHIEF

CYNFAEL (m)
Wel. <u>cyn</u> – chief + <u>mael</u> – iron/metal.

Magnificent CHIEF

MEREDITH/MEREDYDD (m)
Wel. <u>mawredd</u> – greatness/magnificence + <u>iudd</u> – chief. MEREDITH is the anglicised version.

Offshoot of a CHIEF

CYNFRIG (m)
Wel. <u>cyn</u> – chief + <u>brig</u> – offshoot or scion.

Son of a CHIEF

CYNGEN (m)
Wel. <u>cyn</u> – chief + Lat. <u>geni</u> – born, son of.

✳ ✳ ✳ ✳ ✳

CHOSEN

MUSTAFA (m)
Arab. <u>safa</u> – to be pure/select. This is one of the most popular Islamic names. 'Al-Mustafa' is an epithet of Muhammad.

✳ CHRIST ✳

Bearer of CHRIST

CHRISTOPHER (m)
Gk. <u>Khristos</u> – Christ + <u>pherein</u> – to bear. A metaphor for one who carries Christ in his heart, based on the legend of a giant who was in search of the strongest master and who bore the young Christ over a stream on his shoulders, and so became a saint. (There was also a real martyr of that name). The mere sight of his image was said

to afford protection from fire, sickness, earthquake and flood for the rest of the day! Huge statues of the saint were carved and painted outside churches and houses in Italy, Spain and

Germany. He is the patron saint of travellers, and, these days, also of truck drivers, and his feast day is July 25th.

CHRISTIAN

CHRISTIAN (m), CHRISTINE (f)

Lat. <u>Christianus</u> – follower of Christ; from Gk. <u>chrio</u> – to touch, rub, anoint (note the word <u>chrism</u> – holy oil, which is still in use). The title Christ comes from the Gk, <u>Khristos</u> which is a translation of the Hebrew term <u>Messiah</u> meaning 'anointed'. The feminine, Christine, is a form of <u>Christina</u> and not much used until the 19th century. St Christina was a Roman patrician virgin and the first to be baptised, after Jesus himself. People tried to martyr her by throwing her into a lake with a millstone around her neck, but the deadly weight was supported by angels and she floated. Finally she was shot to death with arrows. She is the patroness of the Venetian states and her feast day is July 4th.

CHRISTABEL (f)

A literary coinage by Samuel Taylor Coleridge (1772-1834) in his poem of that name.

✳ ✳ ✳ ✳ ✳

CIRCLE

RHODRI (m)

Wel. <u>rhod</u> – circle, disc, orb. It may refer to a coronet or finger-ring, and is probably a symbol of loyalty (<u>rhi</u> – ruler). It is an ancient name which has been latinised and equated with <u>Roderick</u> though there is probably no connection.

CLEARER / BRIGHTER

ANWAR (m)

Arab. name of famous Egyptian President, Anwar-al-Sadat (1970-81) and Nobel Prize Winner (see **BRIGHT, FAMOUS**).

CLEARING (in a wood or stony field)

STANLEY (m)

OE. from a surname made up of <u>stan</u> – stone + <u>leah</u> – wood or clearing. The surname is that of one of the oldest English aristocratic families, dating back to the Norman Conquest. It is the family name of the earls of Derby who were once kings of the Isle of Man.

COLOURS

AUBURN

AUBURN (f)

One of the rarer colour names.

AZURE (see **SKYLIKE**)

BLACK

KERRON (m)

Manx, from Ir. <u>ciar</u> – black.

MELANIE (f)

Gk. <u>melas</u> – black, dark-complexioned. From Greek name <u>Melania</u> who was named after the Greek winter goddess, an altered form of Demeter, dressed in mourning black for her lost daughter, Persephone, who had been taken to

Hades. Interestingly, St Melanie's feast day is in the middle of winter, on New Year's Eve, December 31st.

MELONY (f) Old Cornish

NIGEL (m)

Lat. nigellus – a dimutive of niger – black. It was recorded in the Middle Ages but was not in common everyday use until revived by 19th century antiquarians.

BLACK WATER

DOUGLAS (m)

Gael. dubh – black + glas – stream.

BROWN

BRUNO (m)

Ger. from Old German brun – brown, i.e. 'with brown hair'. The feast of St Bruno is October 6th.

BROWN WARRIOR

DUNCAN (m)

Gael. implying brown (or possibly black)-haired warrior (see **ARMY** and **BATTLE**).

FLAME-COLOUR

EIROS (m)

Wel. eiros – bright/flame colour (see **FIRE**).

GREEN

ORAN (m)

Ir. diminutive of odhar – green or 'dun'. May refer to a sallow complexion. The name of several

Irish saints, including a famous 6th century Abbot of Meath who went to Scotland with St Columba.

GREY BATTLE-MAIDEN

GRISELDA (f)

Scot. and Eng. Probably not a name you would want to give your daughter! From Ger. gris – grey + hild – battle. Chaucer (in 'The Clerk's Tale') who got the story from Boccaccio (who took it from Petrarch) told the tale of 'patient' Griselda. The name became popular in the Middle Ages, as the model of a patient and long-suffering wife. She actually put up with outrageous testing, humiliation and abuse from her husband, who put their daughter out with foster parents, informing his wife that she was dead, then, when the girl was grown up, re-introduced her into the house, telling Griselda that he was going to divorce her in favour of this young woman. When Griselda made no complaint, her husband finally informed her of the truth and congratulated her on her steadfast patience! Though it has been cited as a popular name in Scotland, in fact it has hardly been used since 1858. It has appeared in various forms, such as GRIZEL. The short form ZELDA is more fashionable and was the name of F. Scott Fitzgerald's wife.

GREY-HAIRED

LLOYD (m)

Wel. from a Welsh surname which was originally a nickname. The Welsh spelling is Llwyd and the meaning includes a range of colours, including browns as well as greys.

COLOURS

COLOURS

GOLDEN

ANEURIN (m)
Wel. modern spelling of old Welsh name Aneirin, which may come from Lat. Honorius or from an old Welsh root, meaning 'little one of pure gold'. The initial 'A' was only added to the name, which was originally Neirin, in the 13th century. This was the name of the first known Welsh poet.

AURELIA (f)
Lat. family name – Aurelius, from aureus – golden. Charlotte Yonge said that this is the old name for a chrysalis, because of the golden spots on the butterfly casing. This was the name of the mother of Julius Caesar. There are a number of variations. ORLA is the Irish equivalent (see below).

AURIEL (f)
Lat. feminine dimin. of aureus – golden.

EURLIW (f)
Wel. eur – gold + lliw – colour

ORIANA (f)
From Old French or, from Lat. aurum (also see **MORNING SUN**).

GOLDEN LADY

ORLA (f)
Ir. from Orfhlaith; or – gold + flaith – lady / princess.

GOLDEN LINK

AURDDOLEN (f) Wel.

GOLD-FAIR

EURWEN (f) Wel. eur – gold + (g)wen – fair.

GOLD-SWEET

EIRLYS (f) Wel. aur – gold + llys – sweet.

RED

FLANNAN (m)
Ir. diminutive of FLANN (lit. 'blood-red' and implying 'ruddy'), which is still in use today. Flann O'Brien (pen name of Brian O'Nolan) was a well-known Irish writer who died in 1966. St Flannan is the patron saint of a diocese in Co. Clare whose feast day is December 18th.

RORY (m), ROY (m)
Gael. Ruairidh from ruadh – red. Rory is the modern form of Ruairi (Irish) – the name of the last High King of Ireland. ROY is the anglicised version of this name, and Roger and Roderick are sometimes used to anglicise these names (see **FAME**).

ROWAN (m) Ir. 'little red one' (see **TREES**).

RUFUS (m)
Lat. from a nickname meaning 'red-(haired)'.

RUSSELL (m)
Fr. Old French equivalent of Rufus (from roux – red). RUSS was originally a short form of this name, but is now a name in its own right.

RED EARTH

ADAM (m), ADAMINA (f)

Heb. adamah – red earth (and also, possibly, complexion). The name of the first man in the Judaeo-Christian tradition; created by God from earth into which He breathed life. Adam was also the first man to practise the art of naming, for this was the first task given him by God – to name all the animals and plants which had been given into his care. The four letters of his name were considered to have talismanic power – representing each of the four directions of the earth from which God had fashioned him: A stood for the east – Anatolia, D for the west – Dysis, A for the north – Arctos and M for Mesembria in the south. According to an old custom, the letters of the name A.D.A.M. were written on the four corners of pigeon houses to protect from attack by reptiles! The feminine, Adamina is an 18th century Scottish invention. Adamnan is an Irish version of this name which means 'little Adam'. This was the name of an important 6th century Irish saint, who became abbot of Iona and was the biographer of St Columba and a friend of the Venerable Bede (see **DOVE** and **PRAYER**). He is also known for making the first recorded sighting of the Loch Ness Monster!

SCARLET

ALLA (f)

Russ. derived from diminutive of Alienka – scarlet.

SILVER

EIRIAN (f)

Wel. arian – silver (see also **GOLD**)

SILVER DISC

ARIANRHOD (f)

Wel. arian – silver + rhod – circle, disc. A legendary heroine and a dawn or moon goddess, related to Venus, as an esteemed paragon of beauty. In Celtic tradition she is the mistress of the Spiral Tower – a place of initiation in the Otherworld. She is the goddess of destiny who carries her symbol of the silver wheel and wears silvery robes. She is the Muse of inspiration and divination (see **MOON**).

SILVER WHITE

ARIANWEN (f)

VIOLET

VIOLA (f) (see **FLOWERS**)

WHITE

ALBAN (m), ALBINIA (f)

Lat. Albanus – of Alba, a town on a 'white hill'. This was the capital city of the earliest Roman kings. St Alban was the first Christian to be martyred on British soil at the place now known as St. Alban's where a Benedictine Abbey was built in his memory. His feast day is June 22nd. Alba was an ancient name for Scottish highlands (Cel. alp) – this was extended to Albion which became the ancient name for the whole of Britain. ALPIN (m) is a Gaelic name.

BANAN (m) Ir.

BIANCA (f)

Ital. bianca – white, pure. Shakespeare gave this name to two of his characters.

COLOURS

BLANCHE (f)

Fr. originally this was a nickname for a woman with blonde hair.

CANDIDA (f)

Lat. 'glowing white'. This name was associated by early Christians with purity and salvation. The word 'candid' originally meant 'unblemished' and the word 'candidate' derives from the white robes worn by Roman politicians when standing for office. This name was given to Roman girls and was the name of several early saints, one of whom was healed by St Peter. St Candida's day is June 6th. The name was revived by Bernard Shaw for his play Candida in 1897. The recent bad press given to the candida albicans (usually referred to as 'candida') which is the most common agent for the fungal infection candidiasis, will probably discourage the use of this name for some time to come.

FIONA (f)

Gael. fionn – white/fair. This name was adopted in the 19th century by the Irish romantic writer, William Sharp, for a pen-name – Fiona Macleod, under which pseudonym he wrote a number of 'Celtic' books. So although associated with Scotland and fairly popular in that country, it is not really a Scottish name.

LABAN (m)

Heb. It has been suggested that this may have been a name given to an albino child as, when named as a baby, it would not have been possible to name the child according to blonde hair or beard.

WHITE BREAST

BRONWEN (f)

Wel. bron – breast + (g)wen – white/fair/ blessed. It could be interpreted as 'fair-bosomed'. The Welsh legendary daughter of the sea-god (see **GODS & GODDESSES**).

WHITE BROW

ELWYN (m) Wel.

WHITE FIRE

AODHFIN (m)

Ir. an early name from Aodhfionn (see **FIRE**).

WHITE SHOULDER

FENELLA (f)

Ir. Fionnghala – fionn fair or white + guala – shoulder. This ancient Irish name was in common use until the end of the 17th century. Now sometimes shortened to Nuala. Sir Walter Scott used the name FENELLA in 1823 for a character in 'Peveril of the Peak' which led to the name being considered Scottish. Finela or Finola are the more usual Irish forms, which were sometimes anglicised as Penelope.

WHITE SNOW

EIRWEN (f) Wel. (see **SNOW**)

WHITE and FLAXEN

GWENLLIAN (f)

Wel. (g)wen – white/fair + llaian – flaxen.

COLOURS

Indicating perhaps a pale skin and blonde hair (see **FLAX – FLOWERS** and **LINEN**).

WHITE and SOFT

GAYNOR (f)
Eng. medieval form of Guinevere (see below).

WHITE TRACK

OLWEN (f)
Wel. ol – track or footprint + (g)wen – white, blessed etc. A Welsh legendary woman in whose departing tracks flowers sprang up wherever she went. The following description of how Olwen came to be so named is from the Mabinogion:

The maiden was clothed in a robe of flame-coloured silk, and about her neck was a collar of ruddy gold on which were precious emeralds and rubies. More yellow was her head than the flower of the broom, and her skin was whiter than the foam of the wave, and fairer were her hands and fingers than the blossoms of the wood anemone amidst the spray of the meadow fountain. The eye of the trained hawk, the glance of the three-mewed falcon, was not brighter than hers. Her bosom was more snowy than the breast of the white swan, her cheek was redder than the reddest roses. Whoso beheld her was filled with her love. Four white trefoils sprang up wherever she trod, and therefore was she called Olwen.

YELLOW

AMBER (f) (see **JEWELS**)

FLAVIA (f)
Lat. flavus – yellow/yellow haired/golden. Flavius was an old Roman family name. The name of several early saints. The feast of St Flavia is May 7th. Flavius is one of the masculine forms of this name, which are no longer in use.

XANTHE (f)
Gk. xanthos – yellow. Referring to a fair-haired or complexioned child.

YELLOW-HAIR

BOYD (m)
Gael. a surname from the nickname Buidhe – yellow, (i.e. blond-haired). Sometimes used as a first name.

Servant of St COLUMBA

MALCOLM (m)
Gael. mael – devotee / disciple / 'shaveling' + coluim – Columba. St Columba founded the Iona Monastery in 563, which became the centre of Celtic Christianity. His feast day is June 3rd (see **DOVE**).

COMELY

KEVIN (m)
Ir. Caoimhin, from caomh – comely/mild; 'handsome at birth'. This was the name of fifteen Irish saints. St Kevin, who died c. 618, founded a monastery at Glendalough, famous for its beautiful location and the quality of its learning. He is one of the patron saints of Dublin. His feast day is June 3rd. Sometimes this name was

Latinised and translated as <u>Pulcherius</u> (beautiful). This name usually indicated that the bearer was Irish, until the 1940s when it was adopted into more general use (see **HANDSOME**).

COMPASSION

'ATIF (m) Arab. from '<u>atafa</u> – to sympathise.

COMPENSATION

SETH (m)
Heb. The name is interpreted as 'compensation' or 'substitute', as it was given to a son of Adam and Eve born after the death of Abel. It has also been interpreted to mean 'appointed' or 'placed', but others say it means 'a cutting' – from the original seed. In Scotland, the name is sometimes used as an anglicised form of <u>Seaghdh</u>. The saint's day is March 1st.

CONFIDANTE

SAFIYYA (f)
Arab. <u>safa</u> – to be pure or select. It has the meaning of a closest friend or the best part of something.

CONQUEROR (see **VICTOR**)

CONSOLATION

SALWA (f) Arab. <u>sala</u> – to comfort or distract.

Son of CONSOLATION

BARNABAS (m)
Gk. from Aramaic word meaning 'son of consolation' or 'son of exhortation'. The name of the travelling companion of St Paul, whose feast day is June 11th. He is described in the Acts of the Apostles (XI.24) as 'a good man, full of the Holy Ghost and of faith'. The English variant, <u>Barnaby</u> is from a mediaeval vernacular form.

CONSTANT

CONSTANCE (f)
CONSTANTINE (m)
From Lat. <u>constans</u> – constant or steadfast. One of the Christian virtues. Constantine was the first Christian Emperor of Rome. Charlotte Yonge said that the Celtic peoples readily adopted this name as they loved to prefix names with <u>con</u> – wisdom or <u>cu</u> – hound. The mediaeval name <u>Constant</u> was revived by the Puritans. St Constantine's day is July 27th and September 19th is dedicated to St Constance.

CONTENTMENT

RIDA (m/f)
Arab. <u>radiya</u> – to be content. Implies satisfaction and the approval of God.

CONTRARY BIRTH

ANTIGONE (f)
Gk. <u>anti</u> – against/contrary + <u>gen/gon</u> – born. A difficult name to fit into a correct meaning. It is a pity that such a beautifully melodic name in English has such an unfortunate meaning in Greek. This mirrors the arduous and tragic life of the classical heroine who bore this name. It has come to be associated with strength and integrity. ANTIGONE was the daughter of the incestuous marriage of Oedipus and his mother Jocasta. After her father was blinded and disgraced, Antigone tended him as he wandered as

an outcast through Greece. Then her brothers killed each other, and, in defiance of her uncle's orders, she administered funeral rites to them. In 'punishment', her uncle had her buried alive (see **BIRTH**).

COUNSEL-PEACE

RENFRED (m)
OG. regin – advice, decision, might or counsel + frithu – peace. The name came to England with the Normans. Remfry (m) is the Cornish version (see **PEACE**).

COUNSEL-WARRIOR

RAYNER (m)
Eng. Norman origin, from Germanic ragin – advice, decision, counsel + heri/hari – army or warrior. The name implies 'wise warrior' (see **ARMY, WARRIOR**).

CREATION

GENESIUS (m)
Gk. genesis – creation, generation. The name of two Roman saints and martyrs: Genesius the Actor was converted to Christianity whilst in the middle of doing a satirical stunt which mocked Baptism. He is the patron saint of actors and his feast day is August 25th. The second was a clerk, Genesius of Arles, who refused to write down an imperial edict against Christians.

CROWN

ATARAH (f)
Heb. Old Testament wife of Jerahmeel.

STEPHEN (m)
Gk. stephanos – crown/garland. He was the first Christian martyr and his feast day is December 26th. In the famous Christmas Carol, Good King Wenceslas of Bohemia looked out and saw the poor man in the snow on this date. Wenceslas also means 'crown-glory'. St Stephen is the patron saint of stonesetters and bricklayers.

CUP-BEARER

HEILYN (m)
Wel. heilyn – old word for cup-bearer (see also **YOUTH**).

CURLY

CRISPIN (m)
Lat. from a Roman family name – Crispus – curly haired (note the modern word 'crisp'). St Crispin is the patron saint of shoemakers and leatherworkers, as he went with his brother, St Quentin, to France to preach the gospel. They lived in Soissons and supported themselves as shoemakers. 'Un crispin' was the French name for a shoemaker's last. He was martyred with his brother c. 285. His feast day is October 25th. This is the same date as the Battle of Agincourt (as mentioned in Shakespeare's famous speech in Henry V) and was a universal holiday.

DAINTINESS/delicacy

TRYPHENA (f)
Gk. popular name in 16th and 17th centuries, and source of the gypsy name <u>Truffeni.</u>

DAIRYMAN

MEIRION (m)
Wel. <u>meirion</u> – dairyman. Associated with pleasant pasture land.

DAMSEL

LODES (f) Wel. <u>lodes</u> – damsel/maiden.

DARKLY BEAUTIFUL

BRANWEN (f)
Wel. <u>bran</u> – raven + <u>(g)wen</u> – beautiful. 'Raven' here is figuratively used to indicate very dark (see **BEAUTIFUL** and **BIRDS**).

DARK STONE

DUNSTAN (m)
OE. <u>dun</u> – dark + <u>stan</u> – stone. This name is sometimes rendered as 'dark hill'. The name of a very famous 10th century saint who was Archbishop of Canterbury. He was an adviser to kings, instigated the revival of monasticism and designed the coronation service which is still used in England to this day. His feast day is July 11th.

Little DARK ONE

KIERAN (m)
Ir. an Irish bishop and hermit, who may have pre-dated St Patrick and also the name of another saint who founded the monastery of Clonmacnoise. His feast day is September 9th (see also **COLOURS**).

DARK STRANGER

DOUGAL (m)
Gael. name applied by the Irish to the invading Danes; comparable to the nicknames 'Paddy' (for an Irishman) and 'Taffy' (for a Welshman) today.

DAWN

AURORA (f)
Lat. 'dawn', and the name of the Roman goddess of the dawn.

ROXANA (f) from Pers. <u>Roschana.</u>

SAHAR (f) Arab. in the early morning.

DEAR

ANWYL (f) Wel.

CARA (f)
Eng. 20th century coinage from Ital. <u>cara</u> – dear / beloved, and Irish vocabulary word for 'friend' (see **BELOVED, CHARITY**).

CHÈRE (f) Fr.

DAYS OF THE WEEK

Egyptian astrologers were the first to distinguish the days of the week by giving them names. Many cultures name the days after the planets and the gods and goddesses who rule them.

Most of our weekday names derive from the names of Scandinavian gods:

Sunday   – Sun
Monday   – Moon
Tuesday   – Tiw, the god of war
Wednesday – Odin or Wodin, the god of magic, inventor of the arts
Thursday   – Thor, son of Odin, god of thunder
Friday   – Frigga, wife of Odin
Saturday   – Saturn

It is fairly common in some cultures to name children after the days of the week on which they are born. Here are a few such names:

SUNDAY

NYIMA (m/f) Tib. nyi-ma – the sun

MONDAY

DAWA (m/f) Tib. dawa – moon

TUESDAY

MIGMAR (m/f)
Tib. mig-mar – lit. 'red eyes' – from Mars, the planet of war.

WEDNESDAY

LHAKPA-BU-TI (f)
Tib. Lhakpa – Mercury. Lit. 'one who will bring the son'. This name was sometimes given to Tibetan female children. The same disappointment and hope of parents was expressed in the Puritan name (given to a little girl in 1646, by parents wanting a son) of Hopestill.

THURSDAY

KHAMIS (m), KHEMISSE (f) Arab.

PHURBU (m/f)
Tib. from the Sanskrit god, Brihaspati, the equivalent of Jupiter and Thor.

FRIDAY

ADINA (f)
Pers. (and see **DISPUTED NAMES**)

JUM'A Arab.

PASANG (m/f) Tib.

SATURDAY

PENBA (m/f) Tib.

SABBATI (f)
SEBTI (m) Arab. (see **MONTHS**)

DECISION-Strong

REYNARD (m)

OG. This name came to England with the Normans, from ragin – advice, decision + hard – hardy, brave, strong. The French word renard – fox is derived from this word (see **COUNSEL** for wider sense of the Old German word ragin, and also see **MIGHTY**).

DECISIVE

HASIM (m)

Arab. hasama – to decide / separate / cut off / distinguish. The ability to distinguish clearly and quickly between right and wrong is a much-prized Muslim quality.

DEFENDER (or Protector) of MEN

ALEXANDER (m), ALEXANDRA (f)

Gk. from Alexandros; alexein – to defend + aner – of men/warriors. This name was probably first coined in the feminine as a title for Hera, the consort of Zeus, the father of the gods. The name may even derive from a more ancient Hittite name – a clay tablet dated 1300 B.C. bears the name King Alaxandus. Alexander was the name of several very famous historical personages. Alexander the Great, famous throughout the world in 340 B.C. gave his name to Alexandria in Egypt. There is a story that all children who were born in the year of his conquest of India were named after him. It was also the name of several saints and martyrs and eight popes. The saint's day is February 26th. This is also a favourite name in Scotland. ALEXANDRA was one of the first two recorded European girls' names, discovered in Mycenae in 1948.

ALASDAIR (m) Scot.
ALISTAIR (m) Eng. spelling

ALEKSANDR, ALEXEI, ALEXIS, SACHA (m)

Russ. St Alexius was a 5th century popular Greek Orthodox and Catholic saint, whose feast day is July 17th.

There are many other variations of this name and it was a title given to the Greek hero, Paris, for his skill in repelling robbers from the flock. It was the favourite name for the kings of Macedon.

DELIGHT

ADINA (f) Heb. (see **JOY** and **DISPUTED NAMES**)

DELICIA (f) Lat.

LAETITIA (f)

Lat. LETTICE is the Middle English form of this name.

THIRZA (f)

Heb. Tirzah, also possibly means 'acceptance'.

My DELIGHT IS IN HER

HEPHZIBAH (f) Heb.

Of St DENIS

SIDNEY (m and occasionally f)

This was a Norman baronial surname, transferred to a first name. One English branch of the name seems to have come from OE – 'wide meadow', from sidan – wide + eg – island-in-a-river or riverside meadow.

SIDONY (f)

This is the real female name behind the feminine use of Sidney. It comes from Lat. Sidonius, Sidonia – a person from Sidon in Phoenicia. Then it came to be associated with the Greek word sindon – winding sheet, and so was given to girls born on the feast day of the Holy Shroud (the 'sacred Sendon'). It was the name of two medieval saints. The female saint Sidonia is honoured on August 21st.

DESIRED

DESIRÉE (f)

Fr. but now commonly used in English-speaking countries. Given by early Christians to a longed-for child, in its Latin form Desiderata, but now given to indicate a desirable woman.

DEW

AVITAL (f)

This is a modern Jewish form of a biblical name; a wife of King David.

ERSA (f) Gk

NADYA (f)

Arab. nada – to be moist. Like rain, dew was a prized substance among desert peoples (see **RAIN**).

DEW DROP

GWLITHYN (f) Wel.

✱ The four DIRECTIONS ✱

NORTHMAN / WOMAN

NORMAN (m)

Ger. nord – North + man – man; i.e. a 'Norseman'.

NORMA (f)

Used as a feminine form of Norman, but it was apparently coined for Bellini's opera of this name (first performed in 1832). In Latin, the word norma means 'rule' and refers to the carpenter's 'square' or 'pattern' and therefore implies unrebellious, and peaceful – one who keeps to the 'norm', but there is no evidence that this is the origin of this name. In the Scottish Highlands NORA is also used as a feminine form of Norman.

EAST

ASIA (f)

This name implies 'of the East' and sunrise (see **DAWN, SUN**).

Man from the EAST

CADMUS (m)

Semitic name. The founder of Thebes and introducer of letters of the Greek alphabet (see also **SUNRISE**).

WEST WIND

ZEPHYRINE (f)

Zephyros was the Greek name for the west wind, possibly from zophos – darkness. St Zephyrinus was the name of one of the early popes.

✱ ✱ ✱ ✱ ✱

DISCRETION

PWYLL (m)
Wel. pwyll – discretion/prudence.

DISTINGUISHED

SHARIF (m), SHARIFA (f)
Arab. sharafa – to be high-bred or distinguished.

DIVINELY BEAUTIFUL
(see **BEAUTIFUL**)

DORIAN MAN

DORIAN (m)
Coined by Oscar Wilde in 1891 for his 'Picture of Dorian Gray', and probably derived from Lat. Dorianus from Gk. Dorieus – a member of the Dorian tribe (see below).

DORIAN WOMAN

DORIS (f)
Gk. The Dorians were one of the classical tribes of Greece, who gave their name to 'Doric archi-tecture' and whose name derived from Doros, which may have come from doron – gift. Doris was a goddess of the sea and mother of the fifty or more Nereids – sea-nymphs.

DREAM

AISLING (f)
Ir. Aisling – dream, vision or daydream.

AHLAM (f)
Arab. from Lalama – to dream. Implies dreams, visions, fantasies and perfection or a state of bliss.

DUDDA's CLEARING

DUDLEY (m)
Anglo-Saxon name, originally a place name and well-known family name.

DUSKY

GETHIN (m)
Wel. cethin – dusky/swarthy.

DWELLER at the triangular hill estate

GORDON (m)
Scot. & Eng. from a Scottish surname, used as a first name since the last century. It has been interpreted as 'spacious fort'.

EARNESTNESS

ERNEST (m), ERNESTINE (f)
Ger. originally from Old High German vocabulary word <u>eornost</u> – seriousness; implying the willingness to do battle to the death. The name has come to be associated with the adjective <u>earnest</u> and to indicate earnestness or vigour. The name was introduced into England in the 18th century with George I and the Hanoverian royal family.

✳ EARTH ✳

EARTH

EARTHA (f)

GAIA (f) Gk. the goddess of the Earth.

RHEA (f) Gk.

EARTH GODDESS

MODRON (f), MADRON (m)
Wel. from <u>Matrona</u> – matron, ancient Celtic Earth-goddess, who later became the triple deity of the <u>Matronae</u> (see **GODS & GODDESSES**).

EARTH-MOTHER

DEMETER (f)
Gk. <u>de</u> (or ge) – earth + <u>meter</u> – mother. The goddess of Earth and harvest, whose name meant either 'Earth-mother' or 'barley mother'.

DEMETRIOS (m)
Popular Gk. name and name of several saints in the Eastern church.

DMITRI (m)
Russ. from the Greek name <u>Demetrios</u>. The most famous St Demetrius was martyred in the 4th century and many legends have grown up around him.

EARTH WORKER

GEORGE (m)

Lat. Georgius, from Gk. <u>Georgios</u>, from <u>georgos</u> – a farmer (<u>ge</u> – earth + <u>ergein</u> -to work). In tradition, St George helped St Paul escape in a basket and was later put to death. The popular legend of the dragon-slaying saint is a medieval Italian invention. He was adopted by the Crusaders as their champion and no saint has had more chivalrous orders established in his name. The festival of St George is an example of Christianity overlaying a more ancient celebration with a Christian one, in an attempt to stamp out 'paganism' – in this case the festival of the Spring Equinox, when the sun moves from the astrological sign of Aries into that of Taurus. The symbology, therefore, of the heroic knight slaying and impregnating the waiting Earth with the dragon's blood and fiery breath relates to the need to introduce new warmth and life into the Earth for the reception and growth of new seed in the spring. St George is the patron saint of England (since the 14th century), though for a long time he was a more important saint in the Orthodox church than in the west, and he is often depicted in eastern icons. If he existed at all, he may have been martyred in Palestine during Diocletian's last persecutions of the Christians in the early 4th century. He is also the patron saint of Germany and Portugal and his feast day is April 23rd. He is remembered in the saying 'As bright as St George'.

GEORGI (m) Russ.

GEORGIA (f)

GEORGETTE (f) Fr.

GEORGINA (f)

Scot. originated in Scotland in 18th century.

YORICK (m)

The name of the famous dead jester in *Hamlet*. This is a version of the Danish form of <u>George</u>.

YURI (m) Russ.

✳ ✳ ✳ ✳ ✳

EASE

YASIR (m)

Arab. <u>yasira</u> – to make easy/facilitate. Implies a rich and easy life.

YUSRA (f)

Arab. <u>aysara</u> – to be or become rich or lucky.

ELEVATED

ALI (m)

Arab. '<u>ala</u> – to rise/ascend. The name means elevated, 'sublime', or the highest. <u>Al-'Ali'</u> – 'The Sublime', is one of the 99 Names of God (see p. 257). This was the name of Muhammad's cousin who was the first male convert to Islam and who married the Prophet's daughter, <u>Fatima</u>. After Muhammad's death he became the fourth Caliph to rule the Islamic world and his opposition to the Prophet's widow and followers led him to become the leader of a new Islamic group, now known as the <u>Shiite</u> Muslims who regard him as the only legitimate successor to Muhammad. He was assassinated in 661.

SAMI (m), SAMYA (f)
Arab. <u>sama</u> – to rise up high (see **HIGH**).

ELF

Man attacked by elves [9]

Be it Aesir* shot,
Or be it elf shot,
Or be it witch's shot,
Now will I help thee.

The Lacnunga [8]

* Aesir = small elf.

In Norse tradition the <u>alfar</u> was a benevolent nature spirit who assisted mankind. (In Old Norse the word for 'sound' was <u>dvergmal</u> – lit. 'dwarf-talk'. The Norse dwarves were mountain gnomes who answered shouts.) The word <u>alfar</u> derives from the Sanskrit <u>rbhu</u> which means 'skillful artist', referring to the three skilled spirits in Vedic myth. In Norse myth the most skillful of the smiths is the leader of the elves (see **SMITH**). In pre-Christian northern lands elves were associated with healing, as were smiths by the Celts. It was auspicious to have the favour of the elf kingdom on your side. This is the reason for the many Old English names which include the element <u>elf</u>: such names indicated wisdom, skill and authority and probably derived from Norse or were coined before the reputation of the elves degenerated! A common poetic phrase was 'aelf-sciene' – shining like an elf. To the Anglo-Saxons,

however, the elf was a troublesome and mischievous creature who was considered to cause many forms of illness, and who was adopted into Christian demonology as a relative of Cain, the rejected brother of Abel. 'If anybody has got elf-disease, his eyes are yellow where they should be red' said one Anglo-Saxon medical text. From 1864-66 the Rev. Oswald Cockayne translated many Anglo-Saxon medical manuscripts under the wonderful name of 'Leechdoms, Wortcunning and Starcraft of Early England'.

Here is a recipe for ELF-SALVE:

EALF WI AELFCYNNE
Make a salve against the race of elves and against spirits walking about at night and against women with whom the devil has sexual intercourse: hop, wormwood, bishop's wort, lupine, vervain, henbane, harewort, viper's bugloss, heathberry, leek, garlic, cleavers seed, cockle, fennel. Remember to boil it in butter and sheep's fat, say nine masses over it, strain it and fumigate the patient. (!)

ELF

ELF

AGAINST ELF-SHOT [10]

If a horse is elfshot, take that knife of which the handle is made from
the fallow horn of an ox, and let there be three brass nails on it.
Then inscribe a cross on the forehead of the horse,
so that blood flows from it; then inscribe a cross on the forehead
of the horse and on all limbs into which you can prick.
Then take the left ear and pierce it in silence.
This you shall do: take a rod, beat the horse on the back, then it is cured.
And write these words on the horn of the knife:
Benedicite omnia opera domini dominum.
Whatever elf has taken possession of it, this will cure him.

Elves were said to cause illness by discharging tiny projectiles into the body of their victim (a Middle Low German name for eye-disease is aelfschot) or by actually entering the body of their prey. The term <u>ylfig</u> referred to mental derangement and probably meant epilepsy. <u>Aelfthona</u> was the name given to a plant (possibly Solanum dulcamara or woody nightshade) which was said to cure elf disease.

ELF

ALLOW (m)
Manx. elf or fairy, common in 16th century.

GWION (m) Wel. <u>gwion</u> – elf.

ELF ARMY

ALVAR (m)
OE. <u>aelf</u> – elf + <u>here</u> – army. This name occurs in the Domesday Book and was revived in Britain in the 1940s.

ELF COUNSEL

ALBREDA (f) Ger.

ALFRED (m), ALFREDA (f),
ALVERDINE (f)
OE. <u>aelf</u> – elf + <u>raed</u> – counsel.

ALURIC (m) OE.

ELF FRIEND

ALVIN (m), ALVINA (f)
OE. <u>Aelfwine</u> – elf friend + <u>Aethelwine</u> – noble friend. These names combined to become <u>Alwine</u>. There are many variants, including ELVIN and ELVIS. As well as the famous rock and roll singer, <u>Elvis Aaron Presley</u> (1935-1977), this was also the name of a 6th century Irish saint whose feast day is on February 22nd.

ELF POWER

AUBREY (m)
From OG. Alberich into Old French and introduced to Britain from Normandy by the de Veres, Earls of Oxford. Ric implies ruling with elf-power.

ELF SPEAR

ALGAR (m) OE. Aelfgar – elf spear.

ELF STRENGTH

ELFREDA (f) OE.

ELOQUENT

ANARAWD (f) Wel.

EUPHEMIA (f)
Gk. This is a Latin form of a late Greek name, from eu – well, good + phenai – to speak. N.B. the English word 'euphemism'. The name of several early saints, notably one who was martyred in 307 AD. The legend tells she survived several attempts on her life, but was finally thrown to wild animals. Her feast day is March 20th. The name may also refer to the *absence* of speech – the stillness which is associated with spiritual power or religious rites. This name has been more popular in Scotland and the Gaelic form is Oighrig. Effie is one of the more common short forms (see **SWEET SPEECH** and also **FLOWERS – Lotus**).

EMBRACE

HABAKKUK (m)
Heb. name of minor Old Testament prophet and popular with the Puritans.

EMINENT

HYWEL (m)
Wel. hywel – conspicuous/eminent. Anglicised to Howell.

ENDURING

DANTE (m)
Ital. Durante – steadfast/enduring, from Lat. durare – to endure. This name was given as an honour to the mediaeval poet Dante Alighieri (1265-1321).

DURAND (m)
Lat. durare – to endure/last.

ENRAPTURED

TARUB (f)
Arab. tariba – to be moved with joy by music or to be delighted. The name implies merriness.

ENVY-FREE

DERMOT (m)
Ir. Diarmaid, from the Old Irish name Diarmait, composed of di -without + fharmait – envy; thus 'a freeman'. This is a very common name in Ireland and is the name of eleven saints, as well as the name of an Irish mythological figure. St Dermot's day is January 18th.

ESTEEMED

ESMÉE (f)

Fr. from old French verb <u>esmer</u> – to love and from Lat. <u>estimare</u> -to esteem. <u>Esmer</u> changed to <u>aimer</u> in modern French, but has survived in the English word <u>aim</u>, which originally meant to 'estimate or reckon'. In the 16th century it was introduced into Scotland as the male name, <u>Esme</u>.

EXALTED RULER

RHYDDERCH (m)

Wel. <u>rhi</u> – ruler + <u>dyrch</u> – exalted (see **RULER**).

EXCELLENCE

JETHRO (m)

Heb. Carries the meaning of pre-eminence and abundance and, in the Old Testament, was the name of the father of Moses' wife. It was possibly used as a title: <u>Ithra</u> – 'Excellence'.

EXCELLENT

SARAID (f)

Ir. <u>saraid</u> – excellent. This name has been anglicised as <u>Sarah</u> (see **PRINCESS**).

STERLING (m)

Eng. transferred use of surname, which may originally have been <u>Starling</u> (see **BIRDS**). Chosen as a first name because of its association with worth, as in the phrase 'sterling qualities'. It derives from a Middle English word <u>sterrling</u> – little star – some Norman coins had a star on them (see **STAR**).

May he EXPAND!

JAPHETH (m)

Heb. the name indicates extension or expansion and was given to Noah's son, one of the eight people to survive the Flood in the Ark.

EXPERIENCED

ENOCH (m)

Heb. biblical name of disputed meaning, which has been variously translated as 'experienced, skilled, trained, initiated'. He was the son of Cain and father of Methusaleh and was said to have lived 365 years, being then transported straight to heaven, without passing through death. It is possible that the stories about him actually relate back to a Babylonian sun-god. This name was popular with the Puritans.

EYE-CATCHING

RAN(Y)A (f)

Arab. <u>rana</u> – to gaze at or look at i.e. an eye-catching beauty.

EYES

MAHA (f)

Arab. this name actually means 'wild cow' but, rather than being an insult, the name refers to the large and beautiful eyes of that animal!

NAJLA (f)

Arab. this name also means having large and beautiful eyes.

FAIR

FINN (m) Ir. and Manx – fynn.

GWEN (f)
Wel. from (g)wyn – fair, white, blessed.

ISOLDE (f)
Wel. Esyllt – original form of name which probably meant 'of fair aspect'. The name of the tragic Arthurian heroine and lover of Tristran. She is a symbol of undying and unhappy love.

FAIR BROW

AELWYN (m) Wel.

FAIR HEAD

MOELWYN (m)
Wel. moel – head + (g)wyn – fair/white.

PENWYN (m)
Wel. pen – head + (g)wyn – fair.

FAIR LANCE

RHONWEN (f)
Wel. rhon – lance (or, maybe, rhawn – hair) + (g)wen – white, fair, blessed. The name carried the meaning of tall (like a lance) and beautiful. Medieval Welsh poets used this as a form of Rowena. Rowena was said to be the daughter of the Saxon invader, Hengist.

FAIR RING (or bow)

GWENDOLEN (f)
Wel. (g)wyn – fair + dolen – ring or bow. May have been the name of an ancient moon goddess, and was traditionally the name of Merlin's mother (see **MOON** and **WHITE**).

FAIR and GOOD

GWENDA (f)
Wel. a combination of (g)wen – fair + da – good. There are many, many Welsh names which begin with the word gwyn or gwen, meaning fair, white, blonde and also, secondarily, blessed – such as Gwynfor, a name coined in this century from gwen + mawr – great or large.

FAIR and YIELDING

GUINEVERE (f)
The French version of the Welsh name Gwenhwyfar; from (g)wen – white/fair/blessed + hwyfar – soft/smooth. The beautiful name of the beautiful wife of King Arthur who falls in love with Sir Lancelot and is unfaithful to her husband. This name first came to Britain via Cornwall in the Anglo-Norman form of Guenievre.

JENNIFER (f)
Corn. form of Guinevere (see above) which was not in wide use until the 1930s. This is the only Cornish name which has been widely adopted further afield, and the older spelling of Jenifer is still retained in Cornwall.

FAIR VALOUR

FINGAL (m)
Manx from Ir. This is what the ancient Irish called the Norwegians, because of their fair hair and complexion. It means 'fair valour', or 'fair stranger'.

FOND FAIR

EIDDWEN (f)
Wel. eiddun – desirous/fond + (g)wen – fair.

FAITH

FAITH (f)
Along with Hope and Charity one of the Christian virtues and a popular name with the Puritans.

FAY (f)
Eng. A late 19th century coinage and possibly from an archaic word for 'fairy' or from a short form of Faith. Associated with Morgan le Fay, King Arthur's sorceress half-sister.

IMAN (f)
Arab. amana – to believe (in God)

VERA (f)
Russ. vjera – faith, co-inciding with the Lat. fem. of verus – true.

FAITHFUL

AMNON (m)
Heb. mainly Jewish name and the name of King David's eldest son but has unhappy associations, because he raped and abandoned his half-sister, Tamar, and was killed by her brother, Absalom.

✳ FAME/FAMOUS ✳

Name and fame is a union which is indissoluble.

S. Moody[11]

The Old English word beorht, meaning 'bright' also carried the meaning of 'famous' – in other words, to be famous meant to be shining before other men. This forms the basis of many names (see **BRIGHT**).

FAME

CLYDAI (m) Wel. clod – fame.

FAME-BRIGHT

ROBERT (m), ROBERTA (f)
Ger. hrod – fame + berht – bright. Introduced into England by the Normans.

ROBIN (m/f), ROBINA (f)
This name started as French pet form of Robert, for which it is still a male diminutive in Scotland. In the U.S.A. Robin is a girl's name and is so used in England sometimes.

RUPERT (m)
Ger. name introduced into England by Prince Rupert of the Rhine, who was the nephew of Charles I and came to help in the Civil War.

FAME-DEVOURER

CLYDNO (m)
Wel. clod – fame/renown + cno – devourer.

FAME-RULER

CLYDRI (m)
Wel. clod – fame + rhi – ruler.

RODERICK (m)
Ger. hrod – fame + ric – ruler or power.

RURIK (m) Russ.

FAME-SPEAR

ROGER (m)
OG. hrothi – fame + ger – spear.

FAMOUS in Battle

ALOYSIUS (m)
Lit. 'famous warrior'. Most likely the Latinised form of a Provençal version of Louis. St. Aloysius Gonzaga, the patron saint of students, was a famous 16th century Spanish saint who was born in Italy and was originally called Luigi. His feast day is June 21st. German scholars attribute the name to Old High German Alwisi – 'the very wise'.

LEWIS (m)
Eng. version of Louis after introduction to Britain by the Normans.

LOUIS (m), LOUISA (f), LOUISE (f)
This name indicates a famous warrior and literally means 'hear fight'. Fr. from Ger. hlud – fame + wig – warrior, corresponding to the German name Ludwig. Popular with French royal families since the Middle Ages. The name was Latinised as Ludovicus then turned into Clovis by the Franks (modern feminine, Clova), the name

of the 5th century leader who regained Gaul from the Romans. He married a Burgundian princess and founded the Frankish monarchy, from which the modern word France derives. He was converted to Christianity in 496. The name later became Louis. Louis I was the son of Charlemagne and both king of France and Holy Roman Emperor. It was the name of sixteen kings of France, in particular Louis XIV, 'le Roi Soleil' (the Sun King) who reigned for 72 years.

(also see **BATTLE**)

FAMOUS in the LAND

ORLANDO (m)
Ital. form of ROLAND (see below), occasionally given in England

ROLAND (m)
From Ger. hrod – fame + land – land/territory. Introduced to Britain by the Normans; and the name of the famous Frankish hero of the Chanson de Roland.

FAMOUS in the NORTH

NORBERT (m)
Ger. nord – north + berht – bright. The name of an 11th century saint, whose feast day is June 6th, who founded an order of monks known as the Norbertians. This name was brought to England by the Normans (see **BRIGHT** and **DIRECTIONS**).

✳ ✳ ✳ ✳ ✳

FARMER (see EARTH WORKER)

FATHER OF ABUNDANCE

ABIATHAR (m)
Heb. biblical name (see **GOD**).

FATHERLY

PADARN (m)
Wel. from Lat. paternus – fatherly.

FATHER'S GLORY

CLEO (f) (see below).
More commonly used short form of Cleopatra

CLEOPATRA (f)
Gk. Kleopatra – kleos – glory + pater – father. This was a popular name in the Ptolemaic royal family of Egypt. Has come to be the model of a passionate woman of great beauty, due to the famous lover of Julius Caesar and Mark Antony.

FATHER of LIGHT

ABNER (m)
Heb. He was the cousin of King Saul. Another popular Puritan name.

FATHER of a MULTITUDE

ABRAHAM (m)
Heb. Although this name is of uncertain meaning, it is explained in the Bible as meaning av hamon (goyim) – 'father of a multitude' (of nations). The name of the first Patriarch. Popular among 17th century Puritans. In Hebrew the word abba means 'father'. Jesus referred to heaven as 'Abraham's bosom'.

FATHER of PEACE

ABSALOM (m)
Heb. The third son of King David (see **PEACE**).

'My FATHER REJOICES'

ABIGAIL (f)
Heb. the wife of king David. A popular Puritan name. In 17th century it became the name for a lady's maid in England after Beaumont and Fletcher gave the name to the character of a servant in their play *The Scornful Lady*. The wife of king David also referred to herself as his 'hand-maid'. Charlotte Yonge explained that it was also the name of a waiting lady of Queen Anne who exerted a 'backstair influence' over her.

GAIL (f)
Originally the short form of Abigail and now a name in its own right.

FATHER SKY

JUPITER (m)
Gk. the king of the Gods (see **GOD, GODS & GODDESSES, SKY**)

High FATHER

ABRAM (m)
Heb. This was Abraham's original name in the Bible, before it was changed by God.

FAVOUR

ANN(E) (f)
Traditionally the name of the mother of the Virgin

Mary. From Gk. <u>Anna</u>. St Anne is the patron saint of Prague and her feast day is July 26th.

HANNAH (f)
Heb. '(God) has favoured me'. The name of the mother of the prophet Samuel. Carries the other meaning of 'grace'.

NANCY (f)
Many popular foreign forms of this name exist, such as ANNETTE (Fr.), ANITA (Sp.) and ANUSHKA (Russ).

FEARLESS

JIGME (m) Tib. <u>jig-me</u> – without fear.

✳ FESTIVALS ✳

CHRISTMAS – (see BIRTH)

EASTER CHILD

PASCAL(m), PASCALE (f),
PASCOW (m) Corn.
(see **DAYS OF THE WEEK, MONTHS** and **SEASONS**)

EPIPHANY

THEOPHANIA (f)
Gk. lit. 'manifestation of God', i.e. when Jesus manifested himself to the Gentiles in the form of the Three Magi who came from the East to pay him homage and present their gifts of gold, frankincense and myrrh. These Magi may be symbolic of the three races of man descended from those who survived in Noah's ark. There is also a tradition that the three royal visitors were kings of Tarsus, Saba and Nubia, that they were later baptised by St Thomas, and martyred, and that their relics were preserved at Constantinople and then moved to Milan. In Mediaeval paintings they came to be identified by the names <u>Caspar</u>, <u>Melchior</u>, and <u>Balthasar</u>. According to one Andalusian biblical tradition, parents would sometimes protect a child from epilepsy by naming him after one of the three Wise Men. The name <u>Theophania</u> was sometimes given to girls born on the festival of the Epiphany (January 6th – 'Twelfth Night'). <u>Tiffany</u> is the English short form of this name (see **DAYS OF THE WEEK, GOD, SEASONS**).

WHITSUNTIDE

PENTECOST (f/m), PENCAST
(19th century Cornish). This name was sometimes given to children born around Whit Sunday, so-called because the newly baptised had to attend Mass dressed in white on that day.

YULE

JOLE (m)
Manx. from ON. <u>Jolfr</u> – Yule (see **CHRISTMAS**)

✳ ✳ ✳ ✳ ✳

FIERY

IGNATIUS (m)

Late Lat. from old Roman family name Egnatius, whose meaning is uncertain – it may be Etruscan. Associated with Lat. ignis – fire, and Gk. agnos – purity/flame. Thus the name links the two ideas of purification and fire. In legend, the first Ignatius was a child whom Jesus placed in the centre of his teaching circle. It was the name of the early 2nd century bishop of Antioch who was a popular saint in the Eastern church. St Ignatius Loyola (1491-1556) was a Spanish nobleman who read the lives of the saints while recovering from battle wounds and was so inspired that he went on to found the Society of Jesus (the Jesuits). Inigo is the Spanish form of this name.

Little FIRE

AIDAN (M), EDANA (f), EITHNE (f)

Cel. aidu-s – of fire, Old Irish Aed. Aodh was the old Celtic fire and sun god. This is an ancient and very common name, popular in the 8th and 9th centuries. The famous St Aidan, who died in 651 was a monk at Iona, became bishop of Lindisfarne and converted much of northern England to Christianity.

EGAN (m)

Ir. Aodghan. More common as a surname.

FLOURISHING

OMAR (m)

Arab. 'amara – to thrive, prosper and live long. One of the most popular Arabic names.

FLOWERS [12]

There's ROSEMARY, that's for remembrance.

W. Shakespeare: *Hamlet*, Act IV, scene 3

Flower names for girls were most popular between 1850-1900. In 1890 a clergyman wrote:

'It was my good fortune recently on a railway journey to make the acquaintance of a perfect nosegay of children, all members of one family and all justifying the sweetness of the names that had been given them – **DAISY, MAY, LILY, VIOLET** and **OLIVE**. There had also been a sixth, **PANSY** but she, I was informed, had been transplanted to a better and brighter garden than any on earth. There is, I may mention, a strong prejudice existing in some minds against naming children after flowers, on the grounds that the children so called are supposed, like flowers, to be short lived. I hope my little travelling companions may, at any rate, belie the superstition.' [13]

Some of these flower names are ancient and others have quite unromantic origins, being called, for instance, after the name of their discoverer. Unless designated (m), all these names are feminine.

ANGELICA

ANGELICA

This name is also the feminine form of Angel. The angelica plant was said to be a preservative against witchcraft, evil spirits and 'supernatural' cattle diseases, such as elfshot (Ger. Hexenschuss – hag-shot). It is the plant of inspiration (see **ANGEL** and **ELF**).

Devotee of ARTEMIS

ARTEMISIA
Gk. Has also been interpreted as 'perfect one'.
This was considered to be a power-plant and was
burned or hung up on the door to protect against
witches. There was an old German custom of
making hats and girdles of artemisia, which were
known as 'St John's girdles' and were thrown
into the fire on St John's day and set light to on
the main street (see **VIGOROUS, MOON** and
GODS & GODDESSES).

AZALEA

AZALEA
Gk. dry or parched. The symbol of temperance.

BLOOM

THALIA
Gk. The name of one of the Three Graces (see
GRACES).

BLOOMING

CHLORIS (m)
Gk. meaning fresh or blooming.

BLOSSOM

BLODYN Wel.

BLOSSOM OE. blostm – blossom.

ZAHRA
Arab. zahara – to shine or blossom. This was the
family name of Muhammad's mother and carries
the additional meaning of 'radiant'. ZUHAYR
was the name of a well-known pre-Islamic poet.
His name also means 'blossoms', being a
diminutive of ZAHR.

BLUEBELL

BLUEBELL
Eng. The flower
of constancy

BREATH

ANEMONE
From Gk., meaning 'frail wind flower'.
Associated with expectation (see **BREATH**).

CAMELIA

CAMELIA
This flower was named after the 18th century
Moravian Jesuit missionary, Georg Josef Kamel,
who first discovered it. It is the flower of perfec-
ted loveliness.

CASSIA

KEZIAH Heb. A fragrant shrub.

CELANDINE

CELANDINE
Gk. cheladon – swallow (the bird). One of the
more usual flower names. Both Pliny and Aris-
totle reported that celandine was an eyesight
restorer and the yellow juice of the plant was
used for treating jaundice.

FLOWERS

FLOWERS

CLEMATIS

CLEMATIS

Gk. klematis – climbing plant. This plant was named in the 16th century and is an unusual flower name. It used to be called 'Devil's Thread', and was referred to by the famous 16th century herbalist Gerarde as 'Virgin's Bower'. Wild clematis is often called 'old man's beard', because of the downy trailing seed heads that it produces.

CLOVER

CLOVER

OE. clafre – clover. The four-leafed clover (because of its cruciform) was endowed with magical properties and said to grant success and give the power to detect evil spirits. The plant was sacred to the Germans, especially the two-leaved and four-leaved forms. There was an old German legend that if you carried a four-leafed clover on Christmas Eve, you would see witches. A two-leafed clover charm was said to indicate a future lover: if a lover placed it under his pillow he would dream of his beloved. A maiden would sometimes put a leaf into her lover's shoe before he set out, without him knowing, to ensure his safe return. It was also credited with the power of stopping the wearer from being drawn into military service, and said to cure diseases and madness.

COLUMBINE

COLUMBINE

Eng. from Lat. Columbina – little dove (see **BIRDS**). The name of Harlequin's girlfriend in the Italian theatrical tradition of the Commedia dell' Arte. The flower is so-named because its curled petals are said to resemble five doves clustered together. It was sometimes associated with deserted lovers and (in Shakespeare) with cuckolds (because of the horned appearance of the petals).

CROCUS

CROCUS

Gk. from Semitic

Little CROWN

CORONELLA

Lat. Given the meaning of 'success crown your wishes' (also see **CROWN**).

DAFFODIL

DAFFODIL

From Dutch de affodil, the asphodel, originally from Lat. and Gk. This flower was introduced into England by the Romans and used to be called 'neckwort', because of its long stem and because it was used to heal diseases of the neck.

NARCISSUS (m)

Gk. <u>Narkissos</u> – the name of the youth who fell in love with his own reflection. Possibly from the root word narkao – to put to sleep, cf. modern word <u>narcotic</u>. This word is still in use in the words <u>narcissism</u> and <u>narcissistic</u>. This was a common name among the Greek slaves of Romans and was the name of a saint and bishop of Jerusalem in 195. He presided at the Council that changed the Resurrection day from the traditional full moon to the first Sunday after the full moon. His feast is March 18th.

NARKISS (m) Russ.

DAHLIA

DAHLIA

This flower was named after the 18th century Swedish botanist Anders <u>Dahl</u>. It has been called the flower of instability.

The DAY'S EYE

Men by reason well it calle may
The Daisie, or else the Eye of Day,
The Empresse and the flowre of flowres all.
Chaucer

DAISY

AS. In older flower books the daisy took the place of the primrose as the flower of the Spring. It was said not to be spring until you could put your foot on 12 daisies! The daisy was considered magical on the Continent. Starlike flowers, such as the daisy and chrysanthemum, have been attributed with heavenly qualities. This flower is associated with innocence and used to be the emblem of fidelity. It is consecrated to early infancy and is the flower of the new-born. In a Celtic legend Malvina's lost baby was later described as being seen in a shower of flowers as 'one with a golden disc surrounded by silver leaves: a sweet tinge of crimson adorns its delicate rays.' Daisies were worn by knights in mediaeval tournaments, and by ladies in their scarves or as head wreaths.

DEW of the SEA

ROSEMARY

Lat. <u>ros</u> – dew + <u>marinus</u> – of the sea. This plant grows well near the sea and is associated with remembrance. It used to be customary to entwine sprigs of rosemary into a bridal wreath and wedding garments – in memory of the former home of the bride. Because of its association with remembrance it was also used in funerals – to adorn the corpse, carry in the hand and strew or plant on the grave. It was also used widely against witchcraft (see **NAMING AND HEALING**).

FLOWERS

Rosemary is good in cooking and has useful medicinal properties. In a poem to his God-child, E.C. Stedman wrote:

> *Rosemary! could we give you*
> *'Remembrance' with your name,*
> *Ere long you'd tell me something*
> *Of Heaven, whence you came...*

EGLANTINE

EGLANTINE Lat. <u>acus</u> – needle.

FERN

FERN
OE. <u>fearn</u> – fern. This is a recently-introduced name. I have read that it may also derive from a Sanskrit word meaning 'wing' or 'leaf'. The Royal Fern was dedicated to St Christopher. This plant was sacred to the Norse gods. On the Eve of St John, the legend tells, wearing fern will make you invisible.

RHEDYN
Wel. <u>rhedyn</u> – fern. This flower has been linked with fascination.

FIRST ROSE

BRIALLEN – Wel.

PRIMROSE
Lat. <u>prima</u> – first + <u>rosa</u> – rose. The flower of early youth.

PRIMULA
Lat. botanical Latin name for the primrose and a separate girl's name in its own right (see **ROSE**).

FLAX

LINUS (m)
Lat. form of a Gk name <u>Linos</u>. May originally have meant 'flaxen-haired' i.e. blond. From this we get the word 'linen'.

LLIAN Wel. (see **LINEN**)

FLOWER

AZHAR Arab. 'flowers'.

FFLUR Wel. <u>fflur</u> – flower.

FLEUR Fr.

FLORA
Lat. The Roman goddess of flowers. The Floralia was celebrated between 28th April and 1st May to express pleasure and joy at the reappearance of spring. This festival was kept by the Phocians and Sabines before the Romans.

GOLD FLOWER of QUEEN MARY

MARIGOLD
Also 'Mary's gold' i.e. the gold of the Blessed Virgin. This flower was chosen as the symbol of the apothecaries and is still used as a symbol by many herbalists.

FLOWER FAIR

BLODWEN
Wel. <u>blodyn</u> – flower + <u>(g)wen</u> – fair/white.

BLANCHEFLEUR
The same name in French, lit. 'white' flower.

FLOWERS

FLOWERING

FLORENCE
Eng. and Fr. mediaeval form of Latin *masculine* name Florentius, from florens – blossoming / flourishing. In the Middle Ages this was a man's name and continued to be used for both sexes in Ireland until the 20th century. Florence Nightingale (1820-1910), the founder of modern nursing, who organised a group to go to help the dying and wounded during the Crimean War, was so named because she was born in the city of Florence (see **FLOURISHING**).

FLOWERLIKE

BLODEUWEDD
Wel. blodau – flowers + (g)wedd – form. The legendary wife of Lleu Llaw Gyffes, fashioned from blossom of broom, oak, and meadowsweet. Her name was originally Blodeuedd. After she was unfaithful she was changed into an owl and her name was changed to 'flower face' – BLODEUWEDD. The petals of her flowers can still be seen radiating in that bird's eyes...

FLOWERY

ANTHEA
Gk. anthos – flower, antheios – flowery. An anthology is literally a 'collection of flowers'!

FOXGLOVE

FFION Wel.

HEATHER

ERICA
Lat. this is the Latin word for heather, still used by gardeners. The name is also the feminine form of Eric which is a Viking name (see **RULER**).

HEATHER

HYACINTH

HYACINTH
This was the Roman name for what we call 'iris' and was the name of a handsome Spartan youth whom Apollo accidentally killed with his own discus. The hyacinth is said to have sprung from his blood, with Apollo's cries of 'Ai, Ai' (alas!), at the death of his friend, on each petal. It was originally a male name. It has been linked with sport, perhaps because Hyakinthos was killed at the games. It was a Greek custom for bridesmaids to wear hyacinth wreaths instead of orange blossom and the flower has also been associated with the dead. It was the flower used to strew the couch of Zeus, the king of the gods in ancient Greece. Its true blue has been linked with fidelity and it has also been taken as the symbol of sorrow and sadness. In the 19th century it was used as a female name.

FLOWERS

IRIS (see **RAINBOW**)

IVY

IVY
OE. <u>ifig</u>. The plant is associated with friendship and fidelity. It is another name which was introduced in the 19th century, and has been used at funerals to indicate immortality. Bacchus, the Roman god of wine, was hidden in a cradle of ivy by his aunt, Ino, so that Juno would not find him; and the spears of the Bacchanalians (the revellers at Bacchus' ecstatic celebrations) were decked with ivy. Crowns of ivy were given at Spartan festivals, in honour of the youth Hyakinthos.

JASMINE

JASMINE From Pers. <u>Yasmin</u>.

JUNIPER

JUNIPER
Lat. <u>juniperus</u> (see also **TREES**)

LARKSPUR/Delphinium

DELPHINIA
Gk. <u>delphis</u> – dolphin. The flower was so named because the shape of the nectary resembles a dolphin (see **ANIMALS – Dolphin**).

LAUREL

The laurel symbolises victory and success. In Rome, the <u>laurus pacifera</u> referred to the 'peace-bringing laurel', as branches of laurel were carried between opposing armies to signify the end of war. The Romans adopted guardian spirits from the Etruscans, who were said to reside in the hearth and were called <u>lars</u> – lord and master. The spirits of good men and infants who died within 40 days of birth became the guardian spirits of home and family. The images of these guardians were draped in dogskins and placed with a figure of a dog in the hearth (this is the origin of the word 'firedogs'). These guardians were included centrally in household festivals and cups were set aside for them. A young bride honoured these household guardians on the nones, ides and calends of the Roman month, and when her master returned from war. At other celebrations these <u>lars</u> were crowned with wreaths of laurel. 22nd December, the time of the winter solstice, was the special feast of the <u>lars</u>. At that time a dog was sacrificed to the female deity, <u>Lara</u>. In Greece, heralds carried branches of laurel (or olive). <u>Laurentia</u> was also the name of a Greek nymph.

DAPHNE
Gk. The Greek word for 'laurel' and the Sanskrit for 'the redness of dawn' – <u>ahana</u> are related. Myths surrounding both Daphne and Phoebus describe the sunrise and sunset. <u>Daphnis</u> was a Sicilian hero who was placed in a laurel grove as an infant and so was named after the plant. In another myth <u>Daphne</u> is saved from Apollo by her mother, the Earth, who turns her into a laurel tree.

FLOWERS

LABHRAINN (m) Gael. <u>Labhrainn</u>.

LABHRAS (m) Ir. <u>Labhras</u>.

LAURA

Lat. This was the name of a 9th century Spanish nun who died in a cauldron of molten lead, and also the name of the heroine of Petrarch's love poems.

LAUREL a 19th century adaptation.

LAUREN Eng.

LAWRENCE (m)

Anglicised spelling of <u>Laurence</u> which comes from Latin <u>Laurentius</u> – man from Laurentum. Laurentum was a town in Latium which may have got its name from the laurel plant, or it may be of even earlier origin. A popular name in the Middle Ages. St Laurence was a 3rd century saint who was martyred in 258 by being roasted on a gridiron, so he is the saint who is invoked against burns. When he was asked to hand over the Church's treasures, he assembled the poor and sick and presented them to his oppressors. The Emperor Constantine built a church over the site of his tomb. The feast of St Lawrence is August 10th. Shooting stars seen on the night of the saint's feast are known in Germany as 'St Lorenz's sparks'.

LEAFY

PHYLLIS, PHYLLIDA

Gk. <u>phullis</u> – foliage/leafy branch. The name of a Greek maiden who hanged herself when her lover did not return and who was changed into an almond tree. The classical poets used the name to denote a country wench.

LILY

SUSAN

Heb. <u>Sushannah</u>, from <u>shoshan</u> – lily. <u>Shushan</u> was the Assyrian 'royal city of lilies', so named because of the radiant flowers which covered the surrounding plain. This also means 'rose' in modern Hebrew, the symbol of purity. The ancient Jews believed that the lily protected against enchantment and witchcraft. As it is a native of the Holy Land it became the emblem of the Virgin Mary. It comes into bloom around July 2nd, the feast of the Visitation, when Mary visited her cousin Elizabeth and announced her pregnancy.

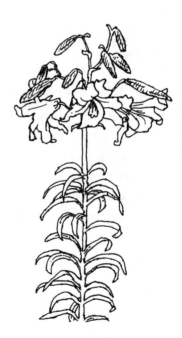

FLOWERS

LILY

Lat. <u>lilium</u> – lily. At Greek weddings, the bride and groom were crowned with lily and corn, to symbolise purity and abundance.

LILIAN

Consider the LILIES how they grow; they toil not, they spin not; and yet I say unto you that Solomon in all his glory was not arrayed like unto one of these.

The New Testament:
St. Luke, chap. XII, line 27

LILY of the VALLEY

GWENONWY Wel.

SAWSUN Arab.

LOTUS

NILUFAR (f) Arab.

PEMA (f/m)
Tib. (<u>padma</u> in Sanskrit). This is a very common Tibetan name and refers to the symbol of enlightenment, which depends for its resplendent and translucent beauty on having its roots firmly out of sight in the mud. It has also been taken as the symbol of eloquence (see **ELOQUENT**).

MAGNOLIA

MAGNOLIA
Named after 18th century French botanist, Pierre <u>Magnol</u>. It is said to symbolise a love of nature.

MARJORAM

MARJORAM Lat.

FLOWERS

MARSHMALLOW
(The Rose of Sharon)

ALTHEA
Gk. refers to the shrub with healing properties and the name is derived from the Greek word 'to heal' and has been interpreted as 'wholesome' (see **HEALER**).

MAY

MAY
Lat. a Roman Earth-goddess. Indicates the vigorous and flowering month.

MIMOSA

MIMOSA From Lat word for 'mime'.

MYRTLE

Myrtle flowers were formerly carried by brides, to be later replaced by orange blossom. The myrtle was used as a badge of office by magistrates in ancient Athens.

ESTHER
Pers. Of this lovely name, Sophy Moody wrote in 1863: '...[imagining] those walls of sculptured alabaster, those gorgeously painted ceilings... with eagle-headed human figures and winged bulls of gigantic size on either side, we shall, in one of Assyria's magnificent palaces, be where the name of **ESTHER** was first heard in its original formation, <u>Sitareh</u> – the Star. It was no doubt bestowed on some lustrous-eyed Assyrian princess privileged by her birth to claim relationship with the heavenly bodies.' (See **STAR, MOON** and **VENUS**)

HADASSAH

Heb. This is the equivalent of the name <u>Esther</u>.

MYRTLE

POPPY

POPPY

Lat. <u>papaver</u> – poppy, via OE. <u>popaeg</u>. Most popular in 1920s, now returning to use. The flower of consolation. It was a Swiss custom for a girl to put a poppy petal into her lover's left hand and strike it with her right. If it burst with a loud noise it was taken as an indication that he loved her. If there was no noise, this was a sign of no love. Poppies were used (with barley and wheat) to adorn statues of Ceres in Rome. Sometimes the flower is considered the symbol of death, because of its sleep-giving properties. Somnus, the god of sleep, was depicted lying in a bed of poppies or crowned with them.

RAINBOW

IRIS

Gk. goddess of rainbow. She was the messenger of the gods who used the rainbow as her bridge between heaven and earth.

REED

JONQUIL

Lat. <u>juncus</u> – reed, from which Fr. name <u>Jonquille</u> derived. Popular name in 1940s and 50s.

RIPPLING STREAM

AMARYLLIS

Gk. rippling or sparkling stream, possibly from <u>amaryssein</u> – to sparkle. It was the name of a shepherdess in Vergil's Eclogues.

ROSE

A rose by any other name would smell less sweet.

Anon 20th century scholiast

JARED (m)

Heb. An unusual *masculine* flower name. The biblical name (of Enoch's father, who is said to have lived for 962 years). Popular with the Puritans and now again in the U.S. and Australia, with several variations.

RHODA

Gk. <u>rhodon</u>, Lat. <u>rosa</u>. Or this name may come indirectly from 'woman of Rhodes'. The name of a servant girl in the New Testament, this name has been in use since the Middle Ages.

ROSE

Lat. <u>rosa</u>. There is a Roman legend which says that Venus was running through the woods in despair at the loss of Adonis when she pierced her foot with a thorn. A red rose sprang from her blood, and a white rose sprang from her tears. The white rose is symbolic of silence, the

FLOWERS

yellow of jealousy or decreased love, and a rose-leaf used to denote that the recipient may continue to have hope in his or her love. The Romans did not use flower names, but they have given us many words which have become floral names. Chaplets of flowers were very popular with the Greeks and a quarter of the market in Athens was devoted to selling them. Roses were much used in weaving chaplets and garlands. Later the Romans legislated against the indiscriminate use of of these decorations and one man was imprisoned for sixteen years for using a rose chaplet! This name has been in use since the Middle Ages and is symbolic of the Blessed Virgin – the 'rose without a thorn' (she is given various titles related to roses in the Catholic Litany, such as 'Mystical Rose'). In the 12th century St Dominic invented the rosarium – the 'rosary'. This was originally a string of nuts or berries which were used to count prayers, now replaced with beads. Rosarium means 'rose garden' and the name referred to the delights of devotion. The rosary is given a special place of veneration in the Catholic calendar. Roseria is the feast of Our Lady of the Rosary and is celebrated on October 7th. The rose is also symbolic of love and of England. Rose leaves were used in divination: a girl would write the names of her suitors on the leaves and float them: the last to sink would indicate the name of her future husband. In the French village of Salency it was the custom to bestow an annual rose crown on the girl considered to have been the most amiable, modest and dutiful throughout the year. She was called the 'Rose Queen'. The name first occurred in England in the 12th century as Rohais or Roesia. The word probably originally derives from OG. (h)ros, meaning 'horse', as does the name Rosamund (see **ANIMALS – Horse**).

Between 900 and 1200 the names Rosel and Rosette appeared in France.

There are several variations of this name, such as:

ROSEN Corn.

ROISIN Ir.

ROSALIE

Fr. from Lat. Rosalia which was an annual ceremony in which garlands of roses were hung on tombs. St Rosalia is the 12th century patron of Palermo. She lived as a hermit in the mountains and was known as 'the darling of each heart and eye'. Her feast day is August 30th.

There are also many Arabic names which contain the element Gul – rose, such as Gulbadan – 'Rose body', Gulrukh – 'Rose face', Gul-ir'na – 'Lovely rose', and many other modern Turkish nicknames associated with Rose names.

Fair ROSE

ROSENWYN Corn.

SAFFRON

SAFFRON

Arab. za'faran – saffron. Name derived from the plant whose orange stigmas provide an aromatic orange powder for flavouring and colouring food, and which was used medicinally. The name has been in use since 1960s (see also **COLOURS**).

SNOWDROP

EIRIOL

Wel. eiriol – snowdrop, may also mean splendid/ bright/beautiful. Sometimes described as the flower of hope.

SWEET BRIAR

BRYONY

Gk. Bryonia – sweet briar plant. Medieval witches would sometimes use the roots of this plant, like those of the mandrake, for making images.

TANSY

TANSY

Short form of Gk. Athanasia or Anastasia – immortal, (anastasis means 'resurrection') and also the name of the flower Tanacetum vulgare. For some reason, some writers have said that this flower means 'I declare war on you' (see **IMMORTAL**).

THOUGHTFUL

PANSY

Fr. pensée – thought, indicates a pensive girl.

TRUE ICON or Image

VERONICA

Lat. verus – true + Gk. ikon – icon or image. The flower veronica (speedwell) offers a true image of the blue sky. This flower derives its name from the legendary St Veronica who was so named because she is supposed to have been standing by the roadside among the crowd when Jesus passed by her, carrying his cross to Calvary. Taking pity on his wretchedness, she stepped forward and wiped his blood-smeared face with her scarf. When she returned home, the image of Christ's face was imprinted onto the cloth. There is an Old English poem on the life of Pilate, written pre 1305, which recounts that when the Roman Emperor heard of Veronike and her handkerchief, he sent for her to heal sickness.

VIOLET FLOWER

IANTHE Gk.

VIOLET

from Old Fr. violete, the diminutive of Lat. viola. The violet is associated with modesty and faithfulness. The Greek word for violet is ion, because these flowers formed a garland around Ion, the founder of the Ionians. One Greek legend tells that the violet sprang from the blood of the dying Adonis. The golden violet was the troubadours' prize in the French medieval courts of love, following the same custom at the ancient Greek games. One of the first popular flower names, established by the middle of the 19th century. The flower became the symbol for Napoleon's supporters, as, when he left for imprisonment on Elba, he said he would return in the violet season.

FLOWERS

WHITE FLOWERS

BLODWEN (f)
Wel. blawd – flowers + (g)wen – white, fair etc.

WHITE HEATHER

GRUGWYN (m)
Wel. grugwyn – white heather.

YARROW

YARROW
Known as Venus' tree. It was customary to take a bit of this plant and sew it into a piece of flannel and then put it under the pillow to help a young girl dream of her future husband. Another herb with useful healing properties and occasionally used as a name.

YOUNG GREEN SHOOT

CHLÖE
From a late Greek name Khloe, which was given to Demeter – the goddess of earth and fertility. In Greek mythology Chloris (a name in its own right) was a minor goddess of vegetation, from Gk. khloros – green. Notice the derivation of the modern word 'chlorophyll'.

ZAYNAB

ZAYNAB
Arab. the name of a flowering plant. One of the most popular Arabic names – the name of a daughter, wife and cousin of Muhammad. It was also the name of his revered granddaughter.

ZINNIA

ZINNIA
From the 18th century German botanist, Johann G. Zinn.

FOLIAGE (leafy branch) –
(see FLOWERS)

Little FOOLISH ONE

BAETHAN (m) Old Irish

FOREIGNER

BARBARA (f) [14]
Eng. from Lat. barbarus – foreign/strange. This name was originally a Greek word which was used to refer to any foreigner or stranger, whose unfamiliar language sounded like 'bar-bar'. It has been translated literally as 'stammerer'. St Barbara was imprisoned in a tower and be-headed by her father after she ordered that her new bath-chamber be built with three windows, thus revealing that she was a Christian (the windows being symbolic of the blessed trinity of Father, Son and Holy Spirit). Her father was later struck by thunder and lightning. She is considered (with Agnes, Catherine and Margaret) to be one of the four great virgin saints, each of whom symbolises a specific idea. St Barbara stands for artistic devotion. She is the patron saint of artillerymen, and the powder room in French artillery ships used to be called 'la sainte Barbe'. She is also the patron saint of architects, stonemakers, firework makers and prisoners, as

FLOWERS

well as affording protection from thunder storms. Her feast day is December 4th.

BAIRBRE (f) Ir.

VARVARA (f) Russ.

FORGIVENESS

GHUFRAN (m) Arab. ghufara – to forgive.

FORTUNATE

FAUSTA (f), FAUSTUS (m)
Lat. fortunate (see **LUCKY** and **HAPPY**)

MADOG (m)
Wel. mad – fortunate/good + suffix.

FOUNTAIN OF LIFE

'AYN AL-HAYAT (f) Arab.

FRAGRANCE

'ABIR (f) Arab. modern.

KETURAH (f)
Heb. from the word meaning 'incense'. The name of Abraham's second wife, whom he married after Sarah's death. Another name which was adopted by the Puritans.

FREEMAN

FRANCIS (m)
From Italian Francesco, introduced into England in the 16th century. The Franks were a 5th century group of Germanic tribes who took over Gaul from the Romans and so it came to be called France. The word Frank came to be a synonym for 'free' – 'Frenchman' equalled 'freeman'. The Late Latin word francalia meant lands held by the Franks, therefore lands not subject to taxes! This was the *nickname* given to St Francis of Assisi (1181-1226) whose merchant father was in France in 1182 when he was born. Francis was actually given the baptismal name of GIOVANNI. St Francis is the patron saint of merchants and the protection of animals is given to him, due to his particular sensitivity to and love for all creatures and his ability to communicate with birds. It was in honour of this remarkable saint that the name became popular from the 13th century onwards. His feast day is October 4th.

FRANK (m)
Ger. Originally referred to a member of the tribe of the Franks, who were named after a type of spear which they used. They gave their name to Gaul, which became France, after they settled there in the 4th century, so the name came to mean 'Frenchman'. This is a short form of Francis, but is now used as a name in its own right.

FRANKLIN (m)
Eng. surname transferred to personal name, from frankeleyn – freeman, indicating a class of non-noble freeholders. Now quite a common name, especially in the United States.

FREEWOMAN

FRANCES (f), FRANCESCA (f) –
(see **FREEMAN** above)

FRIEND

AMICA (f)
Lat. feminine form of Amicus. A name used by Roman slaves (see **BELOVED**).

KHALIL (m)
Arab. 'Al-Khalil' is a name applied to the prophet IBRAHIM (Abraham). The name is often given as 'Khalil-Allah' (friend of God).

Fortunate FRIEND

EDWIN (m), EDWINA (f)
OE. ead – riches, prosperity, good fortune + wine – friend. This name implies 'happy friend', it belongs to the Old English group of names which begin with Ed (ead). (See **PROSPERITY**.) St Edwin was the first Christian king of Northumbria and Edinburgh supposedly is named after him. His feast day is October 12th. The feminine form Edwina was coined in the 19th century.

Old FRIEND

ALDWYN (m)
OE. eald (old, great) + wine – friend.

FRUITFUL

ANONA (f)
from Annona – corn supply – the Roman goddess of fruits and harvests. It probably arose as a combination of existing names and was not recorded before the 1920s.

EPHRAIM (m)
Heb. Still a common Jewish name, after one of the sons of Joseph and one of the tribes of Israel. The name probably means 'fertile' or 'doubly fruitful', as Ephraim received the double blessing normally bestowed on the elder son, from his grandfather, Jacob. St Ephrem was a popular Russian saint, whose feast day was January 28th, and also a Roman Catholic feast day on June 18th.

EUSTACE (m), EUSTACIA (f), STACY (f. pet form)
From the Old French form of late Greek names Eustakhios and Eustathios. The first was formed from eu – well/good + stakhys – grapes, meaning 'good harvest', 'fruitful', 'plentiful'. The name came to Britain with the Normans. St Eustace (whose story parallels that of St. Hubert) was a 2nd century Roman general who had a vision of a cross hanging between the antlers of a stag while he was out hunting. He became converted to Christianity, lost his job and was plunged into poverty and misfortune. He and his family were later roasted to death. This was a very popular medieval story and the feast of St Eustace is September 20th.

FULFILMENT

ANNICE (f)
Eng. form of Gk. Anysia – fulfilment/completion.

GAME-PARK KEEPER

WARREN (m)
From La Varenne – the Norman name for a game-park; and it could refer to someone who lived near, or who looked after, a 'Warren'. Also associated with the Old German folkname Varin – watch/guard. Originally this was a surname, but has been in use as a first name since the 17th century.

GEMS (see JEWELS)

GENEROSITY

KARAM (m/f)
Arab. karuma – to be noble or generous. Also relates to precious stones and has the meaning of 'valuable'.

NADA (f)
Arab. This name means 'moist with dew', 'morning dew' or 'generosity' (see DEW and RAIN).

GENEROUS

HISHAM (m)
Arab. 'generous by nature', from hashama – to crush. This refers to the crushing and sharing of bread by Arabs when travelling in a caravan from the Levant to Yemen. Crushing therefore implies generosity.

WAHIB (m), WAHIBA (f)
Arab. wahaba – to give. 'Al-Wahib' is one of the 99 Names of Allah, a quality which a Muslim would seek to cultivate.

GENEROUS LORD

ITHEL (m)
Wel. iud – lord + haelm – generous.

GENTLE

GARETH (m)
Wel. gwaredd – gentle, benign. The name was introduced by Sir Thomas Malory in the 15th century for the name of an Arthurian hero.

GENUINE

DILYS (f)
Wel. dilys – certain/genuine/sincere/steadfast. This name was first used in 1857 and probably taken from Edmund Prys' version of the 23rd Psalm:

> *Er mwyn es Enw mawr dilys,*
> *fe'm tywys ar yr union.*

(For the sake of Thy sure, great Name, lead me in the straight way.)

GIFT

ARMAGHAN (m) Arab. (Pers.)

DORA (f)
Originally a short of form of Theodora and Dorothy.

DORINDA (f)

This name was coined in the 18th century from Dora + suffix inda.

HIBA (f)

Arab. wahaba – to give or donate.

JESSE (m)

Heb. probably means 'gift' or 'wealthy', from yishai – riches, or a gift. The name of the biblical father of King David, from whom Jesus was descended. 'Jesse windows' in medieval churches depicted this lineage. Popular Puritan name (see **GIFT OF GOD**).

NAWAL (f)

Arab. nawala – to donate or bestow.

GIRDLE

ZONA (f)

American name from the Gk. for 'girdle'.

GIRL

COLLEEN (f) Ir.

GIVEN

DYNAWD (m)

Wel. from Latin name Donatus.

More GLORIOUS

AMJAD (m)

Arab. from majada – to be praiseworthy. There are many such comparative names in Arabic.

GLORY

GLORIA (f)

Lat – gloria. Not used until 1898 when it appeared as the name of a character in George Bernard Shaw's *You Never Can Tell*. Gloriana was a poetic title given to Queen Elizabeth I.

JALAL (m), JALILA (f)

Arab. jalla – to be great/illustrious. Implies greatness, veneration and glory.

STANISLAS (m)

From Slavonic stan – government + slav – glory. The name of an 11th century martyr who was bishop of Cracow and whose feast day is August 15th. STANISLAV is the Russian form of this name.

GOD

We have in the Veda the invocation 'Dyaus Pitar', the Greek 'Zue Pater' and the Latin 'Jupitar'; and that means in these three languages what it meant before these three languages were torn asunder: 'Heaven Father'.

M.F. Müller[15]

The name, Zeus (the Greek king of the gods) relates to the word theos, which means God, just as the name Jupiter (the Roman king of the gods) comes from the words Deus Pater – God Father and relates to the word deus, the Latin word meaning simply God. Both names come from the Sanskrit word deva which is connected with the open sky, light and our word for 'day'. Therefore, etymologically, God is indeed Light; or rather, light, openness, all-seeingness have come to be recognised as the nature and essential attributes of God. In the Avesta (the sacred writings of Zoroastrianism), <u>Mithra</u> was not a specifically sun-god, but rather Lord of heavenly <u>Light</u>. He appears on the mountain before sunrise to mount a chariot drawn by four white horses, which he drives across the heavens by day and which glimmers by night. So he is not the sun or moon or stars, but rather *shines through* them. He is said to have a thousand ears and ten thousand eyes through which he perceives everything and keeps watch over the world.

The meaning of the most sacred name of God is therefore derived from the Hebrew verb, <u>hayah</u>, to be, and the name of God therefore signifies self-existence. [16]

For more information about the Names of God see p. 257. (Also see **GODS & GODDESSES**, **LIGHT**, **SKY**, **SUN**)

GOD ANSWERS

ANAIAH (m) Heb.

GOD BLESSES

BERECHAIAH (m) Heb.

GOD-GIVING

THEODOSIA (f)
Gk. <u>theos</u> – God + <u>dosis</u> – giving. The name of several saints in the early Christian church. Feast day April 2nd.

GOD HAS CREATED

BERAIAH (m) Heb.

ELKANAH (m) Heb.

GOD HAS HEARD

AZANAIAH (m) Heb.

GOD HAS HELPED

AZARIAH (m)
Hebrew name from the Old Testament, borne by 23 men.

ELISHA (m) Heb.

GOD HAS REMEMBERED

ZACHARY (m)
This is the anglicised version of <u>Zachariah</u>, from Gk. <u>Zacharias</u>. The name of the father of John the Baptist, who was struck dumb until after his birth for not believing that his elderly wife, Elizabeth, had conceived.

GOD HAS SHOWN HIMSELF

ANANAIAH (m) Heb.

GOD HEALS

RAPHAEL (m)
Heb. this is the name of the Archangel who restores Tobias' sight in the Book of Tobias. He is the patron saint of the blind (and also of lovers) and his feast day is October 24th.

RAFAELLA, RAPHAELA (f)
(see **HEALER** and **MESSENGER**)

GOD

GOD

GOD HEARS

ISMAIL (m)
Arab. this name means 'God will hear' or 'hearkening to God'. This is the Arabic version of the Hebrew ISHMAEL. He was the son of Abraham (Arabic IBRAHIM) and Hajar, the Egyptian concubine given to Abraham by his wife, Sarah. Sarah's jealousy made Abraham take Ismail and Hajar to the desert. A bird sent by God bored the well of Zamzam, so they survived. Other travellers settled in the area. Later Abraham and his son built the Ka'ba – the temple at Mecca, which is the centre of Muslim prayer. Ismail is said to be the father of the Arabs and the Jews are said to be descended from Sarah's son, Isaac.

GOD is GOOD

TOBY (m)
Eng. form of Gk. <u>Tobias</u>, from Heb. <u>Tobijah</u>. In the apocryphal 'Book of Tobit', <u>Tobias</u>, a rich Jew from Nineveh, with the help of <u>Raphael</u>, the Archangel, sets out with his dog, wins a wife and cures his father's blindness. This was a popular painting subject and so the name became transferred to the dog! There was also a 4th century St Tobias who was martyred in Armenia and whose feast day is November 2nd.

GOD is GRACIOUS

IAN / IAIAN (m) Gael

IEUAN (m) Wel.

IVAN (m) Russ.
(VANYA (m) is the pet form of this name.)

JACK (m)
Eng. from the Middle English <u>Jankin</u>, it was originally a pet form of <u>John</u>, but now a name in its own right.

JANE (f)
Eng. (JEANETTE and JEANNINE are both diminutive forms of Fr. <u>Jeanne</u>.)

JANET (f)
Eng. This is a diminutive of <u>Jane</u>, but now used as a separate name and popular in Scotland.

JANICE (f) Eng. Derivative of <u>Jane</u>.

JOAN (f)
Eng. This is the contracted form of the Old French <u>Jo(h)anne</u> and was the usual feminine of <u>John</u> from the Middle Ages until the 16th and 17th centuries when it was superseded by <u>Jane</u>. This is also the name of the famous French saint <u>Jeanne d'Arc</u>, burned at the stake as a witch for following her inspirational voices which led her to take up the life of a soldier and to head the French armies in battle against the English. Her feast day is celebrated on May 30th.

JOANNA (f)
Lat. Form of Gk. <u>Ioanna</u> (feminine of <u>Ioannes</u> – John). The name of a New Testament follower of Jesus. In medieval Europe it was used as a feminine equivalent of John. Only in common use in England since the 19th century.

JOHN (m)
Eng. From Latin <u>Iohannes</u>, originally from Heb. <u>Johanan</u> – 'God is gracious'. It was the name of 3 very important saints – John the Baptist, John the Apostle, the brother of James and John, the

beloved apostle and Evangelist. It has been the name of many other saints and of 23 popes.

SEAN (m)

Ir. In the Middle Ages from Anglo-Norman <u>Jehan</u>. Given as a name in its own right by those with no Irish connections.

SINEAD (f)

Ir. Form of <u>Janet</u>, from Anglo-Norman <u>Jeannette</u>.

SIOBHAN (f)

Ir. Form of <u>Jane</u>, from Anglo-Norman <u>Jehanne</u>. Now a popular given name in its own right.

There are many short forms, pet names and variations of these names, all of which come from the Hebrew root <u>chaanach</u> – grace, favour, mercy. This is the same root word that produced the <u>Hannah</u>, <u>Anne</u> series of names.

YAHYA (m) is the Arabic form of this name.

GOD is LIGHT

URIEL (m) Heb. <u>uri</u> – light + '<u>el</u> – God.

GOD is RIGHTEOUS

ZEDEKIAH (m) Heb.

GOD is my FATHER

ABIAH (m) Heb. (see **FATHER**)

GOD is my HELP

AZRIEL (m) Heb.

LAZARUS (m)

Heb. (<u>Lazaros</u> in Gk.), from Aramaic <u>Lazar</u> and a short form of Hebrew <u>Eleazar</u>. The biblical beggar Lazarus was covered with sores, which led to the name being used in the Middle Ages as a word for a leper, and so one who was avoided.

GOD is my JUDGE

DANIEL (m)

Heb. the name of the biblical prophet whose story is told in the Book of Daniel. He is the famous Daniel of the 'lion's den', into which he was thrown by his enemies when a slave of the Assyrian king, Nebuchadnezzar. He gained great favour with this king through his wisdom and ability to interpret dreams. The tale of his being thrown to the lions and his rescue by God was popular in the Middle Ages and a favourite subject in miracle plays.

DANIELLE (f) Fr.

DANIELLA (f) Ital.

DEINIOL (m) Wel.

DANIIL (m) Russ.

GOD is my OATH

ELIZABETH (f)

Heb. This name also carries the meaning 'God's promise', 'God has sworn' and 'God is my satisfaction, my perfection, my plenitude'. In the Authorised Version of the New Testament, and in most European languages this name is spelt <u>Elisabeth</u>. She was the saintly mother of John the Baptist and cousin of the Virgin Mary whose

GOD

111

visit to her during her pregnancy is recorded in the song of the <u>Magnificat</u> in which Mary sings to her cousin of her joy, exaltation and awe at being chosen as the mother of the 'Saviour'. She has the peculiar distinction of sharing her feast day of November 5th with the annual 'celebration' of the death of Guy Fawkes. There are many European variations of this name as well as many English short forms, such as <u>Bess</u>, <u>Betty</u>, <u>Liz</u> etc. The life of St Elisabeth of Hungary includes the inspiring tale of the saintly queen who used to carry food down the hill from her castle to feed the poor who lived below in the village. Her angry husband, the king, caught her one day, but when he looked under the cloth covering her basket, he found nothing but roses.

ELISAVETA (f) Russ.

ISABEL(LE) (f)
Eng. and Fr. form of <u>Elizabeth</u> which was originally Spanish and was imported to France in the Middle Ages, and thence to England.

GOD is my REWARD

GAMALIEL (m)
Heb. another popular Puritan name (because of the Old Testament prince of the tribe of Manasseh at the time of the Exodus). This was also the name of a New Testament Pharisee and teacher of St Paul.

GOD is SALVATION

ISAIAH (m)
Heb. One of the three most important Old Testament prophets. This name was popular for a while with the Puritans.

GOD is STRONG
AMAZIAH (m) Heb. (see **STRONG**)

GOD is WITH ME

ITHIEL (m) Heb.

GOD is WITH US

EMMANUEL (m)
Heb. <u>Emm</u> – with + <u>an</u> – us + <u>El</u> – the old Hebrew word for God. The name of the future Messiah.

GOD MAKES HAPPY

MEHETABEL (f) Heb.

GOD-NOURISHING

AMALTHEA (f)
Gk. This name has been interpreted as 'god nourishing'; it was the name of the goat which suckled <u>Zeus</u>, the father of the gods.

GOD SHALL ADD (another son to the family)

JOSEPH (m)
Heb. from <u>Yosef</u>, and interpreted as 'increase' or 'addition'. The name of the famous favourite biblical son of Jacob, by whom he was given the 'coat of many colours', who was exiled into Egypt as a slave and rose to become the Pharaoh's chief steward. Also the name of the husband of Mary (his feast day is March 19th), the mother of Jesus, and of Jesus' uncle, Joseph of Arimathea who is supposed to have brought the young Jesus to England along one of the tin-trading

GOD

sea routes, via Cornwall to Glastonbury. This same Joseph removed the body of Jesus from the cross after the crucifixion and prepared it for burial in a sepulchre (a rock tomb on his land). He is said to have returned to Britain after Jesus' death, bringing with him the Holy Grail (the chalice out of which the apostles drank at the Last Supper, and symbol of spiritual enlightenment – later to become the goal of the Quest of the Knights of King Arthur's Round Table). He is said to have planted his staff on Wearyall Hill, an ancestor of which still flowers annually in the winter – the famous 'Glastonbury Thorn'.

JOSEPHINA (f)

OSIP (m) Russ.

GOD SPEAKS

AMARIS (f)
Heb. feminine of Amariah.

GOD STRENGTHENS

EZEKIEL (m)
Heb. the name of a major Old Testament prophet. A rare name, but the diminutive Zeke is more common.

Appointed by GOD

JEREMY (m)
Heb. Jeremiah. The name of the great 6th century Old Testament Prophet. The feast of St Jeremy is May 1st.

Asked for from GOD

SAUL (m)
Heb. the name of the First King of Israel whom the people had asked God to provide. A name to give to a much wanted, long-awaited child. This was another popular Puritan name.

Belonging to GOD

LEMUEL (m) Heb.

Beloved of GOD

AMADEUS (m), AMADEA (f)
from Lat. Amadeo. Principally famous as the second name of the composer Wolfgang Amadeus Mozart (1765-91). (See **GIFT of GOD** below.)

Gift of GOD

'ATA ALLAH (m) Arab.

MATTHEW (m)
From Old Hebrew Mattaniah. This was the name of the tax collector disciple of Jesus and Evangelist. He is the patron saint of tax collectors (!) and his feast day is September 21st.

MATHIAS (m)
This is the Greek name of the disciple who was chosen to replace Judas Iscariot.

MATFEI (m) Russ.

THEODORE (m), THEODORA (f)
Gk. theos – God + doron – gift. This was a popular name among Christians, especially in the

GOD

113

Eastern church. This was the name of a young soldier who was martyred for setting fire to the temple of Cybele. The Venetians loved him and adopted him as one of their popular patrons. St Theodore's feast day is November 9th.

THEODORA was one of the first two recorded girls' names, discovered in Mycenae in 1948.

DOROTHY (f)

This combines but reverses the above elements of <u>theos</u> + <u>doron</u>. In a legend about St Dorothy, she is said to have sent an angel with roses to earth from heaven after her death. Consequently, she is the patron saint of florists and gardeners and her feast day is February 6th.

FEODOR (m) Russ.

TUDOR, TEWDWR (m) Wel.

Glory of GOD

THEKLA (f)

Gk. <u>Theokleia</u>, from <u>theos</u> – god + <u>kleia</u> – glory. Charlotte Yonge interpreted this name as 'divine fame'. The name of the 1st century first female martyr, details of whose gory death are recorded in the apocryphal 'Acts of Paul and Thecla'. She is supposed to have been converted to Christianity by St. Paul, and when she was turned over to the lions at Antioch to be torn to pieces, the legend says that they crouched at her feet in submission. It was considered the highest praise to be compared to her. Her feast day is September 23rd. It was also the name of an 8th century Anglo-Saxon abbess who was a missionary in Germany. Another lady by the name of <u>Thekla</u> is believed to have been the scribe for the copy of the Gospels which were given to Charles I and which are now in the British Museum.

He is my GOD

ELIHU (m) Heb.

Hidden by GOD

ZEPHANIAH (m)

Heb. usually occurs in short form – <u>Zeph</u>.

Honouring GOD

TIMOTHY (m)

Gk. Timotheos; <u>time</u> – honour + <u>theos</u> – God. The name of the companion of St Paul who in legend was stoned to death for denouncing the worship of the Roman goddess, Diana. His feast day is January 24th. This name is sometimes used in Ireland to replace <u>Tadhgh</u> (see **POET**).

TIMOTHIA (f)

This name was found in 1702 in Lancashire.

House of GOD

BETHEL (m) Heb.

Light of GOD

URIAH (m)

In the Bible, the name of the Hittite warrior husband of the beautiful Bathsheba. This name was popular with the Puritans and again in the 19th century. Despite its beautiful meaning it has become discredited because of Dickens' unpleasant character, <u>Uriah Heep</u> in David Copperfield (1849-50).

GOD

114

Lion of GOD (see **ANIMALS – Lion**)

The Lord (Yah) is GOD

ELIJAH (m)
The Hebrew name <u>Eliyahu</u> means 'Jehovah is God'. <u>Elijah</u> was the famous fiery Israelite prophet who did much to safeguard the Jewish monotheistic religion. His story is told in the First and Second Book of Kings. A popular name among the early Puritan settlers in New England and now being adopted by Black Muslims.

ELIAS (m) Gk.

ELLIS (m)
Eng. Originally a surname, derived from <u>Elias</u>. Used in Wales as an anglicised form of Elisud, which really derives from <u>elus</u>, meaning kind or benevolent.

Only Yahweh is GOD

JOEL (m), JOELLE (f) Fr.
Heb. <u>Yah</u> + <u>El</u> – both the names of God combined into one name; i.e. only the Hebrew god <u>Yahweh</u> is God. Could be translated as 'only God is God'. The name of an Old Testament prophet. It came into use in England with the Puritans who took it to North America.

Loved by GOD

THEOPHILUS (m)
Gk. <u>theos</u> – God + <u>philos</u> – friend, indicating one who loves God or one who is beloved by God. <u>Theophilus</u> was the person to whom St Luke's Gospel and the Acts of the Apostles were addressed.

Manifestation of GOD –
(see **EPIPHANY**)

Name of GOD

SAMUEL (m)
Heb. This was the Hebrew prophet (11th century BC) who established the Hebrew monarchy and who anointed Saul as the First King of Israel, and later David. The name has been popularly translated as 'the Name of God', but, more accurately, it is probably a contracted form of Hebrew '<u>sha'ul me'el</u>' – 'asked of God'.

SAWYL (m) Wel.

SAMUIL (m) Russ.
(see **SEASONS – Summer Wanderer**)

Requested from GOD

SALATHIEL (m)
Heb. originally from the Babylonian <u>Salti-ila</u>.

Servant of GOD

'ABD'ALLAH (m)
Arab. <u>abd</u> – servant + <u>Allah</u> – the one true God. This name is very popular in the Arab world and was the name of Muhammed's father. It is rendered as slave or servant of Allah.

OBADIAH (m)
Heb. The name of several biblical characters. This name is the Hebrew equivalent of the Arabic <u>Abdullah</u>.

GOD

115

Strong MAN / WOMAN of GOD

GABRIEL (m), GABRIELLE (f) Fr.,
GABRIELLA (f) Ital.
Heb. The name of the famous Archangel who
announced the birth of Jesus Christ to the
Virgin, Mary (see **ANGEL, MESSENGER**
and **STRONG**).

Who is like GOD

MICHAEL (m)
Heb. the name of the Archangel, defeater of Satan
and captain of the Church militant. The feast of
St Michael (the old festival of Michaelmas, which
corresponds to the pre-Christian celebration of
the Autumn Equinox) is September 29th. St
Michael is the patron saint of seafarers.

MICHAELA (f)
Ger. but popular in England.

MICHELE, MICHELLE (f) Fr.

MIKHAIL (m) Russ.

GODS & GODDESSES

Devotee of ARTEMIS

ARTEMAS (m)
Gk. Artemis was the goddess of hunting, the
equivalent of the Roman DIANA (see **MOON**
and **FLOWERS**).

BAAL PROTECT THE KING

BALTHASAR (m)
Traditional name of one of the Three Kings (the
Magi) from biblical name Belshazzar. Baal was a
god common to the many Near Eastern peoples,
it is a Semitic word meaning 'lord' or 'owner'. It
was even used as an alternative to El – or Yahweh
– the names of God. Later, though, this was considered to be a corruption of Jewish belief. Baal
was also a separate god of distinct character,
particular to the Canaanites. He was the god of
fertility of field and cattle, the Rider of the
Clouds and the deity of rain and storm.

Of DIONYSIUS

DENIS (m), **DENNIS** (m) **DENISE** (f)

DIONISSIJ (m) Russ.
Dionysus was the Greek god of wine. St Denis was a 3rd century evangelist who converted the Gauls and became the patron saint of Paris. His feast day is October 9th.(Also see **WINE**).

Of FREYA (see **NOBLE LADY**)

GODDESS

LHAMO (f) Tib. lha – god + feminine suffix.

RHIANNON (f)

Wel. rhianon – nymph/goddess. A heroine of the Mabinogion stories. The old name of this famous Celtic heroine is Rigantona which means 'great queen'. She was the daughter of the king of the Underworld and the goddess of horses and of the sacred land. She is the protectress and helper of the wrongfully accused, those overburdened with responsibility, and women who have suffered miscarriages (she was once accused of killing her child and then later vindicated). (See **ANIMALS – Horse** and **LADY**.)

Beautiful under protection of ING

INGRID (f)
Ing was the fertility god of peace and plenty, also known to the Anglo-Saxons. The name has also been explained as meaning 'Ing's ride or steed' (referring to his sacred golden boar). (See **BEAUTIFUL**.)

Dedicated to HERMES

HERMIA (f) (see **MESSENGER**)

GODS AND GODDESSES

Goddess - Rhiannon [17]

GODS AND GODDESSES

Gift of ISIS

ISIDORA (f), ISIDORE (m)
Gk. <u>Isis</u> – the name of the Egyptian goddess + <u>doron</u> – gift. It has also been interpreted as 'gift of strength'. It was the name of the Spanish 6th century writer, St Isidore of Seville, who wrote one of the first encyclopaedias upon which much medieval learning was founded. The American dancer, Isadora Duncan (1878-1927) brought this name into popularity. Despite its roots, it was popular among early Christians and then later came to be regarded as a Jewish name, having been adopted as a Christian version of <u>Isaiah</u>. The feast of St Isidore is April 4th.

THOR

The Viking settlers brought to Northern England, Scotland and Ireland a set of names based on the name of their chief god of thunder and fighting – THOR. He was represented as a middle-aged man of great strength; a personification of the perfect warrior, a foe to the giants, but friend to man. He was the eldest son of Odin (the creator of the world), but worshipped more than other gods. He had equal status to the Roman god, Jupiter, and close affinity to the Lithuanian god, <u>Perkunas</u>, whose name also means thunder. His name continues to be used in the name of the weekday – THURSDAY – 'Thor's day' (see **DAYS OF THE WEEK**). The English had a similar god, called THUNOR.

Dedicated to THOR – 'The Thunderer'

THORA (f)

Isis

Like THOR

TURLOUGH (m)
Ir. <u>Toirdhealbhach</u>; lit. 'tower-like', meaning a tower of strength. The name has been associated with the god, <u>Thor</u>.

THOR'S CAULDRON

TORQUIL (m)

THOR'S STONE

DUSTIN (m)
Transferred use of the surname, which has become known largely because of the talent of the American actor <u>Dustin Hoffman</u>. The name is probably the Norman form of THURSTAN (see below).

THURSTAN (m)

From Danish <u>Thorstein</u> (<u>stein</u> – stone + <u>Thor</u> – the name of the Norse god). Several surnames derive from this name.

THOR'S STRENGTH

THOROLD (m) <u>Thor</u> + <u>weald</u> – strength.

VENUS

ESTHER (f)

Pers. The biblical Esther was originally a Jewish orphan called HADASSAH – myrtle (see **FLOWERS**) – the plant sacred to the Roman goddess of love, <u>Venus</u>. She was taken into the harem of King Achashverosh – the Hebrew version of the later Greek <u>Xerxes</u> (see above). Her name was changed to ESTHER to disguise the fact that she was Jewish, and she became the king's favourite and displaced his wife, Vashti. Esther derives from <u>aster</u> which means 'star' in both Arabic and Greek, from the ancient word <u>satarah</u>. In so naming her, the association with Venus and love was continued (also see **SEA** and **STAR**).

Of VENUS

VENETIA (f)

Lat. May also mean 'from Venice' in N. Italy (the modern name for which is <u>Venezia</u> in Italian). The name of a famous 17th century beauty who set up house on her own in London and married her childhood friend, who mourned her death so heavily that he spent the rest of his life in seclusion.

Daughter of ZEUS

ZENAIDA (f) Russian form of a Greek name.

Gift of ZEUS

ZENO (m)

Gk. A short form of Zenodorus – 'gift of Zeus'. This was the name of two important Greek philosophers, one of whom was <u>Zeno of Citium</u> who founded the Stoics in the 2nd century BC.

ZEUS-LIFE

ZENOBIA (f)

Gk <u>zeno</u> – root word for <u>Zeus</u> – the Greek king of the gods + <u>bios</u> – life. The name of the 3rd queen of Palmyra and of a 4th century martyr and occurs as <u>Zenobe</u> in a 17th century will in Somerset. Also occurred in 16th century Cornwall and sometimes as <u>Zonoby</u> (see **GOD**).

GODS AND GODDESSES

GOOD

AGATHA (f)

Gk. agathos – good. The name of a 3rd century saint who was very popular in the Middle Ages. She suffered as part of her martyrdom the appalling torture of having her breasts cut off. She is sometimes depicted as holding them on a platter and, because in some versions they look more like loaves, this led to the tradition of blessing bread on her feast day, February 5th. Because of the nature of her torture and death, she is invoked against diseases of the breasts. Another confusion arising from the portrayal of the manner of her death has led to her being associated with bell-ringers and campanology.

HASAN (m)

Arab. hasuna – to be good (and beautiful). The name of Muhammad's grandson who was said to resemble him. Husayn is the diminutive which expresses endearment. Very popular because of its religious associations.

GOOD LUCK

PHUNTSOG (m/f)

Tib. refers to the accumulation of all good luck and merit (accumulated spiritual power from wise actions of body, speech and mind). Also carries the idea of prosperity.

TASHI (m/f)

Tib. This word occurs in the Tibetan greeting 'Tashi deleg!' which confers auspiciousness and beneficence on the listener or reader.

GOODNESS

CUNEDDA (m)

Wel. cynnedd – natural quality + dda – good. This name indicates 'natural goodness'.

SALAH (m)

Arab. from saluha – to be a religious or good person. Very popular short form of Salah-al-Din – Righteousness of Religion. Another form of this name is Salih. This was the name of a famous Islamic prophet who was sent to call the people of Thammud back to God. To test his authenticity as a bona fide prophet the villagers asked that he manifest a large red-skinned, black-eyed female camel which could produce milk for the whole village. The saintly prophet met their demand, but cautioned the disbelieving villagers to guard the safety of the miraculous beast, as, if any harm should come to her, God would destroy the village. Disbelievers plotted and killed the camel. The village was destroyed in an earthquake, which only Salih and his faithful followers survived.

SIVE (f)

Ir. from Sadhbh. This is equated with Sabia (sometimes Sabine) and Sophia and generally anglicised as Sally (see **SABINE WOMEN**).

GOOD NEWS

EVANGELINE (f)

Eng. from Lat. evangelium – gospel and Gk. euangelion, from eu – good + angelma – tidings /news.

GOVERNOR

GLYWYS (m) Wel. glyw – governor.

GRACE

CHARIS (f)

Gk. kharis – grace. This was an important word for the early Christians, but was not used as a given name until the 17th century. This may have been to endow with the quality of grace or charity (part of its original meaning), or it may have been in honour of the Three Graces of classical mythology (see below).

CHARISSA (f) is a modern version of this name, which was originally created by Edmund Spenser for 'The Faerie Queene'.

GRACE (f)

Lat. grates – thanks, gratus – thankful, grateful. This meaning of grace survives in the 'grace' before meals. The modern word 'gratis', meaning done for no payment, derives from the original idea that the task in question was done only for thanks. In early Latin writing gratia indicated a divine favour. This was first used as a given name by the 17th century Puritans (see **BEAUTY, CHARITY**).

GRACEFUL

GHADA (f)

Arab. ghayada – to walk gracefully. The name means 'a graceful young woman'.

MAYSA (f)

Arab. mayasa – to swing from side to side or walk proudly.

GRACE PROTECTION
(also see **PROTECT**)

ESMOND (m)

OE. east – grace/beauty + mund – protection. This was a surname in the Middle Ages and re-adopted in the late 19th century as a first name, when it was popular to revive Old English names.

The three GRACES

AGLAIA (f) –
(see **BRIGHTNESS/SPLENDOUR**)

EUPHROSYNE (f) –
(see **CHEERFULNESS**)

THALIA (f) – (see **FLOWERS – BLOOM**)

The names of the Three Graces – kharites – of classical Greece (see **FAITH, HOPE, CHARITY**).

GRATEFUL

SHAKIR (m) Arab. shakara – to thank.

GRIEF (Release from)

ANGARONA (f)
Gk. goddess who releases mortals from secret grief (see also **GODS & GODDESSES**).

GUARDIAN

AYLWARD (m) OE.

HAFIZ (m)
Arab. hafaza – to guard or memorise. This was used as an honorific title for anyone who knew the Koran (Qur'an) by heart.

GUIDE

HADI (m), HADYA (f)
Arab. hadi – one who leads or guides, from hada – to guide (in a religious sense).

Rightly GUIDED

RASHAD (m), RASHID (m), RASHIDA (f)
Arab. all from rashada – to follow the right course. These names imply good sense and guidance, especially in spiritual matters.

***Rainbow** – Iris (f)*
Greek goddess of the rainbow (see FLOWERS)

HALO

HALA (f)
Arab. this is an ancient pre-Islamic name which refers to the halo around the moon (see **MOON**).

HANDSOME

KENNETH (m), KENNA (f)
Gael. this derives from two different names, one of them – Cainnech was a byname, meaning 'handsome, fair one'. The other name, Cinaed meant 'born of fire' (see **FIRE**). Kenneth Mac Alpine was the first king of the Scots.

COINNEACH (m)
Scot. from old name Cainnech.

WASIM (m)
Arab. wasama – to distinguish or mark.

HAPPIEST

AS'AD (m)
Arab. From sa'ida – to be happy or lucky: 'happiest / luckier'. This is another example of a popular Arabic comparative name form.

HAPPY

ALIZA (f)
Modern Hebrew name used as translation of Yiddish name Freyde.

ASHER (m)
Heb. biblical son of Jacob. The name means 'happy' or 'fortunate'.

DEDWYDD (m)
Wel. dedwydd – happy/blessed.

FELICIA (f), FELICITY (f), FELIX (m)
Lat. felix – lucky or happy. To the Romans Felicitas was the goddess of happiness and good fortune. Felicity was first used as a given name in the 17th century. The name of several saints, including one famous slave who was martyred with her mistress Perpetua in 203 AD. Another St Felicitas was a Roman widow who, after witnessing the torture and agonizing death of her sons, is reputed to have said 'Be strong of heart and look to the heaven where Christ and His saints awaited their coming'. She herself was later tortured and thrown into boiling oil. Felix was used as a Roman byname, notably for the dictator Sulla (138-178 BC) who believed that he was especially lucky and blessed by the gods. He named his children Fausta and Faustus, which have the same meaning as Felix. It is the name of many saints. Feast day is May 30th.

HANI (m), HANIYYA (f)
Arab. hani'a – to be happy/contented.

HAPPY/PROSPEROUS

ADA (f)

This was originally the short form of German names beginning Adal, e.g. Adalheid (Adelaide). Became independent name from mid 19th century and very popular 1875-1900 (see **FORTUNATE, PROSPERITY**).

She who makes HAPPY

BEATRICE (f)

Ital. and Fr. form of Beatrix. This name means 'bringer of joy and blessing'. The name of the famous beloved of Dante and very popular in the 19th century. (See **BLESSED**)

BEATRIX (f),

Lat. beatus – blessed. The original form of this name was Viatrix, from Viator – a 'voyager through life'. This later became altered by association with beatus. This was the name of an early saint and martyr of the 4th century.

HAWK (see BIRDS)

HAY MEADOW

HAYLEY (f)

Eng. originally surname, from Hailey in Oxfordshire, from OE. heg – hay + leah – clearing or meadow.

HEALER

ASA (m)

Heb. lit. 'physician'. The great-grandson of King Solomon (see **FLOWERS – Marshmallow**).

JASON (m)

Gk. probably from iasthai – to heal. IASO was a Greek goddess of healing. This is also the Greek form of the Hebrew name JOSHUA (see **GOD SAVES**). It was also the name attributed to the author of the biblical book of Ecclesiastes. The name of the famous classical hero, who, with his Argonauts, sailed in search of the golden fleece. Medea, the sorceress, fell for him and helped him win the fleece. When Jason betrayed and deserted her, Medea killed the woman who had ousted her, but Jason lived into old age, when, ironically, he was killed by the fall of a rotting timber from his old ship, the Argo.

HEALTHY

VALENTINE (m/f)

Lat. from valens – strong/healthy. Used for men and women since the 17th century. The Festival of Juno Februata on 15th February was a Roman fertility festival of early spring when people drew lots for lovers; and this custom became transferred to the Feast of St Valentine's Day – February 14th. He was a 3rd century Roman Christian priest who tried to give new meaning to the old custom. His name was added to the English and French custom of choosing a 'true valentine' or of receiving as such the first person of the opposite sex encountered on the morning of 14th February, so he has now become not only the patron saint of lovers, but also of greetings! Some attribute the patronage of lovers to St Raphael whose feast day is October 24th. (See **STRONG**)

VALERIE (f)

from Roman family name <u>Valerius</u>, from <u>valere</u>
– to be strong, healthy and flourishing. This was
one of the oldest and noblest Roman clans who
were allowed to bury their dead within the city
walls. It was also the name of several saints, who
spell the name differently and have different
feast days. The feast day of St <u>Valerie</u> is June 5th.

VALERY (m)

Feast day April 1st.

HEARKENING

SIMEON (m)

Heb. <u>sehama</u> – to hear. The name of the old
man who performed the circumcision and
blessed Jesus in the Temple, declaring: 'Now let
Thy servant depart in peace, now that mine
eyes have beheld my Saviour.' His feast day is
February 18th.

SIMON (m)

The Gk form of <u>Simeon</u>, and the name of
several New Testament characters and Jesus'
chief disciple (<u>Simon Peter</u>). A Greek personal
name, which meant 'snub-nosed' contributed to
the alteration in the spelling from the original
Hebrew. This was also the name of a sorcerer
who tried to buy the gifts of the Holy Spirit,
hence the word <u>simony</u>: the offence of offering
or accepting any kind of payment from
nomination to a position in the church office.
The feast day is October 28th.

SIMONE (f)

SIOMON (m) Ir.

SIMIDH (m) Scot.

SEMYON (m) Russ.

HEART

CORCAN (m) Manx.

CORDELIA (f)

Lat. <u>cordis</u> – of the heart.

HUGH (m)

Ger. <u>hug</u> – heart, soul, mind. Anglicised form of
Lat. <u>Hugo</u>, which the Normans introduced into
Britain. There are two very famous St Hughs.
One was the bishop of Lincoln (1186-1200)
who was noted for good works and charity and
the defence of the Church against the state. He
had a pet swan who nestled so close to his
beloved owner that he would put his head up
his sleeve, but was very fierce with everyone
else. The other, Little Hugh of Lincoln, is an
apocryphal figure who was supposed to have
been 'martyred' by the local Jews around 1255,
and so became an excuse for anti-semitism. St
Hugh's day is April 29th.

HUW (m)

Wel. Very popular and regarded as a form of
<u>Hu</u>. <u>Hu Gadarn</u> the Mighty was the legendary
leader of the <u>Cymru</u> (the ancient Welsh people)
across Europe to Wales and who established
that nomadic people as agriculturalists. Later he
was deified as the creator of the Earth.

HUGHINA (f) Scot.

HEARTH

VESTA (f)
Lat. the Roman goddess of the hearth.

(Notice how the names of famous mythological characters and those of gods and goddesses have been adopted in modern times for the names of household products and brand names of food!). (Also see **GODS & GODDESSES.**)

HEAVEN

CELESTE (f)
Fr. from Lat. caelistis – 'heavenly'. The feast of St Celeste is April 16th.

SELINA (f)
From Fr. Celine, from Lat. caelum – heaven. It has also been associated with the Gk. Selene – the goddess of the Moon, or considered to be a derivative of Celia. It was the name of a 5th century saint whose feast day is September 22nd (see **MOON**).

HEIGHT

ALVA (m/f) Heb. a biblical name.

Brave HELMET

KENELM (m)
OE. cene – brave, bold, keen + helm – helmet. This name was popular in the Middle Ages and was the name of a 9th century saint and martyr.

Divine HELMET

ANSELM (m)
Ital. Anselmo from Ger. ans – divinity + helm – helmet. A rare name in England, used formerly by Roman Catholics. It was brought to England by a 12th century Archbishop of Canterbury who was born in Italy. His feast day is April 21st.

Will HELMET

WILLIAM (m), WILHELMINA (f), WILMA (f)
OG. vilja – will + helma – helmet. Introduced by the Normans in the 11th century. GWILYM is the Welsh version of this name, and LIAM the Irish. WILMOT is a transferred use of a surname which comes from the medieval pet form of William. VLADIMIR is the Russian form of this name.

HELP/AID

EZRA (m)
Heb. Taken up by the 17th century Puritans and still in use, though more popular in the US.

OPHELIA (f)
Gk. ophelos – help. Used by Shakespeare for the unfortunate heroine of 'Hamlet', adopted from the 15th century pastoralist, Sannazzaro who was the first to introduce this name. The unhappy fate of Ophelia (madness and drowning) has not influenced the name's popularity.

HERO-BRIGHT

GWRGAN (m)
Wel. gwr – hero + can – bright.

HERO-STRONG

GWRNERTH (m)
Wel. gwr – hero + nerth – strong.

HEWER

GIDEON (m)
Heb. May mean 'feller of trees' or simply 'one who cuts down'. The name has also been interpreted as 'having a stump for a hand'. The name of the 5th Judge of Israel, who delivered the Israelites from the Midianites by having his army creep up on the enemy ranks with their torches hidden in pitchers. The story of 'Gideon's Fleece' became confused in the Middle Ages with the Greek myth of Jason and the Argonauts (who went in search of the golden fleece). In the biblical story, Gideon received many signs and miracles from God, among these was a dew which fell but only came to rest upon a fleece and not on the surrounding earth. This was a popular 17th century Puritan name.

HIGH

CONN (m)
Ir. This is a name in its own right or a short form of such names as Connor.

BRIDGET (f)
Ir. Probably derived from brigh – strength. The name may be linked with the Brigantes, a tribe who inhabited the north of England. It has also been interpreted as meaning 'high one' and 'fire'. Brighid was the Celtic goddess of fire, poetry, inspiration, smithcraft and healing, and many healing wells are named after her. Later her qualities and attributes were ascribed to St Brigit (c. 452-523), patron saint of Ireland, whose feast day is October 8th. St Brigit's head was supposed to be in Lisbon, so the name became popular in Portugal. St Brigit's Bell (Clog Bride) was supposed to have belonged to the saint and was taken on exhibition in England and Ireland, but the tradition was stopped by Henry V. It did not become popular as a name until the 17th or 18th centuries.

ELI (m)
Heb. The name of the High Priest who brought up the boy Samuel. It carries the meaning of 'elevated, raised up'. This name was very popular with 17th century Puritans. It is also used as a Jewish short form for names which contain the syllable Eli (see **ELEVATED**).

HIGH-GUARDIAN

HOWARD (m)
Eng. Adopted in the 19th century as a first name from a noble surname. Probably comes from Old Norse ha – high + ward – guardian. It is probably not from the Old English Hereweard – army guardian, as is often claimed. It has also been interpreted as coming from the term hayward, which referred to the occupation of maintaining hedges against cattle, or as coming from an Old Germanic name, meaning 'heart protector'.

HILL

BRIAN (m), BRIANA (f)
Ir. This name may derive from an old Celtic word, meaning 'high' or 'noble'. It was the name of the famous 10th century king of Ireland, Brian Boru, who defeated the Vikings at the Battle of Clontarf. The name came to East Anglia from

Britanny in the Middle Ages and to north west England with Scandinavians from Ireland. The name of the famous 18th century poet from Co. Clare, Brian Merriman, who, in his work, was an early advocator of the emancipation of women. This was also the given name of the writer who used the pseudonym of Flann O'Brien.

TARA (f)

Ir. After the place in Meath which was where the High Kings of Ireland were crowned. More popular in Britain since the 1960s. It is also the name of the female Protectress of Tibet who in that role appears in her green form.

HOLDING FAST

HECTOR (m)

Gk. Hektor – from ekhein – to check or restrain. The name of the Trojan champion who was killed by Achilles, having until then held the city against the Greeks. His name therefore implies 'defender', 'the one who holds in check'.

HOLY

HELGA (f) ON.

OLGA (f) Russ.

SANCHO (m), SANCHIA (f)

Sp. and Provencal. from Lat. sanctus – holy. St Sancho or Sanctus was martyred in Cordoba in 851 by the Moors. His feast day is June 2nd.

SANCTAN (m) Ir.

HOLY AND GOOD

GLENDA (f)

Wel. glan – clean/pure/holy + da – good.

HOLY AND FAIR

GLENYS (f)

Wel. glan – holy/fair + feminine suffix.

Very HOLY ONE

ARIADNE (f)

Gk. ari – very + adnos – holy. She was the daughter of the sun god and honoured as a goddess and the personification of the spring. Also the name of the famous daughter of the king of Minos, who gave Theseus the thread to enable him to return through the Labyrinth after killing the minotaur.

ARIANE (f)

Fr. form of Ariadne and the name of a 2nd century saint whose feast day is September 17th.

HOME

HAMELEN (m), HAMO (m)

OG. gypsy names

HOMECOMING

NESTOR (m)

Gk. possibly from nostos – homecoming. Nestor, was the king of Pylos and one of the most experienced Greek leaders at Troy, thus the name implies longevity and wisdom. It was used a little among early Christians, and there is a feast of St Nestor on February 26th.

HOME RULE

HARRIET (f) Eng. form of Fr. <u>Henriette</u>.

HENRY (m), **HENRIETTA** (f) Fr. OG. <u>haim</u> – home + <u>ric</u> – power/rule. It was introduced by the Normans and became the name of eight kings of England. Until the 17th century, <u>Harry</u> was the normal vernacular form.

Large HOMESTEAD

TREVOR (m)
Eng. form of Welsh name, which existed in Wales since the 10th century, and has been in use in England since the 19th. It is a transferred use of a surname which came originally from a place name: <u>tref</u> – settlement + <u>for</u> (<u>mawr</u>) – large.

HONEST

AMIN (m), **AMINA** (f)
Arab. honest or trustworthy, from <u>amura</u> – to be reliable or faithful.

AMITTAI (m)
Heb. A biblical name, meaning true or honest. The name of Jonah's father.

HONEY

HONEY (f)
OE. <u>honeg</u> – honey. Sugar did not arrive in England until the 16th century, until then honey was the principal form of sweetening and, as well as being a common form of endearment, especially in the US, this is a name in its own right.

MELINDA (f), **MELITA** (f)
derived from names such as <u>Melanie</u> and <u>Melissa</u>.

PAMELA (f) – (see **A-Z** p. 237 and **BEE**)

HONOUR

EMYR (m) Wel.

HONORIA (f), **HONOUR** (f)
Lat. <u>Honorius</u> from <u>honor</u> – honour. <u>Honour</u> was popular with the Puritans and is in use today.

NORA (f)
sometimes used as a short form (especially in Ireland) as well as now being a name in its own right.

More HONOURABLE

ASHRAF (m)
Arab. from <u>sharafa</u> – to be distinguished. This is an example of the popular type of Arabic comparative name which includes names such as 'more commendable', 'luckier' etc.

HOPE

AMAL (f/m)
Arab. The name means hope or 'expectation', from <u>amala</u> – to hope. Usually a female name.

MUNYA (f)
Arab. <u>maniya</u> – to have hope or desire.

NADIA (f)
Fr. and Eng. spelling of Russ. <u>Nadya</u>, the pet form of <u>Nadezhda</u> – hope.

NADINE (f) Fr.

RAJA / RAJYA (f) Arab. 'to anticipate'.

HORN

CORNELIUS (m)
from Roman family name Cornelius – possibly 'war horn' from cornu – horn, implying kingship.

CORNELIA (f)
Lat. The name of the 2nd century mother of two famous revolutionary reformers who became the symbol of all matronly qualities. When asked to show her jewels, it is said she would present her two sons to the enquirer, saying 'These are my jewels'. A statue was erected in her honour. In Egypt talismanic buckles of the cornelian stone were laid on the chest of corpses. This stone was considered to be a protector of the dead (see **JEWELS**).

HORN of EYE-PAINT

KERENHAPPUCH (f), KERENA (f), KEREN (short form)
Heb. Refers to the container in which women kept their kohl – black eye makeup – and so perhaps indicated a dark-eyed beauty. It was the name of one of Job's three daughters.

HOSPITABLE

XENIA (f), ZENA (f)
Gk. xenos – stranger/foreigner.

HOUSE by the WOOD

WOODROW (m)
Eng. Transferred use of a surname, which was originally given to someone who lived in a row of houses by a wood (see **TREES**).

IDOL

EILUNED (f)
Wel. eilun – idol/icon (see **FLOWERS – True Image**).

LYNETTE (f)
Fr. This is the more common form of the name and was invented by Tennyson in his 'Idylls of the King' (see **BIRDS**).

ILLUSTRIOUS

CLARENCE (m)
Derives from the surname Clare which was transferred to the Irish county.

CLARICE (f)
Eng. from Fr. form of Latin name Claritia, from clarus – famous. This name carries the meaning of 'illustrious', which combines the qualities of fame, brightness and clarity (see **BRIGHT, CLEAR, FAMOUS**).

IMMORTAL

AMBROSE (m), AMBROSINA (f)
Gk. Literally: 'belonging to the immortals'. In Sanskrit amrita means 'nectar' (a-mri – against death – notice the relationship between mri and the modern word murder). Amrita or nectar was the water of life which was said to sustain the Indo-European races. Ambrosia was the food of the gods (adopted significantly today as a brand name for a creamed rice pudding!), which had the power to convey and sustain immortality; and nectar was their drink. It was the name of the 4th century scholar and bishop of Milan, whose feast day is December 7th. Ambrosius Aurelianus was the traditional 5th century uncle of King Arthur and Ambrosius was the Latin forerunner of the Welsh name Emrys (see **DISPUTED MEANINGS – Merlin**).

ATHANASIUS (m)
Gk. Thanatos was the god of death, from which the name for the newly revived art and science of death and dying – thanatology – is derived. The name, therefore, means 'against death' – immortal. St Athanasius is a popular saint in the Orthodox Church who is said to have tamed a wolf as a messenger. His feast day is May 2nd.

EMRYS (m) Wel.

KHALID (m), KHALIDA (f) (rare)
Arab. khalada – to last forever/to be long-lived. This is one of the most popular male names in the Arab world. It was the name of Islam's most famous military leader Khalid-ibn-al-Walid who died in 619. Muhammad nicknamed him 'the unsheathed sword of God' (see also **UNFADING**).

INDESTRUCTIBLE
(see **JEWELS – Diamond**)

INDIA

INDIA (f)
The name of the country used as a first name. Probably came into regular use because of a

character in Margaret Mitchell's 'Gone With the Wind' (1936), from which several names were adopted into the language. Also the result of the interest of the 1970s 'hippy' generation in that continent. Popularity spreading from the US to England.

INDUSTRIOUS

AMALIA (f)
Ger. amal – work. A common element of Germanic names which are now no longer in use.

AMELIA (f)
Eng. This is a cross between Lat. Emelia and latinised Ger. Amalia. Amelie is the Fr. form and is sometimes used in England.

INTELLECTUAL

ELFOD (m)
Wel. elfod – this word carries the joint meaning of possessing mental and *spiritual* capacity.

INTELLIGENCE

MACHONNA (m)
Cel. kondos – sense/reason/intelligence.

INTOXICATING

MAEVE (f)
Ir. meadhbh, from a word meaning 'she who makes drunk'. The name of the queen of the Fairies (from whom Shakespeare derived 'Queen Mab'), the 1st century Queen of Connacht and an ancient Irish saint whose feast was on November 22nd.

IRELAND

BANBA (f)
Ir. The name of one of the goddesses identified with the land of Ireland itself.

IRON BROW

AELHAEARN (m) Wel.

Determined as IRON

DERFEL (m):
Wel. der – stubborn/dogged + mael – metal/iron.

Great IRON

MORFAEL (m)
Wel. mawr – great (one) + mael – metal/iron.

IRON LAD

MAELWAS (m)
Wel. mael – metal/iron + (g)was – youth/lad.

IRONLIKE

TRAHAIARN (m)
Wel. tra – whilst/as long as + haiarn – iron. A very ancient name, conveying that the bearer is long lived, enduring and has other qualities like iron. Iron was very important in Celtic society, being better than wood or stone for making tools. The smith was valued as a magician who exercised a very special craft, as the ore was found in meteoric stones and extracting it required special skill. The steel knife was considered to have magical properties and was sometimes

plunged into medicinal potions (such as charms against elves) to activate them or increase their efficacy (see **ELF** and **LONG LIFE**).

Of IRON

BARZILLAI (m) Heb.

ISLAND

INNES (m/f)
Scot. from Gaelic word for 'island', and an anglicised form of the Gaelic name <u>Aonghas</u>

(ANGUS) (see **UNIQUE CHOICE**). A surname which became a clan name and is occasionally used as a first name in Scotland, mainly for boys.

Rough ISLAND

RHONA (f)
Scot. probably from ON. <u>hraun-ey</u> – rough isle. Not in use till end of 19th century (see also **SEAL**).

Servant of JESUS

MALISE (m)
Gael. <u>Maol Iosa</u> – 'servant of Jesus'.

JEWELS [18]

Good name in man and woman, dear my lord,
Is the immediate jewel of their souls.

Othello, Act III (1650)

With very few exceptions, jewel and gem names are feminine. Like flower names, they were very popular in the 19th century in England.

AMBER

AMBER
Arab. <u>ambar</u>. A stone said to possess curative properties and was associated by the early Egyptians with light.

ELECTRA
Gk. <u>elektron</u> – amber:'one who shines brightly'. The daughter of Agamemnon. The word electricity derives from the Greek word for amber (see **COLOURS – Yellow**).

AMETHYST

AMETHYST
Gk <u>amethystos</u> – lit. 'against wine' (<u>a methys</u>); a remedy against drunkenness. We get our word 'mead' from the Greek word for wine – <u>methy</u>. (and also chemical terms 'methyl alcohol' etc.) This gem is associated with the quality of beneficence.

BRILLIANT

BERYL
Lat. <u>berillare</u> – to shine/to be brilliant. Sometimes taken as the symbol of purity.

CORAL

CORAL
Gk. <u>kouralion</u> – probably from an older Semitic word. The symbol of a mother's protection.

Like CRYSTAL

CRYSTAL Gk. <u>krystallos</u>.

DIAMOND

DIAMOND (f)
Gk. <u>adamas</u> – untameable/not to be subdued. Unusual gem name. Came into fashion in 1920s.

DORJE (m)

Tib. This is the Tibetan version of Sanskrit VAJRA – thunderbolt. In Vedic literature the god Indra comes from <u>indhana</u> – lighting/kindling, hence his power of lightning or thunderbolt which is symbolised by the thunderbolt (<u>vajra</u>) that he carries. The name carries the meaning of diamondlike, indestructible, adamantine. It refers to an extremely hard meteorite-type stone and symbolises the absolute indestructibility of the fundamental clarity of consciousness and the teaching of the Buddhas. It also refers to a ritual object which is used in Tibetan Tantric Buddhist practices and held in the right hand, symbolizing the active energy of skillful means. This is a very common name among Tibetans.

Richly GREEN

EMERALD

Gk. <u>smaragdos</u> – possibly 'to twinkle or sparkle'. <u>Maira</u> was a name given to the dog-star. <u>Esmeralda</u> is the Spanish version of this name. In Egypt this stone was considered to provide protection for mother and child. It was considered a good name for a Christian, because in the vision of St John the rainbow was described 'in sight like unto an emerald'. <u>Smaragdus</u> was the name of an early martyr and <u>Meraud</u> was a Cornish version of this name.

JEWEL

JAWAHIR Arab.

JEWEL or JEWELL

From Old French <u>jouel</u>, a diminutive of <u>jou</u> (Latin <u>jocus</u>) – a plaything or delight. N.B. the archaic English word 'jocund'.

NORBU (m/f) Tib.

MASTER OF THE TREASURE

JASPER (m)

Arab./Pers. Traditionally, the name of one of the Three Magi who followed the star from the east to Bethlehem to greet the newborn Jesus and offer him gifts of gold, frankincense and myrrh – symbolic of spiritual and temporal kingship and of death, and whose arrival is celebrated at the feast of the Epiphany. The name of the stone derives from a Semitic word, akin to the Heb. <u>yashepheh</u> – jasper. The stone was associated with courage in Egypt (see **FESTIVALS – Epiphany**).

NAIL (of the toe or finger)

ONYX Gk.

PEARL

PEARL

Lat. pirula – 'little pear'. An Anglo-Saxon name.

MARGARET

From Pers. <u>murwarid</u> – lit. 'a child of light' – the name for a pearl. The legend told by ancient magicians said that the oyster rose nightly to worship the moon and that drops of dew fell into its shell and were transformed by the moon's rays into pearl. St Margaret of Antioch was a legendary early martyr who was swallowed alive

JEWELS

135

by 'the dragon' (Satan) but burst through the side of the monster by making the sign of the cross. Her story provided a popular Christian allegory of feminine innocence and faith overcoming the devil and she is often depicted wearing pearls and holding daisies in her lap. The feast of St Margaret is June 10th.

MARGERY and MARGO are variations. MEGAN and MERERID are Welsh versions. GRETA and RITA are both pet forms of Margaret which are now names in their own right. There are several short forms and variations of Margaret, such as Peggy and Maisie. MARGUERITE is the French form, which also means Daisy (see **FLOWERS**).

PRECIOUS STONE

OPAL
Skt. upala – precious stone. Associated with truth by the Hindus.

TOPAZ

TOPAZ
From Gk. topazos – the name of an island in the Red Sea.

TURQUOISE

FAYRUZ Arab.

JEWESS

JUDITH (f)
Heb. 'Woman of Judaea'. The heroine of the Book of Judith in the Apocrypha, in which she is depicted as a widow who delivers her people from the Assyrians by cutting off the head of their sleeping commander, Holofernes, with his own sword while he is asleep, having been invited to spend the night with him. It was also the name of a Hittite wife of Esau. This was the name of one of Shakespeare's daughters. A consistently favourite Jewish name and adopted by Gentiles in the 18th century. The feast of St Judith is September 14th.

JOINED

LEVI (m), LEVIA (f. modern)
Heb. from a word meaning 'associated' or 'attached', deriving from the hopeful words of Jacob's wife, Leah, in Genesis: 'Now this time will my husband be joined unto me, because I have born him three sons: therefore was his name called Levi'. The priestly caste of the Levites was descended from him. This is also a byname of the evangelist, Matthew, the patron saint of tax collectors (see **GIFT OF GOD**).

After the RIVER JORDAN

JORDAN (m)
Heb. jared – to descend. It used to be popular to baptise children with water brought back from the River Jordan, during a pilgrimage to the Holy Land, and to confer that name at baptism.

JOY

BAHJAT (m), BAHIJA (f)
Arab. bahija – to be glad or happy.

CHARMIAN (f)
Gk. Kharmion, from kharma – delight/joy.

JOY (f)
Fr. joie, from Lat. gaudia – joy. This name was adopted by the 17th century Puritans.

TALAL (m)
Arab. talla indicates dew or fine rain, which were a source of joy to desert dwellers; talalah means joy and rejoicing and good looks (see **HAPPINESS**).

JOYSTONE

WINSTON (m)
This is actually a transferred surname, from the name of the hamlet of Winston in Gloucester-shire. It was first used as a given name in 1620 and was made popular by the Churchill family. There was an Old English name Wynnstan, from wynn – joy + stan – stone, which, if it had survived, would have become the modern WINSTON.

JUDGE

FAYSAL (m)
Arab. 'separator between right and wrong', from fasala – to separate. Faysal means sharp sword.

JUDGEMENT

DINAH (f)
Heb. din – judgement. A biblical woman, the beautiful daughter of Jacob and Leah, who was raped and avenged by her brothers, thus her name means 'vindication', 'avenged' or 'judgement'.

JUNE – (see **MONTHS OF THE YEAR**)

JUST

ADIL (m)
Arab. from 'adala – to act justly. This name is very popular in most Arab countries.

JUSTIN (m), JUSTINE (f)
Lat. justus – just. Justinus was the name of various early saints. The feast of St Justin is April 14th and that of St Justus, November 10th. St Justina is the patron saint of Padua in Italy and her emblem is a unicorn. Her feast day is shared with St Justin.

KERNEL

INEY (f)
Manx name from Old Irish eithne – kernel.

KING

BASIL (m)
Gk. Basileios – royal, from basileus – king. St Basil the Great was a 4th century bishop of Caesarea who is one of the Fathers of the Eastern Church. His feast day is June 14th. The basil plant was used in funerals in Persia and sometimes in Italy. The herb was considered holy by the Hindus, and was sacred to Vishnu and Krishna.

VASILII (m) Russ.

LEROY/ELROY (m)
Fr. le roi – the king; popular black American name. May originally have been used for servants of the king of France.

MELCHIOR (m)
Pers. melk – king + quart – city. The name ascribed by medieval tradition to one of the Three Magi (see **GODS & GODDESSES – Baal**, **FESTIVALS – Epiphany**, and **JEWELS – Master of the Treasure**).

MELEK (m) Heb.

REX (m)
Lat. rex – king. Not used as a given name until the 19th century (see **QUEEN**).

KIND – (see **NURTURING**)

KISS

PHILEMON (m)
Gk. philema – kiss. The name of a poor cottager in Ovid's 'Metamorphoses' who entertains the gods Jupiter and Mercury in disguise. They are so pleased with their treatment that they transform the cottage into a temple and install the elderly Philemon and his wife, Baucis, as priest and priestess, granting their wish to die together. When they die, they are transformed into an oak and linden tree with their branches entwined. This was a popular Puritan name.

KNOWING

ERNAN (m), ERNAIT (f)
Ir. 'my little experienced one'. This name is used as an equivalent of ERNEST in Ireland. It was the name of several Irish saints.

LADY

MARTHA (f)

Aramaic. The name of the sister of Mary of Bethany. While her sister Mary sat at Jesus' feet, enrapt in his teaching, Martha would busy herself with cooking and with the housework. She complained to the Master about this, and he replied: 'Martha, Martha, thou art careful and troubled about many things; but one thing is needful and Mary hath chosen that good part, which shall not be taken away from her' (St. Luke 10:41). Thus poor Martha was told that she had chosen the less important role and she became the symbol for the hardworking, rather than the contemplative life; from the 16th century the name was given to girls to encourage them to become conscientious housewives! St Martha is the patron saint of cooks and her feast day is July 29th.

NERYS (f)

Wel. Ner – lord + feminine ending.

The LADY Who Weans Her Children

FATIMA (f)

Arab. from the root yaftum. The name of Muhammad's daughter. The name carries the meaning of a prayer that the girl will live to see her children healthy and grown to maturity (also see **WOMANLY**).

LAME

CLAUDE (m), CLAUDIA (f)

Lat. Claudius, a Roman family name, from claudus – lame; the traditional interpretation referred to a past, presumably lame, ancestor of this family. The feast of St Claude is June 6th.

LAMP of AUSPICIOUS ENERGY

YANG-DRON (f/m)

Tib. This name derives from pre-Buddhist Bonpo influences (the indigenous, shamanic religion of Tibet). Yang is difficult to translate exactly, but relates to 'lung-ta' (lit. 'wind-horse'), which is a particularly auspicious form of energy + dron – lamp (see **AUSPICIOUS**).

LAND-BRIGHT

LAMBERT (m)

Ger. land – land + beorht – bright/famous. It could be interpreted as 'famous throughout the land' or 'pride of the nation'. It was the name of the 7th century saint, Lambert of Maastricht, whose feast day is September 17th (also see **BRIGHT** and **FAMOUS**).

LAUGHTER

ISAAC (m)

Heb. yitzchak – laughter. Three angels disguised as men visited Abraham and his ageing wife, Sarah, to announce that she was to have a child. Abraham received them well and Sarah was so amazed and delighted at the news that she laughed aloud, thus foretelling the name of her future son, Isaac. This was the name of several Orthodox saints and St Isaac is the patron of the

Cathedral of St Petersburg. His feast day is 30th May (and September 9th in the Catholic Church).

LIFE

BEATHAN (m), BEATHAG (f)
Gael. beatha – life.

EVE (F)
Heb. hawwah – breath of life. She was given this name by Adam, because she is 'the mother of all the living'. The name of the mythical first woman (see **BIRDS – Screech Owl**). Sometimes used to translate the Irish legendary name Aoife.

VIDA (f) Sp.

VITALIS (m)
Lat. vitalis – of life/vital. The name of several early saints.

ZOE (f)
Gk. This began as an affectionate nickname among the Romans. It was sometimes used by Greek-speaking Jews as a substitute for Eve, and then became popular among the early Christians, indicating their faith in eternal life. It was the name of a woman whom St Sebastian cured of dumbness, who died in the same bout of perse-cution with him c. 286 BC. It was a favourite among royal women in the Eastern church. In the 1880s ZOIA was a common name in Russia. Not used in England until the 19th century. It was the name of several early martyrs. St Zoe's feast day is July 5th.

Long LIFE

'AMMAR (m) Arab. 'amara – to live long.

TSERING (f/m) Tib. tse – life + ring – long.

LIGHT

FINLO (m)
Ir. 'fair Lugh'. Lugh, (Lat. lux – light), was the ancient Irish and Manx sun-god (see **GIVER OF LIFE** and **SUN**).

LUCIUS (m), LUCY (f)
Lat. lux – light. A name sometimes given to girls born at daybreak. St Lucy, because of her assoc-iation with light, and the legend that her eyes were put out when she was martyred under Diocletian, is invoked against blindness and diseases of the eyes. In early paintings St Lucia is sometimes shown carrying her eyes on a plate or holding the awl with which they are supposed to have been gouged out, or carrying a shining lamp. On the night of December 13th (the feast of St Lucy, also known as 'Little Yule'), an old celebration survives in Sweden which remains from the ancient winter solstice celebrations. Every year each village elects a 'Lucia Queen' and on this special night the little girl dresses in white and wears a crown of lighted candles on her head. She carries trays of food and drink to each house in the village, followed by a procession of candlebearers. This symbolises the strength of the returning sun. Santa Lucia is the patroness of Italian fishermen. Lucille (Fr.) and Lucinda are variations of this name which are used in their own right (see **BRIGHT** and **SUN**).

NUR (m/f)

Arab. <u>nawara</u> – to illumine. This is unusual in being used for both men and women. 'Nur-un-nisa' meant 'Light of the Women'. <u>Nurten</u> – Body of light, is a Turkish name (see also **SHINING**).

LIGHTBEARER

SVETLANA (f)

Russ. 'bearer of light' or 'light one', from Slavonic <u>svet</u> – light. This is a pre-Christian Slavic name but it is not found in Old Church Slavonic or Old Russian. It has been suggested that it was coined by the poet Zukovskij.

LIGHT of GOD – (see **GOD**)

LIGHTHOUSE

MANAR (m/f)

Arab. lighthouse or beacon, from <u>nawara</u> – to illuminate.

LIGHTNING

BARAK (m)

Heb. lightning flash, or flash of light.

LINEN

LLIAN (f)

Wel. <u>lliain</u> – linen. Perhaps refers to 'flaxen' or the whiteness of linen or simply its value (see **FLOWERS – FLAX**).

LISPING

BLAISE (m)

Lat. <u>Blasius</u>; from <u>blaesus</u> – lisping, or babbler/stutterer. St Blaise was a popular medieval saint and bishop of Sebaste in Armenia. He was martyred in the 4th century. His relics were brought from the East during the Crusades. An iron comb was his symbol, because of the manner of his death. He once healed a child who had a thorn in his throat and so he is invoked to heal diseases of the throat. His feast day is February 3rd. Another 4th century saint, St. <u>Blasius</u>, was the favourite saint of the English raw wool dealers. This is also the name of Merlin's secretary who is supposed to have written down his sayings. The name became popular in France because of the 17th century philosopher, <u>Blaise Pascal</u>.

LITTLE

VAUGHAN (m)

Anglicization of Wel <u>Fychan</u>, which is a mutation of <u>bychan</u> – little (see **SMALL**).

141

LITTLE DARK ONE (see DARK)

LITTLE LAD

GWESYN (m)
Wel. gwesyn – little lad or servant.

LIVELY

ALLEGRA (f)
Italian fem. of allegro – lively/merry. Known as the name of a musical tempo. Seems to have first been coined by Byron for his illegitimate daughter.

VIVIAN (m), VIVIEN (f)
Lat. vivus – alive. The saint's day is August 28th (also see above LIFE).

LORD

ADONIS (m)
Phoenician name from adon – lord, adopted by the Greeks, where it became the name personifying male beauty. Adonis was the god of agriculture, born from a tree. In one of his legends Aphrodite and Persephone both love him; and the king of the gods, Zeus, rules that he will live with each of them for 6 months of the year. In the other he is the lover of Aphrodite and is killed by a wild animal when hunting. The annual Phoenician festival of the Adonia honoured and mourned his death (also see GODS & GODDESSES).

CYRIL (m)
Gk. kyrillos, from kyrios – lord. The name of many early saints, including the famous theologians Cyril of Alexandria and Cyril of Jerusalem. The Cyrillic script is named after St Cyril, the 9th century missionary who brought Christianity to Russia and devised an alphabet to provide written translations of the Bible for converts.

KIRILL (m) Russ.

IVOR (m)
Wel. ior – lord. This is the anglicization of the Welsh name, Ifor.

Of the LORD

DOMINIC (m), DOMINIQUE (f)
Fr. from the Latin name Dominicus, from dominus – lord. St. Dominic (1170-1221) founded the order of Dominican monks. His feast day is August 4th and he is the patron saint of astronomers. These names may originally have been given to children born on a Sunday (Domenica) but are now more commonly given in honour of St Dominic (see DAYS OF THE WEEK).

LORDLY

ERMIN (m) Wel. from Lat. Herminii.

From LORRAINE

LORRAINE (f)
Fr. An Eng. and Scot. transferred use of a surname, which denoted a migrant from the French province of Lorraine. First used as a given name in the 19th century.

LOST

PERDITA (f)
Lat. perditus – lost. Coined by Shakespeare for the

abandoned baby princess and heroine of 'The Winter's Tale'. I once had a cat called Perdie, named after this character, as she had staggered, abandoned, hungry and pregnant, into a friend's house out of the snow, shortly after Christmas!

LOVE

CARADOC (m)

Wel. cariad – love. A very ancient name, the same as Caractacos, the British chief who was captured and taken to Rome in 51 AD. The historian, Tacitus, recorded how he impressed the Emperor, Claudius with the dignity of his bearing. Also the name of a character in the Arthurian legends who proved to be the only one at court whose wife was faithful to him.

CARYS (f)

Wel. from root car – love. Modern.

ERENSA (f)

Corn. (cf. Sanskrit karuna – compassion). (See **BELOVED**.)

LOVEABLE

AMABEL (f)

Lat. amabilis – loveable. This is the original form of ANNABEL and MABEL (see below).

AMANDA (f)

Lat. from amare – to love. This name was coined in the 17th century. MANDY is the popular pet form of this name. The masculine form – Amandus – is now out of use, but was the name of several saints from the 4th – 7th centuries. The feast of St Amanda is June 18th.

ANNABEL (f)

Eng. May come from Gael. aine – joy or Ger. Arnhilda, which actually means 'eagle-heroine'! The original meaning probably derives from a misreading (or mishearing) of AMABEL. This name is popular in Scotland.

MABEL (f)

Originally a nickname from AMABEL (see above and also **BELOVED**).

LOVED

AMY (f)

Fr. aimée – loved. St Amy's day is June 10th (see **BELOVED**).

LOVED BY THE PEOPLE

LUDMILA (f)

Russ. from an old Slavonic name, lud – people or tribe + mila – grace/favour. The name of a 10th century duchess of Bohemia who was the grandmother of the famous king of the Christmas Carol, St Wenceslas.

LOVED ONE

ASTHORE (f) Ir. a stoir – loved one.

Much LOVED

ANGHARAD (f)

Wel. an – intensifying prefix + car – to love + ad – suffix – 'much loved' (the syllable an intensifies the second syllable). This was the name of the mother of the famous 12th century chronicler, Giraldus Cambrensis, and of a character in the Mabinogi (see **BELOVED**).

LOVEDAY

LOVEDAY (f)
Corn. Medieval name sometimes given to children born on the 'loveday' which was set aside for the amicable settlement of disputes.

DYDDGU (f)
Wel. dydd – day + cu – dear/fond/beloved

LOVER of MANKIND

PHILANDER (m), PHILANA (f)
Gk. philo – love + andros – man.

Man from LUCANIA

LUKE (m)
Gk. Loukas – 'man from Lucania'. The non-Jewish third evangelist. He was converted to Christianity by St Paul whom he is said to have accompanied on some of his missionary travel. He was a physician and is the patron saint of doctors, and also of painters (he is supposed to have painted portraits of the Virgin Mary). His feast day is on October 18th.

LUCKY

BONAVENTURE (m)
Lat. buona – good + ventura – luck / fortune / adventure. The name of the closest companion of St Francis of Assisi, who is considered to be a second founder of the Franciscan order. Originally his name was Giovanni and it is said that when St Francis first met him he exclaimed 'O buona ventura!'. He was known for his simplicity, wisdom and scholarship and was made a doctor of the church, sometimes being referred to as 'the seraphic doctor'. His feast day is July 14th.

BONIFACE (m)
Lat. bonum – good + fatum – fate. In the Middle Ages this name was sometimes written Bonifacius and explained as a derivative of bonum + facere – i.e. a *doer* of good. The name of several early saints, a 7th century Pope and an Anglo-Saxon missionary. The saint's day is June 5th.

FAUSTUS (m)
Lat. faustus – fortunate. The hero of Goethe's 'Faust' (who sells his soul to the devil) was modelled on the 16th century German astrologer and magician Johann Faust.

FORTUNATA (f)
Lat. fortuna – luck/chance. The Roman goddess of good luck and the bringer of fertility.

GAD (m)
Heb. meaning 'fortunate warrior'. The name of one of 12 sons of Joseph (see **GOOD FORTUNE, FORTUNATE** and **HAPPY**).

Woman of LYDIA

LYDIA (f)
Gk. Lydia was a town in what is now Western Turkey. The name of a convert of St Paul, who is mentioned in the Acts of the Apostles and a popular name since the 17th century. St Lydia, whose feast day is August 3rd, is the patron saint of dyers, which function she shares with St Maurice.

Devotee of ST MAEDOC

MARMADUKE (m)

Ir. Mael-Maedoc – servant or 'devotee of St Maedoc'. Maedoc was the Irish name of St Aidan of Ferns (the Irish aidh – fire is represented in one name by Aid and in the other by aed). Portents surrounded the birth of this saint and many miracles were attributed to him during his lifetime. When a hunted stag was driven into the saint's vicinity, he rendered it invisible and the hounds fled. Another story tells of how, due to the saint's powers, many visitors were fed with only a small jug of milk and a little butter. He is reported to have told the cook: 'Give to everyone generously, as if you had all the mountain pastures to furnish supplies' (Butler's Lives of the Saints). He studied in Brittany where rumours of further miracles accompanied him. He founded a monastery at Ferns in County Wexford. His bell, shrine and satchel are exhibited in the National Museum in Dublin. The name MARMADUKE is completely out of fashion now, and is even considered comical. It used to be common in a small area of North Yorkshire. (I have a particular affection for this name as it was the name of a beloved small panda bear given to me by my father when I was in hospital with pneumonia, aged three – and he accompanied me throughout my childhood; he survived the indignity of being washed in disinfectant by one of the over-zealous nuns at school and hung out by his ears to dry, while I was recovering from chicken pox!)

MAGNIFICENT

MAGDALEN (f) / MADELEINE (f)

The name Magdalen is usually said to mean (woman) 'from Magdala' after the fishing town of el Mejdel in Galilee. However, there is no evidence for this and in Jesus' time it was probably not called that. There was, however, a town in N.E. Egypt called Magdolum. Over recent years new information about the true identity of Mary Magdalene has been recovered[19] confirming intuitions I have had since childhood Religious Knowledge classes and proving that, not only was Mary Magdalene the spiritual equal of Jesus, she was also his wife. She is the only woman mentioned in the Gospels in her own right, not as the wife or mother of a man. Her very special relationship with Jesus is recounted in Chapter 7 of St Luke's Gospel, when she washed and dried his feet and anointed him with precious ointment. In the non-Canonical Gospel of Philip[20] she is referred to as 'the woman whom Jesus loved and kissed often on the mouth'. He also honours her by calling her 'The Woman who knows All'. The name has variously been rendered as 'place of the dove', 'place of the tower' and 'temple tower' and it may not have been so much a reference to a place-name as a *title*. The Hebrew epithet Magdal-eder literally means 'tower' or 'elevated', 'great', 'magnificent'.[21] Madeleine is the French version of this name and this was introduced to England in the Middle Ages when it became contracted to Maudlin. The feast day of St Mary Magdalene is 22 July.

MAIDEN

CORA (f), CORINNA (f)
Gk. <u>kore</u> – girl.

MORWENNA (f) Wel. <u>morwyn</u> – maiden

PARTHENOPE (f)
Gk. <u>parthenos</u> – maiden + <u>ops</u> – face, form. This was an epithet for Athena. It was the name of one of the Sirens in Greek mythology. She drowned herself when Odysseus avoided her seductions by having himself tied to his ship's mast and commanding his sailors to block their ears with wax. Her dead body is said to have been washed ashore at Naples.

Beloved MAIDEN

RHIANGAR (f)
Wel. <u>rhiain</u> – maiden + <u>car</u> – loved

Fair MAIDEN

RHIANWEN (f)
Wel <u>rhiain</u> – maiden + <u>(g)wen</u> – fair/blessed

MAJESTY

AUGUSTUS (m), AUGUSTINE (m), AUGUSTA (f), AUGUSTEEN (f) Ir, AVGUST (m) Russ.
Lat. <u>Augustus</u> (from <u>augere</u> – to increase; note the modern words <u>augment</u> and <u>august</u>). This became the name of the eighth month of the year (see **MONTHS of the YEAR**). Originally a title which the first Roman Emperor gave himself in 27 BC and which he later adopted as a name. The name was brought to England from Germany by the Hanoverian kings, who, in the 16th century, were making it fashionable to adopt all things Roman. AUGUSTINE was the name of two notable saints – the 4th century St Augustine was one of the great Doctors of Christianity and the patron saint of theologians; and St Augustine, a 6th century Benedictine missionary, sent by Pope Gregory to convert the Saxons to Christianity, who became the first Archbishop of Canterbury. The feast of St Augustine is August 28th. Augustinian or Austin friars were once the greatest sheep owners in Britain. AUGUSTA is the name the Romans used for the City of London and it was adopted as a title for women.

MAN

ENOS (m) Heb. <u>enosh</u> – man

MANLY

ANDREW (m)
Gk. <u>andreios</u> – manly. The name of the first Apostle whom Jesus called. His relics were taken to Scotland (though most of the accounts of his life, including his crucifixion, are legend). Hungus, the king of the Picts, had a vision of St. Andrew's cross (the saint was crucified on an X-shaped cross) rendering him victorious. Thus the St Andrew's cross became the national flag of Scotland. In Tudor England the name gathered comic associations.

ANDREA (f) – (see **WOMANLY**)

ANDREI (m)
Russ. St Andrew is the patron saint of Russia, as well as of Scotland. His feast day is November 30th.

CHARLES (m), KARL (m)

from an old Norse word <u>karl</u> and the Old High German <u>karal</u> and <u>carlo</u> meaning 'free man', through OE. <u>ceorl</u> – man. The modern word 'churlish' derives from this, but only gathered its negative meaning later. The Frankish Holy Roman Emperor, Charlemagne was responsible for the initial popularity of this name (see **WOMANLY**).

MARINER

MURDOCH (m), MURDINA (f)

Gael. <u>Murdo</u> is the Scottish form of this name, which derives from <u>Muireach</u> – mariner or <u>Murchadh</u> – sea warrior.

MARRIED

BEULAH (f)

Heb. This was the symbolic name which the prophet Isaiah gave to the land of Israel. Popular Puritan name.

Of MARS

MARIUS (m)

Lat. Roman clan name, probably from <u>Mars</u> – the god of war.

MARK (m), MARCUS (m), MARCIA (f), MARCELLA (f), MARCELLINE (f)

Lat. <u>Marcus</u>, from <u>Mars</u> – see below. <u>Marcus</u> was one of the dozen or so given names in use in Rome in the classical period. The name of the author of the second gospel. He is the patron saint of Venice (it is believed that his relics were brought there in 829), who offers protection from fire and flood, and his feast day is April 25th. The symbol of St Mark is the lion with the eagle's head and this became the stamp on Venetian coinage – the 'marc'. Although long disused, traces of this old currency remained in the 19th century in the old legal fee of 6 shillings and 8 pence. In Arthurian legend, this was the name of the king of Cornwall.

MARTIN (m), MARTINA (f), MARTINE (f)

Lat. <u>Marcus</u> from <u>Mars</u> – the Roman god of war and (earlier) of fertility and agriculture. He was said to be the son of the union of Juno, the queen of the gods and a fabulous flower. He was the father of Romulus and Remus, the founders of Rome. He gave his name to the month of March and to a planet. St Martin of Tours was a 4th century Roman soldier who shared his cloak with a beggar by cutting it in half and eventually left the army and became a missionary, and later Bishop of Tours. His preaching attracted crowds because of his reputation as a miracle worker. He founded two monasteries and is considered the father of French monasticism. His feast day is November 11th. It was the name of 5 Popes, including one who died defending Roman Catholicism against Eastern Orthodoxy and was proclaimed a martyr. Due to Martin Luther (the founder of Protestantism), the name was sometimes used as a symbol for the Protestant Church in 18th century satire. St. MARTINA was a Roman who was martyred under Decius. The maidenhair fern is the plant associated with her. Her feast day is January 30th.

MASTER

SAYYID (m)

Arab. <u>sada</u> – to rule or prevail – (see **LORD**)

147

MEADOW

LEE (m/f)
OE. leah – meadowland or clearing in a wood. Transferred use of a surname.

MEDITATIVE

FIKRI (m), FIKRIYYA (f)
Arab. fikri – relating to the mind, from fakara – to ponder or meditate.

MELODY

ALAW (f) Wel.

MELODY (f)
Gk. melodia – singing of songs; from melos – song + aiedein – to sing.

MERCIFUL

CLEMENT (m), CLEMENCE (f), CLEMENTINE (f)
Lat. Clementius, from clemens – mercy. Clement was the name of several early saints, including the 4th Pope. The feast day is November 23rd. One St Clement was martyred by being thrown into the sea and a coral shrine formed around his head. He became the patron saint of sailors especially among the Danish and Dutch. CLEMENTIA was worshipped as a Roman goddess; she held a cup in one hand and a lance in the other. Roman Emperors were sometimes addressed by the title 'Your Clemency'. Clemency was a popular name with the Puritans.

RAFAT (m) Arab. ra'afa – to show mercy.

MERCY

MERCY (f)
Lat. merces – reward, later came to imply pity and compassion. A favourite 17th century Puritan name.

MERCEDES (f)
Spanish version of Mercy. One of the titles of the Blessed Virgin is Maria de las Mercedes – 'Mary of Mercies' and her feast is celebrated on 10th August and 24th September.

MYGHIN (f) Manx.

MERRY LIVELY YOUTH

GILMERE (m) Old Irish name.

MESSENGER

ANGEL (m), ANGELA (f), ANGELINA (f), ANGELICA (f)
Gk. angelo – messenger (originally this word meant simply 'messenger' in Classical Greek, but later came to mean *heavenly* messenger – an intermediary between God and man). Angels were first mentioned as 'keeping the way of the tree of life' and they were revealed in visions to Ezekiel and St. John. They combined in their being the wisest, bravest, strongest and loftiest qualities in creation. St Angela was a 16th century Italian who founded the first teaching order of nuns – the Company of St Ursula. Her feast day is May 31st. Angel was originally a feminine name, then exclusively a male name, but is now out of fashion for men in English-speaking countries, but is occasionally used for women (see **ANGEL, BURNING ONE**).

ANGELET (f) is a 17th century Cornish form, which may actually mean 'light, brown tawny one'.

HERMIA (f), HERMIONE (f)
Gk. I have included these names here by association rather than by etymology. They probably mean 'dedicated to the god Hermes', who was the messenger of the gods, with wings on his heels; Greek equivalent of the Roman, Mercury, who moved as swiftly and silkily as quicksilver. St Hermione's day is September 4th (also see **GODS & GODDESSES**).

ERMOLAI (f)
Russ. A saint in the Greek Orthodox Church.

MALACHI (m)
Heb. The last of the 12 Old Testament minor prophets, who foretold the coming of Christ. His name means literally 'my messenger'.

MALACHY (m)
Ir. Sometimes used as an anglicization of Maelseachlain who was a disciple of one of St Patrick's companions.

METAL – (see **IRON**)

MIGHTY

REGINALD (m), RONALD (m)
OG. Regenweald – might/power + rule. Implies a great warrior. A popular Norman name. Some say that it derives from the Latin name Reginaldus, from regina – queen. RONALD is an Old Norse form of the same name which was very popular in the Middle Ages and is now popular in Scotland. The feast of St. Reginald is April 9th.

RENOWDEN (m) Corn. (18th century)

REYNOLD (m)
OE. ragin – advice, decision + wald – ruler. Both words imply power, force and might; a strong ruler and the ability to make wise and strong decisions (see also **COUNSEL**).

MILD-FAIR

MWYNWEN (f)
Wel. mwyn – mild/gentle + (g)wen – fair.

MILD POWER

MILDRED (f)
OE. mild – gentle + thryth – strength. St Mildred was a 7th century abbess who was known for her kindness. She was the daughter of the Mercian King Merowald and had two sisters, both of whom also became saints. St Mildred's day is July 13th.

MIND – (see **HEART**)

MIRAGE

SARAB (f)
Arab. sariba – to flow, escape or steal away.

MODESTY

MODEST (f)
Russ. from Lat. <u>Modestus</u> – moderate / restrained / obedient / modest. This word derived from <u>modus</u> – moderation, measure or due. This was the name of a few early saints.

MONARCH

EDERN (m)
Wel. probably from <u>teyrn</u> – monarch, though usually said to come from Lat. <u>eternus</u> (also see **KING, RULER**).

Great MONARCH

MORDEYRN (m)
Wel. <u>mawr</u> – great + <u>teyrn</u> – monarch.

✳ MONTHS of the YEAR ✳

APRIL

APRIL (f), AVRIL (f) Fr.
Lat. <u>aprire</u> – to open, i.e. the month when the buds open.

MAY

MAY (f)
Lat. <u>Maius</u> – month of Maia. This name derives from the month *or* the flower (see **FLOWERS**).

MAIA (f)
The name of a Roman earth-goddess who was worshipped on May day, and the name of the mother of Hermes.

MAYDAY

GWYLFAI (f/m)
Wel. <u>gwyl</u> – festival + <u>Mai</u> – May. Sometimes given to children born on May day.

JUNE

JUNE (f), JUNO (f)
Lat. '<u>month sacred to Juno</u>' – the queen of the Roman gods, consort of Jupiter who took a special responsibility for the lives of women. Her name has been interpreted as meaning 'goddess', 'divine one' or 'young woman'. Coined as a first name earlier this century, it is the most successful and enduring month-name. Sean O'Casey made the name JUNO popular with his play *Juno and the Paycock*, and the name has sometimes been used in Ireland to anglicise UNA.

JULY – (see **JULIAN** in **DISPUTED NAMES**)

AUGUST – (see **MAJESTY** and also **DAYS OF THE WEEK**)

✳ ✳ ✳ ✳ ✳

MOON

The moon is the archetypal and cosmic symbol of the feminine, as the sun represents masculine solar consciousness. The etymology of the word <u>moon</u> weaves together many strands of interconnected meaning: as well as <u>mensis</u> – month, <u>menses</u> – monthly flow of blood, <u>menos</u> – heart /spirit and <u>mania</u> – madness (i.e. <u>lunacy</u>), it also includes the ideas of prophecy (<u>manteia</u>), meditation (<u>menoinan</u>), revelation (<u>menuo</u>), memory (memini), lying or deception (mentiri), wisdom (metis), holding in the mind or dreaming (metiesthai) and measurement (matih).

BADR (m/f)

Arab. 'Full Moon' from badara – to come up unexpectedly or take by surprise. 'Badr-al-Budur' ('Full Moon of the Full Moons') is a complimentary expression used about an outstandingly beautiful woman. The Full Moon is associated with the teaching of Islam.

CYNTHIA (f)

Gk. Kynthia was another name for the goddess Artemis who was born on Mount Kynthus (which is a pre-Greek name) on the island of Delos in the Aegean Sea.

DAWA (f/m)

Tib. – (see also **DAYS of the WEEK**)

DELIA (f)

Gk. Another name for Artemis (after the island of Delos).

DIANA (f)

Lat. originally Diva Jana – the goddess of the night and the moon. The chaste Roman goddess of hunting and later of the moon, she was a protectress of wild animals and equivalent to the Greek Artemis (see **VIGOROUS**). Despite her virginity, she was invoked by women as a goddess/protectress of fertility and childbirth. This is an ancient name, whose origins and meaning are obscure. It may be associated with the Lat. deus – god and share a common root with the name of Dionysius – the Greek god of wine and ecstasy. There are a number of popular variant forms and spellings of this name, such as Diane.

LUNA (f) – Lat. luna – moon.

SELENE (f)

Gk. Yet another epithet for Artemis, and possibly the name of a more ancient goddess, from the root ele – light. She crossed the sky each night in a chariot drawn by two white horses, while her golden crown illuminated the darkness (see **FLOWERS – Devotee of Artemis**).

Artemis

MOON ANGEL

AYMELEK (f) Arab. (Turk.)
(also see **ANGEL** and **MESSENGER**)

MOON BODY

AYTERI (f) Arab

MOON FAIRY

AYPERI (f)
Arab. – (also see **HEAVEN, SKY, STAR, SUN**)

151

MOOR (inhabitant of MAURICIUS)

MAURICE (m)

Lat. Maurus – 'a Moor' – the name the Romans gave to their North African enemies. Used for anyone with a dark complexion. Introduced to Britain by the Normans. The name of a Roman soldier and saint who was martyred in Switzerland in 286, giving his name to the famous ski resort St Moritz. His feast day is January 15th.

MORRIS (m)

This spelling was common as a medieval given name. Some say that it derives from the OE. mor, meaning 'uncultivated, open marshland'. Among Jews, this name has been adopted as an anglicised version of Moses.

MORNING

SABAH (f)

Arab. sabaha – to happen in the morning, or to become morning (see **DAWN**).

MORNING SUN

ORIANA (f)

Lat. oriens – morning/rising sun. Implies the east, or orient, where the sun rises (also see **COLOURS** and **SUN**).

Little MOTHER

'UMAYMA (f) – Arab. (pre-Islamic)

MOUNTAIN

AARON (m)

Heb. Interpreted as 'the most high'. This is a folk etymology from har-on – mountain of strength. The actual meaning of the name is unknown (see **DISPUTED NAMES**).

MOUSTACHED

ALGERNON (m)

from Norman French als gernons – 'with whiskers' or moustaches. This was unusual in Norman France, as most Normans were clean-shaven! Two 11th century Counts of Boulogne, a father and son, were both christened Eustace. According to the story, the son was given the nickname 'aux gernons' (with whiskers) to avoid confusion with his father.

Man of South MUNSTER

DESMOND (m)
Ir. Transferred use of a surname and now popular as a first name (see also **FOUR DIRECTIONS**).

The MUSE

AWEN (f) Wel.

The MUSES
These were the Greek patron goddesses of inspiration and creativity who originally inspired poet-musicians, and later took over the guardianship of all liberal arts and sciences. Their collective name derived from mao – to invent; from which the Latin words musa and musicus and our word 'music' come. A festival of the Muses was held every 4 years and also a contest – the Museia. It was Hesiod who categorised the Muses – limiting them to 9 and allocating certain realms of influence to each. Previously, they had been many in number and rather vague in function. These 9 Muses were: Calliope, Clio ('the proclaimer' – the Muse of History), Euterpe, Thalia (the Muse of Comedy), Melpomene, Terpsichore ('the whirler of the dance'), Erato ('the lovely' – the Muse of love poetry), Polymnia, and Urania ('the heavenly' – the Muse of Astronomy). Mnemosyne was the mother of the Muses. Her name means 'Memory' (from which comes the word 'mnemonic' – a device to aid memory).

CALLIOPE (f)
The chief Muse and in charge of eloquence and poetry. Her name means 'beautiful voiced'.

POLYMNIA (f) 'She of many hymns'

THALEIA (f)
from Gk. thallein – to flourish. The Muse of Comedy and also one of the **Three GRACES**

URANIA (f), URIEN (f)
Wel. from Gk. Ouranos – lit. 'the heavenly'. He was the sky and the father of all from whom we have named the planet Uranus.

The Gift of the MUSES

MUSIDORA (f) 'The gift of the Muses'

NEAT AND FAIR

DELWEN (f)
Wel. del – pretty/neat + (g)wen – fair.

NEW

NOVA (f)
Lat. novus – new, new-comer. In astronomy, the name for a star which suddenly becomes brighter and then returns to its previous brightness some weeks or months later.

The NEW HOUSE

XAVIER (m), XAVIERA (f)
This was the surname of the 16th century Spanish soldier-saint who founded the Jesuits. He was born in what is now Navarre, but was then part of the independent Basque kingdom and his name comes from the Basque place-name Etcheberria – 'the new house'. St Francis Xavier is the patron saint of missionaries and spent much of his life spreading Christianity in the Far East. He visited China and Japan and is buried in Goa in India. His feast day is December 3rd. This is an unusual name, used exclusively by Roman Catholics.

One who comes by NIGHT

TARIQ (m)
Arab. This is the name of the morning star and was the name of a famous Islamic military leader. He was a Berber who led the conquest of Spain.

NOBLE

ADELA (f)
There were many Frankish names beginning with adel, as the nobility were anxious to draw attention to their daughters' noble birth. Adelinde meant 'noble snake' (remember that snakes in those days were associated with wisdom and did not have the often negative connotations that they do today) and Adeliza was the mother of William the Conqueror.

ADELE (f)
Fr. version of ADELA popular in the 19th century.

ALICE (f)
Ger. from Adelheidis. An honorific title for German princesses. Came to Britain with the Normans. The publication, in 1865, of Lewis Carroll's *Alice in Wonderland* restored the name to popularity. ALICIA is a modern Latinate form.

ALISA (f) Russ.

ALISON (f)
This name was particularly popular in Scotland and has returned to use in England this century. The name actually derives from a popular medieval Norman diminutive of Alis (Alice). The name may also have been used as a corruption

of the flower name <u>alyssum</u>, from Gk. <u>a</u> – against + <u>lussa</u> – madness, so-called due to its peculiar healing properties (see **FLOWERS**).

ETHEL (f)

OE. <u>aethel</u> – noble. Originally a short form for several names which began with <u>aethel</u>, which at first could only be borne by the younger sons of hereditary kings or earls. Adopted as a female name in its own right in the 19th century.

MONA (f)

Ir. 'little noble one'. A name in its own right and a pet form of <u>Monica</u>. <u>Muadhnait</u> is the Irish spelling of this name. It was the name of a saint whose feast day was January 6th.

NABIL (m), NABILA (f)

Arab. <u>nabula</u> – to be noble/high born.

NAJIB (m), NAJIBA (f)

Arab. <u>najuba</u> – to be of noble birth. In modern Arabic <u>najib</u> means 'bright/intelligent'.

NOBLE (m)

Eng. especially US, from Lat. <u>nobilis</u> – noble. This was a medieval surname which derived from a nickname.

NOBLE BRIGHT

ALBERT (m), ALBERTA (f)

Ger. <u>adal</u> – noble + <u>berht</u> – bright, famous. This Norman name replaced the Old English name <u>Ethelbert</u>. This died out until it was revived in the 19th century. It has been a popular name in several European princely families. St Albert's day is November 15th. Louise <u>Alberta</u> was the daughter of Queen Victoria and Prince Albert

and the Canadian province was named after her in 1882 (also see **BRIGHT**).

NOBLE EAGERNESS

ALPHONSE (m), Fr.
ALPHONSUS (m) Ir.

OG. <u>adal</u> – noble + <u>funsa</u> – ready, eager, apt. Alphonsine the Wise was a Spanish king who had a set of astronomical tables named after him. The name was adopted in Ireland in honour of St Alphonsus Liguori, a Doctor of the Church, who founded the Congregation of the Most Holy Redeemer and was canonised in 1839. His feast day is August 2nd.

NOBLE FAMOUS

ELMER (m)

OE. <u>Aethelmaer</u> – noble and famous. It is a transferred use of a surname. Mainly used in the US in honour of two leading supporters of the American Revolution. <u>Aylmer</u> is another version of this name.

NOBLE KIND

ADELAIDE (f)

Ger. <u>adal</u> – noble + <u>heid</u> – kind, sort. HEIDI is a pet form of this name. The Australian city was named in honour of Queen <u>Adelaide</u>, the wife of William IV, as Adelaide Bay was discovered on her birthday.

NOBLE LADY

FREYA (f)

ON. <u>freyja</u> – noble lady, female ruler, mistress. The Norse goddess of love and beauty. The male god <u>Frey</u> was god of peace, prosperity, fertility and good weather. Such was Freya's beauty that the myths are full of plots to try to abduct her. This name was traditional in Shetland and is still used in Scotland (see also **GODS & GODDESSES**).

NOBLEMAN / NOBLEWOMAN

PATRICK (m), PATRICIA (f)
Lat. <u>Patricius</u> – a 'patrician' – ie. member of the Roman aristocracy. <u>Padraig</u> (c. 385-461) is the name of the famous patron saint of Ireland. This name was not used in Ireland in early times and St Patrick was not, in fact, Irish, but a Christian native of Briton who was captured as a young man and enslaved by Irish raiders. He escaped and went to Gaul where he studied for 12 years before returning to Ireland to preach at the court of the high kings of Tara. He was largely responsible for establishing Christianity in Ireland and he codified Irish law, grafting Christianity onto its pagan social structure. His feast day is March 17th. This is widely celebrated by the Irish who wear small sprigs of the shamrock on that day – it is said that St Patrick used the trefoil shamrock leaf to demonstrate the Christian teaching of the three persons in one God. The Welsh form of his name is <u>Padrig</u>. St Patricia's day is August 25th. This name came to Britain from Scotland in the 18th century.

NOBLE STONE

ATHELSTAN (m)
OE. <u>aethel</u> – noble + <u>stan</u> – stone. This name implies nobility and reliability. Very popular in the Middle Ages and the name of a 10th century

king of Wessex. Rarely used after the Norman Conquest, but revived in the 19th century.

NOBLE STRENGTH

AUDREY (f)
OE. <u>Etheldreda</u>. St Audrey's day is June 23rd. She died from a tumour in her throat which she attributed to an early love of necklaces. Necklaces sold at 'St Audrey's Fair' were cheap and cheerful and led to the term 'tawdry' (see also **KING, MAJESTY**).

✳ NUMBERS ✳

FIRST

ALPHA (f/m) Gk.

PRIMA (f), PRIMUS (m) Lat.

FIRST PERFECTION

CYNFERTH (f)
Wel. <u>cyn</u> – first + <u>berth</u> – beauty/perfection.

SECOND

SECUNDUS (m), SECUNDA (f)
Lat. sometimes given to the second-born.

THIRD CHILD

TERTIA (f) Lat. feminine of <u>Tertius</u>.

FIFTH

QUENTIN (m)
Lat. quintus (m), quinta (f) – fifth, names given to a fifth-born child. Saint Quentin's day is October 31st.

SIXTH

SEXTUS (m)
Lat. Sextilius. The name for a sixth child. Sextus was one of the sixteen praenomina (individual first names) in common use in ancient Rome (see Roman naming, p. 12). It travelled to Britain with the Romans, where it became the Welsh name Seisyllt and in turn the family name Cecil. The Victorians revived Sextus.

SEVENTH

SEPTIMUS (m), SEPTIMA (f)
Lat. name given to the seventh child.

EIGHTH

OCTAVIA (f)
Lat. feminine of Octavius – 'eighth', a name originally given to the eighth-born and later associated with the Roman imperial family.

NINTH

NONA (f)
Lat. nonus – ninth. Given to the ninth child, or one born on the ninth of the month, or in September.

LAST Child

ULTIMUS (m), ULTIMA (f)
Lat. Ultimus – referred to the last child, also denoted supremacy, meaning 'final, ultimate, the greatest'.

✳ ✳ ✳ ✳ ✳

NURTURING

ALMA (f)
Lat. alma – nurturing, loving, kind, bounteous. The term Alma Mater – 'bounteous mother' was used by the Romans to describe Ceres, the goddess of agriculture and Cybele, the goddess of nature. In the 16th century Edmund Spenser created a character of this name for his Faerie Queene and he derived it from the Latin word for soul – anima. The defeat of the Russians by the British in 1854 at the Battle of Alma during the Crimean War revived the name's popularity. Sophy Moody wrote of this in 1863: 'It will be in the recollection of all how many a fatherless babe but a few years back was baptised in tears by the name of ALMA' The term 'Alma Mater' (loving or nurturing mother) is sometimes used to refer to a person's old college or university.

Daughter of the OATH

BATHSHEBA (f)

Heb. 'daughter of the oath'. King David saw her naked while bathing and arranged for Uriah, her Hittite husband, to be murdered, so that he could marry her. She was Solomon's mother. Some say her name means 'opulent' or 'voluptuous'. It was a popular name with the Puritans, possibly as a warning!

OCEAN

OCEAN (f)

Lat. oceanus – of the ocean. Sometimes given to children born in or at sea. This custom dates at least from the voyage of the Mayflower in 1620. Other names include Neptune – the Roman god of the sea, Atlantic and even Sou'wester!, or the names of ships (see **ANIMALS – Dolphin** and **SEA**).

OCEAN OF TRUTH

CHÖGYAM (m)

Tib. A contracted name, made by combining chokyi – lit. 'the dharma', a Sanskrit word meaning, in this context, the teachings of the Buddha and gyatso – ocean (see **SEA, TRUTH**).

OLD

ALDOUS (m)

Eng. This name is of uncertain origin, but contains the Germanic element, ald – old. It may be a short form of various Norman names. Fairly common in East Anglia in the Middle Ages and now very rare, but mainly known because of the novelist Aldous Huxley (1894-1963). The name implies the wisdom and maturity of age.

GERAINT (m)

Wel. from Gk. Gerontios: geron – old man. The name of a character in Arthurian legend. An early king of Cornwall, who was killed in 530, also had this name (see **ANCIENT**).

ORACLE

PHINEAS (m)

The name of two biblical characters. Folk etymology has associated this name with the Hebrew meaning 'serpent's mouth', i.e. oracle, but it actually derives from the Egyptian Panhsj which meant 'the Nubian' or dark-skinned negro and was a personal name in ancient Egypt. For reasons not clear to me, it has also been rendered as 'Blower of brass'. It was a popular 17th century Puritan name. In use now as a Yiddish name – Pinchas.

SYBIL (f)

Gk. this was a *title* given to the ancient Greek prophetesses who spoke at various religious centres. The word derives from Gk. Sibulla which is probably a Doric form of Attic theoboule – divine will. Originally it was spelled Si byl.

Collections were made of these prophecies from c. 200 BC. by Jews and then Christians. Some took them to foretell Christ's coming and accepted them as one form of divine revelation, and Christians sometimes used the word to indicate any pagan priestess.

ORCHARD

CARMEL (f)

Heb. orchard or garden. This was the name of a mountain in the Holy Land which was famous for its fruitfulness and became the home of early Christian Crusader-hermits. These later became the Carmelite order of monks. 'Our Lady of Carmel' is a title of the Virgin Mary, whose specific feast day is July 16th. CARMEN is the Spanish form of this name (see **SONG**).

ORDER

COSMO (m), COSIMA (f)

Gk. Kosmas, from kosmos – order, beauty. This is the name of a famous 4th century saint who was martyred with his brother Damian. They became the patron saints of Milan. The feast of St Cosmo is September 27th. This name was brought to Britain in the 18th century by the Scottish dukes of Gordon. They had connections with the Italian ducal house of Tuscany whose founder was the famous Florentine, Cosimo de' Medici, who was one of the chief patrons of the Renaissance.

ORNAMENT

ADAH (f)

Heb. 'adornment, ornament or beauty' – referring to a woman's physical beauty and preciousness. One of the earliest Hebrew names to be recorded, and the name of the wives of Lamech and Esau. In use in England since the 16th century.

PARADISE

JINAN (m/f) Arab. Garden or paradise.

Gatekeeper of PARADISE

RIDWANA (f)
Arab. ridwan – God's pleasure.

PATIENCE

PATIENCE (f)
Lat. pati – to suffer. One of the Seven Christian Virtues. An example of a popular Puritan name which survived longer than most.

PATIENT

SABIR (m)
Arab. sabara – to endure, i.e. persevering, patient.

PEACE

Most ancient and modern languages include a name for a man or woman of peace – EIRENEOS in Greek, FRIEDRICH in German, SIMAITH in Celtic and LUBORMIRSKI in Slavic. The Hebrew word schalem (shalom) – peace – is at the root of several names, such as ABSALOM and SOLOMON.

OLIVE (f), OLIVIA (f) – (see TREES).

PEACE (f) Lat. pax – peace.

PEACE-BLESSED

TANGWYN (m)
Wel. tang – peace + (g)wyn – blessed.

PEACEFUL

AMINA (f)
Arab. amina – to be or feel safe. The name of Muhammad's mother.

PEACEFUL AND STRONG

HUMPHREY (m)
Ger. hun – warrior, strong or bearcub + frithu – peace. Implies quiet and solid strength. An aristocratic name in the Middle Ages. The phrase 'to dine with Duke Humphrey' means to go without supper and refers to the son of Henry IV who was starved to death by his political opponents. He was a patron of literature and founded part of the Bodleian Library in Oxford.

PEACEFUL RULER

FREDERICK (m), FREDERICA (f)
Ger. frid – peace + ric – king, ruler. This name was used by the Normans and was reintroduced into Britain by the Hanoverians in the 18th century, one of whom became king George I of England in 1714. There have been many European king Fredericks, most of whom have failed to live up to the meaning of their name! (also see RULER).

Father of PEACE – (see **FATHER**)

Man of PEACE

MANFRED (m)

Ger. man – man + frid – peace. It has been suggested that the first syllable actually derived from magin – strength. The Norman form of the name was Mainfred (as in the phrase 'might and main').

SOLOMON (m)

Heb. shalom – peace. The name of the famous, wise biblical king. He was the son of king David and built the Temple at Jerusalem. He is said to have been the author of the biblical books of Proverbs and Ecclesiastes and his is the famous spiritual love-poem, the Song of Songs. 'Solomon's Seal' is a 6-pointed star, like the Star of David and is an amulet in the shape of a hexagram which is said to possess mystical powers. Charlotte Yonge tells the story of an idiot boy who lived in Auray in Brittany. He dwelt under a tree and only ever uttered two things – 'Ave Maria' or 'Salaum hungry' – when he wandered the village in search of food. When he died, the villagers, believing him worthless, buried him under a tree. A lily grew on his grave, with 'Ave Maria' on every leaf. A church was built on the spot in honour of Salaum the Simple.

SULAYMAN is the Arabic form of Solomon and in tradition he was said to be gifted with the ability to converse with birds and animals.

Woman of PEACE

SALOME (f)

from an Aramaic name (Shalam-zion), related to the Heb. shalom – peace. This was abbreviated to Shalamzu and took the Greek form of Salome. It was common in Jesus' time and was the name of the wife of Zebedee and the mother of James and John – one of the women who mourned him at the foot of the cross, and one of the first to see Jesus after the Resurrection. It was also the name of the infamous daughter of queen Herodias, the stepdaughter of king Herod, who danced before Herod and then, encouraged by her mother, demanded the head of John the Baptist on a plate as her reward. This made the name very unpopular until the 19th century, when Oscar Wilde wrote a play of that name and it returned to very occasional use.

SALOMEA (f) Russ.

SULEIMA (f) Arab.

PEOPLE'S LEADER

LEOPOLD (m)

OG. Leutpold: liut – people + bold – brave, bold. This name came to England from the Continent in the 19th century when Queen Victoria named her third son after her uncle, Leopold of Belgium. The name implies a bold and brave leader of the people, which has been reinforced by the first element having come to be associated with Leo – lion (see also **RULER**).

THEOBALD (m)

Ger. This is the anglicised version of a Norman name which was recorded in medieval manuscripts. It derives from theuda – people/folk + bald – brave/bold. Under Greek influence, names compounded from theu were changed to theo, from Greek theos – God.

TIOBOID (m) Ir.

TIOBAID (m) Scot.

PERFECTION

KAMAL (m)
Arab. kamula – to be or become perfect.

PERPETUAL

PERPETUA (f)
Lat. perpetualis – constant, perpetual, everlasting.
St Perpetua was a 3rd century virgin martyr
(see **IMMORTAL**).

PILGRIM

PEREGRINE (m)
Lat. peregrinus (apparently originally from per –
through + ager – field) i.e. traveller/pilgrim. This
was a common early Christian name, indicating
the transitoriness of mortal life. St Peregrine's
feast day is May 1st and, in Catholic tradition,
he is invoked against cancer.

PIOUS

EUSEBIUS (m)
Gk. eu – well, good + sebein – to worship,
honour. It implies piety, respectfulness and
devotion. It was the name of a noted 4th
century Greek historian and several early saints,
including the reputed founder of the Abbey at
Guadalupe in Spain.

PLAIN

SHARON (f)
Heb. yashar – plain or flat area. This refers to
the rich coastal pastureland on the coastal plain
of Palestine. The so-called 'Rose of Sharon', symbolic of great beauty, may actually have been a
narcissus. The name is an English coinage from
the placename.

PLEASANT

AFFRICA (f) Manx and Ir. from Cel.

LLAWDDEN (m)
Wel. llawdd – pleasant + diminutive suffix.

PLEASANTNESS

AVELINE (f)
Heb. Introduced into England by the Normans.

NAOMI (f)
Heb. She was the mother-in-law of Ruth, the
Moabitesss, who suffered so much that she
wanted to change her name to 'bitter'. A
popular name in the 17th century.

PLEASURE

EDNA (f)
Heb. 'Pleasure, rejuvenation, delight'. The
meaning of the name may be connected with
the Garden of Eden. In the Apocryphal Book of
Tobit, Edna is Enoch's wife and the stepmother
of Tobias. It has been used to anglicise the Irish
name Eithne which means 'kernel' and was the
name of three virgin saints. It was brought to
England from Ireland in the 18th century.

EUNYS (f)

Manx name derived from Gk. Eunice, meaning pleasure or ecstasy.

PLEDGE

GISELLE (f)

Fr. from Ger. gisil – pledge. It was common in medieval Europe to leave children, as pledges for an alliance, to be brought up by a foreign court. The use of the name in English-speaking countries is largely due to the popular ballet Giselle (1841) though it was used in many European courts.

Bright PLEDGE

GILBERT (m)

Ger. gisil – pledge + berht – bright/famous. Introduced into England by the Normans. St Gilbert of Sempringham, (who died at over a hundred years of age in 1189) established the 'Gilbertians' – the only British religious order – which ran orphanages and leper hospitals as well as monasteries and convents. All this was abolished at the time of the Dissolution of the Monasteries. St Gilbert's day is February 4th. In Ireland the name was used to translate Gilbride (Giolla Bhrighde), which actually means 'servant of St Brigid' (see **BRIGHT**).

Little PLUM – (see **TREES**)

POET

TADGH (m)

Ir. implies poet and philosopher. Anglicised forms include Tad, Teague and Thaddeus.

POETRY

AWENA (f)

Wel. awen – the Muse + feminine suffix. The Welsh muse of poetry.

CERIDWEN (f)

Wel. Probably derived from cerdd – poetry. In Celtic tradition she was the goddess of barley and pigs who initiated the poet Taliesin and so is considered to be the goddess of poetic inspiration. She brews the cauldron of wisdom from which shamans drink.

POLISHED

SIXTUS (m)

Gk./Lat. possibly from Gk. xystos – polished, but may be a variant of Sextus – the sixth (child). The name of three early Popes. St Sixtus' day is April 6th.

POWER

WALDO (m), VALDA (f)

Ger. meaning 'great ruler'.

The one with great POWER

WANG-MO (f/m)

Tib. diminutive of Wang-chug-ma and a name in its own right. Wang – power/empowerment.

PRAISE

JUDE (m)

Heb. this is actually the short form of Judas, and is used sometimes to distinguish the apostle, Judas Thaddeus, from Judas Iscariot who betrayed

Jesus to the soldiers of the Sanhedrin in the Garden of Gethsemane, by indicating him with a kiss. The Lennon and McCartney song of 1968, 'Hey Jude' did something to revive the name's popularity. Judas is the New Testament Greek form of the Hebrew Judah. The 1st century St Jude was the patron saint of lost causes. His feast day is October 28th. The celebrated violinist, YEHUDI Menuhin, bears the Hebrew form of this name (lit. 'the Lord praises'). The Irish name, Siobhan (which is actually equivalent to English Joan, is sometimes anglicised as Judith.

MADIHA (f) Arab. madaha – to praise.

THANA (f) Arab. athna – to praise.

Most PRAISED

AHMAD (m)

Arab. hamida – to praise, lit. 'more commendable'. The name Muhammad ('the richly praised one'), as well as several other names, derive from the same root. It is one of the most popular names in Muslim countries and is an example of the common *comparative* type of male name.

PRAISEWORTHY

AENEAS (m)

Gk. from ainein – to praise. This meaning was attributed to the name by the Romans, although its exact origin is unknown. It was the name of the famous Trojan hero and founder of the Roman people, whose adventures are recorded by Virgil in The Aeneid. This name was sometimes used to translate the Gaelic Aonghus

(Angus, which means 'unique choice') and the Irish, Eigneachan, which actually means 'violent fate or death'.

ANTONINA (f), NINA (f)

Russ. originally a diminutive and now a name in its own right.

MAHMUD (m)

Arab. Several names come from the root hamida – to praise and majada – to be glorious / illustrious. This was the name of the first Muslim leader to conquer India. Mahmud of Ghazna, who lived in the 9th century, was responsible for the destruction of many Hindu temples which sowed the seeds of enmity between Muslim and Hindu.

MUHAMMAD (m)

Arab. Muhammad ibn-'Abd-Allah ibn-'Abd-al-Muttalib (570-632) was born in Mecca and received a revelation on Mount Hira at the age of forty, which led to the founding of Islam. This is considered one of the most auspicious Muslim names.

PRAYER

BEDE (m)

ME. bede – prayer. The Venerable Bede (673-735) was a Benedictine monk in Northumbria. He was a historian and theologian and the first known writer of English prose. He was the author of *The History of the English Church and People*. He was made the first English 'Doctor of the Church' by Pope Leo XIII in 1899. His feast day is May 27th.

Moved by PRAYER

ARABELLA (f)
Lat. orabilis (from orare – to pray to) i.e. invokable, or capable of being moved by prayer. This is a folk etymology attributed to the form of the name Orabel. The name may actually be an altered version of Anabella. Sophy Moody said that this is one of the few original feminine Latin names, as most are feminizations of male ones. It first came into use in 13th century Scotland.

PRECIOUS

NADIR (m), NADIRA (f)
Arab. nadara – to be rare/precious.

PREMATURE CHILD

KHADIJA (f)
Arab. pre-Islamic name. This was the name of Muhammad's first wife and the mother of all his children. She was the first convert to Islam and her strength, faith, wealth and maturity (she was years his senior and around forty when she married him) gave him the support he needed to establish his message in the face of much hostility. The Prophet married no other woman while she was alive, and always remembered her with the deepest love and respect. For these reasons the name is obviously very popular with Muslims.

PRESTIGE

ASMA (f)
Arab. the name of the famous daughter of the first 'guided' caliph (Islamic leader), who helped the Prophet and her father to escape from Mecca in 622, when opponents were planning to murder them. She tied parcels of food to her horse by splitting her belt and smuggled these to a cave where they were hiding. She became known as 'The Lady of the Two Belts'.

PRETTY

BONNIE (f)
Lat. bonus – good, but used to imply attractive, fair, pretty. Although this is a Scottish word, it has rarely been used as a *name* in Scotland, but is quite popular in the US, due, perhaps to the character of Eugenie Victoria, in Margaret Mitchell's *Gone With the Wind,* who had eyes 'as blue as the bonnie blue flag... and Bonnie she became until even her parents did not recall she had been named for two queens'. This was also the name of the famous female gangster partner of Clyde.

PRINCE

AMIR (m) Arab. amara – to command.
(see **PROSPEROUS**)

PRINCESS

SADIE (f)
Pet form of SARAH (see below) but now used as a name in its own right.

SARAH (f)
Heb. The name to which God changed that of Sarai ('contentious'), the wife of Abraham as a mark of auspiciousness and blessing. Sara was the legendary handmaiden of Mary Magdalene. She has a tomb in Provence and is believed by gypsies to have been a gypsy. The name's popularity rose with the post-Reformation revival of

biblical names. <u>Morag</u> is the Gaelic equivalent of this name, from <u>mor</u> – great. The Irish name <u>Saraid</u> – excellent, and <u>Sorcha</u> have been anglicised as <u>Sarah</u> (see EXCELLENT).

SALLY (f)

Pet form of SARAH (see above), but now used as a name in its own right (see also **KING, NOBLE, QUEEN**).

PRIVILEGED BIRTH

URIEN (m)

Wel. possibly from Cel. <u>orbo</u> – privileged + <u>gen</u> – birth. The name of a character in the Mabinogion who was identical with a 6th century Welsh warrior (also see **MUSES** and **TOWN-BORN**).

PROSPERITY

ODILE (f), ODETTE (f), OTTO (m)

Fr. from medieval German <u>Odila</u> from <u>od</u> – wealth/prosperity/riches. This is equivalent to the Old English <u>ead</u> – riches, fortune, in such names as <u>Edward</u> and <u>Edmund</u>. St. Odile (8th century) was a Benedictine nun and is the patron saint of Alsace. Her feast day is December 4th. Otto the Great (912-73) was the founder of the Holy Roman Empire. St Otto of Bamburg was a 12th century missionary saint. His feast is July 2nd. The name came to England in the Norman form of <u>Odo</u>, which was the name of the brother of William the Conqueror (see **WEALTH**).

PROSPERITY GUARDIAN

EDMUND (m)

OE. <u>ead</u> – riches, prosperity, happiness, good fortune + <u>mund</u> – protection. There are several ways of interpreting this – 'rich protection', 'happy or fortunate protection', 'guardian of prosperity' etc. The 9th century King Edmund of East Anglia became a saint and martyr because he refused to fight the Vikings, following the example of Christ. He was used by them for target practice, until he was covered with their spears 'like a hedgehog's spines'. He gave his name to Bury St Edmund's where he was interred, and gave rise to quite a cult in Western and Central Europe: many miracles are attributed to him. His feast day is November 16th. This was also the name of the 10th century Edmund I, king of England, who expelled the Danes from Northumbria. Edmund <u>Ironside</u> was king of England from 981-1016 and resisted Knute's invasion. Edmund was the name too of a 13th century Archbishop of Canterbury who wrote 'Mirror of Holy Church', a contemplative, mystical book.

EAMON(N) (m)

Ir. form of <u>Edmund</u>, but now also used to translate Edward.

EDWARD (m)

OE. <u>ead</u> – riches, fortune + <u>weard</u> – guardian, protector (as in the modern word 'ward'). Edward the Elder, the son of Alfred the Great, became king of Wessex and died in 924. Edward the Confessor (1004-66) was king of England, established the monastery and Abbey at Westminster and was famous for his piety, his service to the poor and sick, and his miracles. He was canonised in the 12th century and his feast day is October 13th. This Saxon name continued to be popular after the Norman conquest, not because of its royal associations, but because of its Christian ones. It is the most popular of the Old English names which begin with <u>ed</u> and imply prosperity and good fortune.

PROSPEROUS

AMIR (m)
Arab. amir – flourishing/prosperous (see **PRINCE**).

'I PROTECT'

AMINTA (f)
Gk. feminine version of Amyntas, the name of several ancient Macedonian kings.

PROTECTION

GERDA (f)
ON. garth – enclosure, stronghold. This is the Latinate form of the Scandinavian Gerd who was the wife of the fertility god Frey.

PROTECTOR

'ASIM (m) Arab. 'asama – to protect.

DARIUS (m), DARIA (f)
Persian. This is an ancient royal name.

Wise PROTECTOR/ PROTECTRESS

RAMONA (f) Sp.

RAYMOND (m)
OG. Raginmund; ragin – counsel, advice, decision, wisdom + mund – protection. The name implies guardianship and the ability to give wise advice. It was introduced to England by the Normans and became popular with crusading families, because of two 13th century saints. The feast day is January 23rd.

Good PROVIDER

HARITH (m)
Arab. haratha – to be a good provider/able to make money. This is also a name given to the lion.

PURE

AGNES (f)
Gk. (h)agne – pure/chaste. In Greece, agos denoted an object of religious awe. Women would strew twigs of the plant Agnus Castus on the bed during the festival of Demeter, the goddess of fertility and harvest. This Mediterranean plant is used in herbalism today to heal menstrual problems and to rebalance female hormones. Agnus means 'lamb' in Latin and this animal was consecrated to sacred purposes. Agnes was the name of a young Roman girl who became a saint and martyr in 304; she was driven to her death, veiled only by her hair. She is the patron saint of girls and girl scouts. Constantine built a church in her honour over her burial catacomb in Rome, and she became very popular in both the Eastern and Roman Church. After her death, according to legend, her parents and other Christians were weeping at her grave when she appeared before them, radiant and with a white lamb beside her. She spoke of her perfect bliss and told them not to weep. St Agnes symbolises the triumph of innocence, and her feast day is January 21st.

CATHERINE (f), KATHERINE (f)
Gk. katharos – pure. This meaning has come to be associated with this name through tradition, though its actual meaning is unknown. The 4th century St Katherine of Alexandria, about whom very little is actually known, became the subject

of many legends. A very popular cult grew up, especially among the monks of Sinai whose monastery bore her name. She was considered to be a model of great wisdom, the symbol of intellectual religion, eloquence and literature. The story goes that she rejected the advances of Maximus, refused to give up her Christianity, and then destroyed the wheel upon which she was supposed to have been put to death (hence the name of the popular firework). She was then beheaded with a sword, and milk flowed from her veins. Her corpse was borne aloft by angels and transported to Mt. Sinai. Her name was made popular by the Crusaders who introduced it into England, (where it was spelt with a 'C', as there was no 'K' in the alphabet at that time). The name was further popularised by St Catherine of Siena (1347-80) who was a mystic contemplative, as well as adviser to many of the Church fathers in Rome. She is patroness of Italy and of the Dominican Order. St Catherine's day is commemorated in the Catholic Church on April 30th. This was also the name of several queens, including the first wife of Henry VIII of England – Katherine of Aragon (1485-1536). It was the name, too, of the famous Russian empress, Catherine the Great (1729-96). There are many variations of this name, such as:

      CATRIONA (Gael.)
      KAREN, KATE (short form)
      KATHLEEN (CAITLÍN) (both Ir.),
      and EKATERINA (Russ.).

NESTA (f) Wel.

TAHIR (m) Arab. <u>tahura</u> – to be pure/clean

ZACCHAEUS (m)
Heb. possibly from Aramaic <u>zakkai</u> – pure.

ZAKI (m), **ZAKIYYA** (f)
Arab. <u>zaka</u> – to be pure or righteous.

QUEEN

REGINA (f)
Lat. <u>regina</u> – queen. Sometimes used as an allusion to the Blessed Virgin – 'Queen of Heaven'. There was a 3rd century St Regina whose feast day is September 7th. Also the name of an Irish saint (<u>Rioghnach</u> or <u>Riona</u>) whose feast day was kept on December 18th.

RAINA (f) Russ. – (see **KING**)

RADIANCE

ÖSEL (m)
Tib. 'clear light or radiance'. This refers to a spiritual quality of clarity of being.

SANA (f)
Arab. <u>sana</u> – to gleam or shine (see **BRIGHT, LIGHT** etc).

RADIANT BROW

TALIESIN (m)
Wel. <u>tal</u> – brow. Traditionally the name has been translated as 'radiant brow'. He was one of the three great 6th century bards.

RAIN

GHAYTH (m)
Arab. Names for 'dew' and 'rain' and other names associated with water are common in Arabic, because of the value of water in the desert. TALAL means 'fine rain', MAZIN means 'rain clouds', DIMA means 'thunder-free rain'.

RAINBOW

ENFYS (f) Wel.

IRIS (f)
Gk. She was the messenger of the gods who travelled between heaven and earth on a rainbow. Her name was also given to the 'iris' of the eye, because of its many colours (see **FLOWERS**).

RAMADAN

RAMADAN (m)
Arab. <u>ramid</u> – very hot. The ninth month of the Arab calendar. Considered the holiest month when devout Muslims fast from dawn until sunset. This name is used as a surname as well as a first name.

My RARE ONE

MYFANWY (f)
Wel. <u>Mi fanwy</u>. A medieval name, meaning 'my rare or fine one', revived in this century. Composed of affectionate prefix <u>my</u> and <u>banwy</u> which may be a variant of <u>menyw</u> – woman.

RAVEN – (see BIRDS)

REBORN

RENATA (f), RENÉ (m), RENÉE (f)
Lat. <u>Renatus</u> – reborn. Used by early Christians. RENATA is the original Latin form of <u>Renée</u> which is used a lot in Italy. Apparently, <u>Renata</u> also derives from a Hebrew word for 'joy, song' and from the Arabic for 'sweet melody'. St René is said to have risen from the dead seven days after burial. His feast is February 22nd. St Renata's day is March 16th.

REMEDY

FARAJ (m)
Arab. <u>faraja</u> – to remedy or drive away worries or grief. The name implies improvement.

RENOWNED

CLYDOG (m)
Wel. clod – fame / renown + adjectival suffix og.

SHAHIRA (f)
Arab. shuhira – to become well-known

RESTORATION

EDRYD (m) Wel. edryd – restoration.

RESTORER

JABIR (m)
Arab. jabara – to restore/bring back to normal. The name means a comforter or helper in time of need.

RESURRECTION

ANASTASIA (f)
Russ. feminine form of the Greek name Anastasios, (anastasis – resurrection). This name was used by early Christians as a symbol of their entry into a new life of the spirit. It has been used for babies born around Eastertime or in the spring. The name of a 4th century saint. The name was very popular in medieval England and was considered to be the name of Mary's midwife at the birth of Jesus, which may account for her feast day being on December 25th. Also the name of the daughter of the last Tsar Nicholas II. She was probably murdered, but a woman claiming to be her turned up in Germany in 1920. Her story was the subject of a film made in 1956.

STACEY (f)
Eng. pet form of Anastasia which became very popular in the 1970s and 80s.

REVERED

RAJAB (m)
Arab. rajaba – to glorify/treat with awe. This is the name of the seventh month of the Arab lunar calendar and one of the four holy months in which no fighting was allowed in pre-Islamic times (also see **MAJESTY**).

RICH

TAMIR (m)
Arab. This name literally means 'possessor of many dates' (tamr), which used to be the staple food of the Arabs. The name therefore indicates well-off, prosperous.

RICH and FORTUNATE FRIEND –
(see **FORTUNE** and **PROSPERITY**)

RIGHTEOUS

ZADOK (m)
Heb. 'just' or 'righteous'. The name of 9 Israelites, including a chief priest in the time of David, who anointed Solomon as king of Israel. Its auspicious meaning has led to its continued use.

RIVAL

EMILY (f)
from Lat. Roman family name Aemilius, which probably derives from aemulus – rival. This was made popular in the Italian Renaissance by the poet Boccaccio and revived in the 19th century.

ROCK

ALBION (m), ALBINA (f)
Cel. alp – rock, mountain. The ancient name for England (see **WHITE**).

CRAIG (m)
Gael. creag – crag, rock. Originally transferred use of a Scottish surname, now more widely popular.

PETER (m), PETRA (f), PETRONELLA (f)
Gk. petros – rock or stone. The most famous of Jesus' apostles and the founder of the Christian Church: 'Thou art Petros (stone) and upon this Petra (rock) I will build my church'. Jesus gave the Aramaic byname Cephas (rock) to this apostle to distinguish him from another of the same name. The feast of St Peter is June 29th. This was also the name of Peter the Great, Tsar of Russia (1672-1725) who founded the Russian navy and made his country into a significant European power. PIOTR is the Russian form of this name.

PIERS (m)
OE. from French pierre. In the medieval poem *Piers Plowman,* by William Langland, the character of Piers symbolises hard work, honesty and justice. The form Peter was not adopted until the 14th century.

Pilgrim to ROME

ROMEO (m)
Lat. Romanus – Roman citizen. The hero of Shakespeare's 'Romeo and Juliet' has made this name immortal (see also **PILGRIM**).

ROYAL – (see **KING**)

RULER OF ARMIES

WALTER (m)
Ger. wald – rule + heri/hari – army/warrior. The Old English form of this name was Wealdhere, but it was supplanted by the Norman version.

RULER OF THE PEOPLE

DEREK (m), THEODORIC (m)
OG. theuda – folk/people + ric – ruler. TERRY was the Middle English form which survives now as a separate name. DEREK is the form of this name which developed from one brought to England by Flemish weavers.

RULER of a TRIBE

DYFAN (m) Wel.

DYFNOG (m)
Wel. This name means 'having the qualities of a ruler of a tribe'. There are many Welsh names which include the word dyfn – ruler.

DYFNWAL (m)
Wel. dyfn – ruler of a tribe + (g)wal – defence/wall. This was the name of a 5th century legendary king of Wales.

Eternal RULER

ERIC (m), ERICA (f)
ON. ei – ever, always (or possibly einn – one, alone) + rikr – ruler. The name may mean 'eternal ruler', 'honourable ruler' or even 'island ruler'. Eric the Red was a Norse chieftain who

discovered Greenland. The name was introduced to Britain from Scandinavia before the Norman conquest, but was not used widely until the 19th century. The feminine form was coined towards the end of the 18th century. This is also the Latin word for 'heather' (see **FLOWERS**).

Strong RULER

RICHARD (m), RICARDA (f)

Ger. <u>ric</u> – power/ruler + <u>hard</u> – hardy/brave/strong. The Anglo-Saxons had a form of this name – <u>Ricehard</u>, but the modern form of the name was introduced by the Normans. The name of three kings of England. The 12th century 'Richard the Lionheart' (Richard I) was king for only ten years and spent most of them abroad engaged in expensive wars, yet he became a folk hero, earning his title from exploits in the 3rd Crusade. St Richard was a 12th century bishop of Chichester and his feast day is April 3rd. The feminine form RICARDA is used mainly in Germany. RICHARD is one of the most popular boys' names and many nicknames derive from it. There are several unusual feminine forms of this name.

Sea-born *– Aphrodite*
Greek

SABINE WOMAN

SABINA (f)

Lat. This refers to the women of a tribe who refused to marry into the nearby newly-founded Rome. The Romans invited the Sabines to a feast and captured many women. By the time the Sabines were organised to wreak vengeance, the Sabine women, now living in Rome, felt allegiance to both sides of the quarrel, as their sons and husbands were Roman and part-Roman; so they intervened between the opposing armies and brought the hostilities to an end. St Sabina was martyred around 127 in Rome. Her feast day is August 29th (see **GOODNESS**).

SACRED CAULDRON of the GODS

ASKELL (m)

Manx. from ON. Asketill – sacred cauldron of the gods.

SACRED NAME

JEROME (m)

Gk. hieros – sacred. The name in Greek is Hieronymus (hieros -sacred + onoma – name) and Eusebios Hieronymos Sophronios was the name of a Dalmatian hermit who lived from 342-420. He was a citizen of the East Roman Empire, a scholar (he translated the Bible into Latin) and was adopted as one of the great Church fathers.

The name Jerome was adopted by Christians in his honour. St Jerome is the patron saint of librarians and his feast is September 30th.

SAD

TRISTRAM (m)

linked with Fr. triste – sorrowful, sad; through association rather than certain etymology. Possibly from the Celtic name Drystan, who was mentioned as one of King Arthur's advisers in the Welsh Mabinogi (from the old Pictish name Drust, meaning 'tumult'). The name of the hero of the famous tragic love-story *Tristan and Isolde*. In folk legend, his mother gave birth to him in a forest when she was searching for his father who had been kidnapped by a sorceress. Because of the circumstances, the birth was difficult and Tristan's mother died. Her dying words were to ask her midwife/waiting woman to ask the king to name their baby son Tristram – 'a sorrowful birth'. Tristan's homeland was Lyonesse, which has been interpreted as Lothian, thus linking him further with Scotland. The name was very popular in Perthshire for many years. It is also associated with Cornwall. In Arthurian legend, Tristan was a brave knight and nephew of king Mark of Cornwall. The name seems to occur in the Cornish place name Tredrestan.

SALUTATION

TAHIYYA (f) Arab. hayya – to greet.

SAVIOUR

FADI (m), FADIA (f)

Arab. fada – to redeem, sacrifice. This is an attribute of Jesus Christ, known as 'Al-Fadi' in Arabic.

SCHOLAR

SCHOLASTICA (f)

Lat. from Gk. for 'scholar'. St Scholastica (c. 480-543) was the sister of St Benedict and the first nun in his Order. Her feast day is February 10th. She is the saint invoked in the Catholic church against convulsions in children.

SEA-BORN

APHRODITE (f), APHRA (f)

Gk. Aphrodite was the 'one born of the sea foam' (Charlotte Yonge called her 'foam-sprung'!). The Greek goddess of love equivalent to the Roman Venus, and known as 'The Emerging One'. She renewed her virginity every morning by bathing in the sea of Paphos. As an archetypal symbol of feminine sexuality and sensuality, she is born from and continually returns to the sea of the feminine unconscious (see **GODS and GOD-DESSES**)..

MORIEN (m)

Wel. mor – sea + geni – born.

SEA-BRIGHT

MURIEL (f)

Celtic from Gael. Muirgheal – from muir – sea + geal – bright, meaning 'sea-bright' or 'fair one of the sea'.

VORGELL (f)

Manx. comparable name to Muriel.

SEA-EXPERT

MURCARD (m)

Manx. from Irish muir – the sea + ceart – right.

SEA NYMPH

NERISSA (f)

Gk. nereis – sea nymph or sprite. In Greek myth Nereus was a god of the sea and father of fifty Nereids – the sea nymphs who were Neptune's attendants. The word also refers to a satellite of the planet Neptune. This was the name that Shakespeare gave to Portia's waiting woman in *The Merchant of Venice* (see **GODDESSES**).

Of the SEA

MARINA (f)

Lat. feminine form of family name Marinus – of the sea (originally the name derived from Marius, but came to be associated with marinus). It is the name of several early saints and the feast day is June 18th.

Dew of the SEA

ROSEMARY (f) – (see **FLOWERS**)

✳ SEASONS ✳

SPRING

AVIVA (f)
a modern Jewish coinage from the Hebrew vocabulary word for spring.

VERNA (f) Lat.

SUMMER FULLNESS

HAF (f), HAFWEN (f)
Wel. haf – summer fullness (g)wen – fair)

SUMMER WANDERER

SOMERLED (m), SORLEY (m)
– from ON. Sumarlithr: sumar – summer + lithr – warrior. It was a name used for the Vikings who made raids in the summer sailing season. Somerled is a Scottish Highland name and the name of the founder of the clan MacDonald, Lords of the Isles from the 12th-15th century. The name is sometimes anglicised as Samuel.

AUTUMN

AUTUMN (f)
Lat. autumnus – the month used as a name (see also MONTHS of the YEAR).

ELFED (m) Wel.

✳ ✳ ✳ ✳ ✳

Man from SEBASTIA

SEBASTIAN (m)
Lat. Sebastia was a city of Pontus in Asia Minor which carried the meaning of 'venerable' (from sebas – awe, veneration). St Sebastian (whose feast day is January 20th) was in legend a Roman officer martyred by Diocletian by being shot full of arrows – a favourite subject for medieval artists. It is said that his wounds were healed by a saintly widow, but that he was later beaten to death in the arena by clubs. He was buried in the catacombs by some women, and a hundred years later the Pope built a church over his tomb. St Sebastian is the patron saint of athletes and used to be invoked against the plague. BASTIAN is the Cornish version of this name.

SEER

GWYDDON (m)
Wel. gwyddon – 'one who knows'. Gwyddon ganhebon is the legendary inventor of vocal music.

SELFLESS

ANHUN (f)
Wel. an – negative prefix, meaning without. The name of the 5th century daughter of Vortimer and handmaiden to Madrun.

SERIOUS – (see EARNESTNESS)

SHADE / SHADOW

ZILLAH (f)
Heb. The third woman to be mentioned by name in the Bible and one of Lamech's two wives.

SHELTER

GWARTHEN (m)
Wel. gwarthen – shelter/cover

SHINING

LLEW (m)
Wel. This Celtic god, the son of Arianrhod, was known in Irish as LUGH. His name means bright, shining, warmth, light, sun. He was known as samildanach – the 'many gifted' or 'skilful hand', and was the patron of poets and talented people.

MUNIR (m), MUNIRA (f)
Arab. nawara – to illuminate, i.e. luminous, bright, shining (see **BRIGHT, LIGHT, SUN**).

SILENT

TACE (f)
Lat. tacitum – silent, not speaking. A rather barbed name to give to a girl, but still in use. Tacita was the Roman goddess of silence and this was a popular name with the Puritans. NB. modern word 'tacit'.

SILENT ONE

FIDDA (f) Arab.

LUJAYA (f) Arab. diminutive.

SINGER

SHADI (m), SHADYA (f)
Arab. shada – to sing.

One who loves SINGING

PHILOMELA (f)
Gk. philos – love + melos – song. This was the name of a mythological Athenian princess who was transformed into a swallow or nightingale (see **BIRDS**).

SKILFUL

MAHIR (m) Arab. mahara – to be skilled.

SKY

ASUMARI (f) Arab. (Pers.)

URANIA (f)
Gk. uranos – heaven. The name of the Muse of Astronomy (see **HEAVEN** and **MUSES**). Uranus was the earliest supreme god, who ruled over sky and heaven and after whom the planet, discovered in 1781, was named, having first been called Georgium Sidus after king George III.

SKYLIKE

AZURE (f)
Arab. (Pers.) 'lapis lazuli'. The stone was ground to use as a rich dye and paint and the name refers to the deep blue of a cloudless sky (see also **COLOURS**).

SLENDER-FAIR

MEINWEN (f)
Wel. main – slender + (g)wen – fair.

SMALL

PAUL (m), PAULA (f), PAULINE (f)

Lat. paulus – small. This was a Latin family name, which was later used as a given name. The name which the famous Saul of Tarsus took when he was converted to Christianity after a blinding vision of light on the road to Damascus. It is said that he chose his new name: a) because it was like a Jewish name, when he was enrolling as a Roman citizen; b) after the name of the people who had freed his parents; c) as a compliment to Sergius Paulus who was the deputy ruler; d) to indicate weakness; and e) out of humility – as a counterbalance to his former life. Up to that time he had been a staunch opponent of Christianity (and persecutor of Christians), but during his visionary experience it is said that he heard a voice calling to him 'Saul, Saul, why persecutest thou Me?' He became the newly-founded Church's chief missionary and was the author of the Epistles. His teaching aroused such hostility that he was beheaded in Rome about 65 AD. The feast of St Paul is June 29th. PAVEL is the Russian form of this name. St Paula was a 4th century Roman who founded several convents in Bethlehem. Her feast day is January 26th. PAULETTE is another French variation of the name.

SMILING

BASIM (m)

Arab. basama – to smile.)

GWENOG (f)

Wel. gwenog – smiling.

IBTISAM (f)

Arab. basama – to smile

SMITH

GOFANNON (m)

Wel. gof/gofan – smith. The legendary Gofannon is equated with Jove. The importance of metal in early society made the trade of the smith a noble one. The name was originally given to a man working with a hammer – whether in metal or wood. In Celtic society the smith held an elevated position and was considered to be both healer and magician.

SMOOTH BROW

MALVINA (f)

Gael. mala mhin – smooth brow. This name was invented by James Macpherson, an 18th century Scottish antiquarian poet who composed bogus but convincing and very popular Gaelic epics.

SNOW

EIRA (f)

Wel. eira – snow, but could also be from aur – gold from which several other names were formed.

White SNOW

GWYNEIRA (f)

Wel. (g)wyn – white + eira – snow.

SOLDIER

HERMAN (m)
Ger. lit. 'army man'; from heri/hari – army + man – man.

SON

FITZ (m) Norman Fr.

SONG

CARMEN (f)
Lat. carmen – song. This name is actually the Spanish form of the name Carmel which is a Hebrew word, meaning garden or orchard, but through folk etymology it has come to be associated with song and praise and is linked with the heroine of Bizet's opera of 1875. The character of Carmen was taken from a novel on Prosper Merimee (see **ORCHARD, SINGING**).

SOUL

ENID (f)
Wel. enaid – soul. A Celtic name which includes the ideas of purity and flawlessness. In the Arthurian myth she was the wife of Geraint, who is famed for her loyalty and patience.

SOWER

SHOLTO (m) Scot. from Gael.
Sioltach – sower i.e. fruitful or seed-bearing. Used traditionally by the Douglas family.

SPARKLING

SEIRIAN (f) Wel. seirian – sparkling.

SPEAR

BARRY (m)
Ir. bearach – spearlike: 'he who looks straight at the mark.' In the form of Barra this name is the pet form of Finbar – 'fair head', the name of the patron saint of Cork. St Barry was a 6th century Irish abbot and disciple of St Kevin with whom he later became a missionary in Scotland. His name was said to signify 'one who takes a direct aim at an object, or reaches it, as it were with the point of sword'. The priest who baptised him said: 'Rightly has this name been given to him, for he shall be a saint and his place shall be in Heaven.' His feast day is September 25th.

RHAIN (m) Wel. rhain – spear/lance.

SPEAR of Good Fortune

EDGAR (m)
OE. ead – fortune, riches, prosperity + gar – spear. Edgar the Peaceful who died in 975 was an English king and saint whose feast day is July 8th. It was also the name of the prince who would have succeeded Harold as king of England, had the Normans not invaded in 1066.

Ruling SPEAR

GERALD (m), GERALDINE (f) Ir.
Ger. gar – spear + wald – rule. Introduced to Britain by the Normans, became confused with Gerard and died out at the end of the 13th century. It was revived in the 19th century and is now more common than Gerard. In the 16th century, the earls of Kildare were known as 'Geraldines' which may have been where the name came from. The feast of St Gerald is October 13th.

Strong SPEAR

GERARD (m)

OE. gar – spear + hardu – brave/hardy/strong. A more common name in the Middle Ages than Gerald (see **SPEAR**). St Gerard Majella is the patron of the wrongly accused and his feast day is October 16th.

GERTRUDE (f)

Ger. gar – spear + drudi – strength. May have been introduced by migrant weavers from the Low Countries (there was a much-celebrated St Gertrude in Holland in the 7th century). Popular in the 19th century. It was the name of two 13th century Cistercian nuns who were famous for their mystical writings, and there is a feast of St Gertrude on November 16th.

A SPIRITUAL BEING

ELAETH (m) Wel. elaeth – intellect/spirit.

SPLENDID

EIRIG (m) Wel. eirig – splendid/fine.

LLEUFER (m)

Wel. lleufer – splendid – (see also **BRIGHT, SHINING**)

SPRIGHTLY

GOEWIN (f) Wel. gohoew – sprightly.

Young SPRING

IVAR (m)

Manx. from ON. Yngvarr – young spring.

STAR

ESTELLE (f) Fr., STELLA (f)

Lat. stella – star. Estelle was rarely used until its revival in the 19th century. Sir Philip Sidney popularised the name Stella in the 16th century, in a sonnet. Stella Maris – 'star of the sea', is a title of the Virgin Mary. The feast of St Estelle is May 21st and that of St Stella is on July 10th.

SUHA (f) Arab.

SUHAYL (m)

Arab. refers to the constellation of Canopus.

THURAYYA (f)

Arab. from thariya – to be abundant or to have many in one place. This name refers to the Pleiades, the seven stars in the neck of the constellation of Taurus.

Of the STARS

ASTRA (f) Lat.

Morning STAR

GWENDYDD (f)

Wel. gwendydd – the morning star.

STEWARD

STUART (m)

Scot. from the Gaelic name Stiubhart. Surname meaning 'chief of the royal household'. The title was conferred on Walter Stewart in the 12th century by King David I. The famous house of Stuart ruled Scotland from 1371-1707 and

England from 1603-1714. The name is also spelled STEWART, and is very popular in Scotland.

STONE

CHANTAL (f)

Fr. sometimes used in England, from the Old Provencal word cantal – stone or boulder. This was the name of the very popular 17th century French saint St Jeanne de Chantal, who, after the death of her husband (the Baron de Chantal), became an associate of St Francis de Sales and founded her own order of nuns (see **ROCK**).

STONE OF HELP

EBENEZER (m)

Heb. The name of the place where the Israelites defeated the Philistines. Samuel set up a stone there in commemoration of this victory. It was another popular Puritan name, possibly having been misinterpreted as a personal name. Dickens' character, Ebenezer Scrooge, has somewhat sullied its meaning with miserliness.

STRANGER – (see FOREIGNER)

STREAM

GHADIR (f)

Arab. name indicating favourable fresh water, a much-valued substance in the desert (see **RAIN**).

STRENGTH

BOAZ (m)

Heb. 'strength and swiftness'. The biblical name of the wealthy second husband of Ruth. He recognised her for all the kindness she had shown her mother-in-law, Naomi, and all the hardships she had endured; and he took care of her and eventually married her. Now a very rare name.

ESWEN (f)

Wel. esgwyn – possibly means 'strength'.

Possessor of STRENGTH

THUBTEN (m/f)

Tib. a term applied sometimes to the Buddha, as one of his ancestors, Buramshing-pa, married his cousin. This was considered shameless and requiring great thub-pa – daring, ability or 'guts'.

STRONG

MAYNARD (m)

Ger. magin – strength + hard – hardy/brave/ strong. A Norman name.

SWITHIN (m)

> St Swithin's day if thou dost rain
> For forty days it will remain.
> St Swithin's day if thou be fair
> For forty days 'twill rain na mair...

OE. swith – strong. St Swithin was bishop of Winchester and died in 862. His feast day is July 2nd. When his tomb was transferred to a grand new basilica in 971, miracles were said to accompany the event and a mass of legends arose surrounding revival of interest in the saint, including the still-followed weather myth which seems to date from the 12th century:

VALENTINE (m/f)

Lat. <u>Valentinus</u> from <u>valere</u> – to be strong (compare the English word 'valorous'). The name of a 3rd century saint and martyr, and common among early Christians. St Valentinus was martyred on February 13th, the day before the festival of Juno on which people drew lots for lovers. Hence his feast day is February 14th, and he became the patron saint of lovers. There is an old tale that birds began to couple on this day. Valentine cards only came into use in the 19th century, but St Valentine has nevertheless been adopted as the patron of greetings! (see **HEALTHY**)

STRONG LORD

IDNERTH (m)

Wel. <u>iud</u> – lord + <u>nerth</u> – strong (see also **LORD**).

STRONG WORKER

MILLICENT (f)

Ger. <u>amal</u> – labour + <u>swinth</u> – strength. This is the English form of the French MELISANDE. It was the name of Charlemagne's daughter and was introduced to Britain by the Normans.

SUCCESS

TAUFIQ (m)

Arab. good fortune / prosperity / success, from <u>wafiqa</u> – to be successful or lucky (see **GOOD FORTUNE** and **PROSPERITY**).

SUCCESSOR

ALPHEUS (m)

from a Semitic word meaning 'successor'.

The name of several Old and New Testament characters.

SULLEN

'ABBAS (m)

Arab. '<u>abasa</u> – to frown/look sternly at. This may seem a strange name to call a boy, but it also carries the qualities of austerity and seriousness which are considered desirable for Islamic men. It was the name of one of Muhammad's uncles and is also a nickname for the lion.

SUN

The ancestors of the whole Aryan race, thousands of years it may be before Homer or the Veda, worshipped an unseen being under the selfsame name, the name of Light and Sky. [22]

APOLLONIA (f), APOLLONIUS (m)

Lat. feminine of Gk. masculine <u>Apollonios</u>, meaning 'of the sun-god Apollo' and therefore has come to be associated with the life-giving power of the sun. When a statue of one of the priests of Eleusis was discovered, an inscription on the base read: 'Ask not my name, the mystic rule (or packet) has carried it away into the blue sea. But when I reach the fated day and go to the abode of the blest, then all who care for me will pronounce it.' When the priest died, his sons added these words to the inscription: 'Now we, his children, reveal the name of the best of fathers, which, when alive, he hid in the depths of the sea. This is the famous Apollonius'. APOLLONIA was a 3rd century martyr who has become the patron saint of dentists (and is invoked against toothache) as she suffered the unimaginable death of having all her teeth pulled out. Her feast day is February 9th. Ultimately this name is of unknown meaning, and it may be of pre-Greek origin (see also **BRIGHT, LIGHT, MOON, SHINING,** and **STAR**).

LUGH (m) Manx-Celtic sun-god.

NYIMA (m)
Tib. (see **DAYS OF THE WEEK**)

SUN-BORN

SULIEN (m)
Wel. sul – sun + geni – born. Sul was the ancient Celtic sun-god.

SUN-CHILD

SAMSON (m)
Heb. Lit. 'child of the sun-god Shamash'. The name implies 'strong as the strength of the sun'. As well as being one of the Judges of Israel and famous champion of Israelites, against Philistines, he was a folk-hero equivalent to Hercules in Greek tradition or Gilgamesh in the Babylonian. St Samson was a Welsh bishop who founded an Abbey in Brittany. He passed through Cornwall on the way and gave his name to one of the Isles of Scilly. His feast day is July 28th. The 'p' was added to the spelling – to make Sampson – by the Greeks who could not pronounce the 'sh' in the Hebrew form.

SUN-FAIR

SULWYN (m)
Wel. sul – sun + (g)wyn – fair. The feast of Sulgwyn was Whitsun, i.e. 'sun white' or 'White Sunday' (g)wyn has the triple meaning of fair/beautiful, blessed and white).

SUNRISE

ANATOLE (m) Fr., ANATOLI (m)
Russ. from a Latin personal name Anatolius, from Gk. anatole – sunrise/dawn. The name indicated a 'man from the East'. St Anatolius was a 5th century Bishop of Constantinople, so the name was popular in Russia and the Eastern Church. His feast is July 3rd (also see **DAWN**).

SUNSHINE

HEULWEN (f) Wel. heulwen – shine.

SUPPLANTER

JACOB (m) Lat.,
JAMES (m) Heb. through Gk.,
JACQUELINE (f)
The original Hebrew name Yaakov, from akev, meaning 'heel', was given to the son of Isaac and Rebecca (whom we know as Jacob) because the baby, when born, was said to grab hold of his brother Esau's heel; and then supplanted his elder brother by persuading him to sell his inheritance to him in exchange for a 'mess of pottage'. The name developed in Latin as Iacobus, from which we derive JACOB and Iacomus from which come JAMES. There are many variations of this name: Iago in Welsh, Hamish in Scotland, Seamus in Ireland, Jago in

Cornwall, with <u>Jamma</u> as a Cornish pet form. In the 17th century <u>James</u> was pronounced 'Jammez' in Cornwall. <u>Jamesina</u> is another feminine form and <u>Jakov</u> and <u>Jaschenka</u> (f) are Russian forms. Two of Christ's disciples were called James, as were many famous kings. St James at Compostella in Spain was one of the most popular medieval pilgrimage sites. The feast day is July 25th.

SWARTHY

KEIR (m)
Gael. <u>ciar</u> – swarthy/dusky. Scottish surname occasionally used as a first name.

SWEET

DULCIE (f)
Lat. <u>dulcis</u> – sweet. This is a 19th century version of a medieval name, from the Latin name <u>Dulcia</u>.

SADHBH (f)
Ir. meaning 'sweetness' or 'goodness'.

GLYKERA (f)
Gk. this name is not in use now, but comes from <u>glukeros</u> – 'sweet' which is still in use in the word 'glycerine'.

GLOUKERA (f)
was a 19th century Russian name.

SWEET SPEECH

EULALIA (f)
Gk. <u>eu</u> – well/good + <u>lalein</u> – to talk. This name was sometimes given to Apollo. It was also the name of a 4th century Spanish martyr. She was apparently a 12-year-old girl who was put to death for trying to persuade the authorities to stop persecuting Christians. The legend tells that as she died a dove flew from her mouth and her body was covered with a soft fall of snow. Her cult and the popularity of the name were fairly common in Anglo-Saxon England. The feast of St Eulalia is February 12th.

YANG-CHEN (f)
Tib. The Tibetan name of the goddess called <u>Sarasvati</u> in Sanskrit. She is the consort of <u>Manjusri</u>, the bodhisattva (awakened being) of Wisdom. <u>Yeshe Tsogyal</u> who was the consort of <u>Padmasambhava</u> (the founder of Buddhism in Tibet) is considered to have been an incarnation of the goddess Yang-chen. She is associated with the qualities of Venus, and with melody and sweet and wise speech. Her particular gift is the ability to express perfect ideas in a perfect form (see **ELOQUENT**).

Blessed SWORD

CLEDWYN (m)
Wel. most likely from <u>cledd</u> – sword + <u>(g)wyn</u> – blessed, but may be derived from cled – shelter (see also **BLESSED**).

Flaming SWORD

BRENDA (f)
Scot. Shetland name, and Ir., and used in England since the beginning of the 20th century. Probably of Norse origin, from <u>brand</u> – (flaming) sword.

TALL AND FAIR

ROWENA (f)
Wel. Rhonwen (rhon – pike or lance, meaning tall or slender + (g)wen – blessed/fair). This is one possible interpretation of this name. In tradition, she was the daughter of Hengist – the famous Saxon invader. She is supposed to have used beauty, and possibly magic, to persuade Vortigern to give large areas of Britain to the Saxons in exchange for marriage to her. Some have said that the name derives from AS. hrod – fame + wynn – joy (see **FAIR, SLENDER**).

Son of TALMAI

BARTHOLOMEW (m), BARTHOLOMEA (f) Ital.
Aramaic. 'son of Talmai'. In Hebrew Talmai means 'abounding in furrows'. It was the name of one of Jesus' Apostles whose feast day is August 24th. Little is known about him, but he may have spread the Gospel to India. A 19th century female saint, BARTHOLOMEA, founded a group of Sisters of Charity in Italy. The name was introduced to England by the Normans. It became famous after the founding of St Bartholomew's Hospital (Bart's) in London. This was established by the court jester of Henry I after he had been cured of illness following a vision of St Bartholomew. There are a number of Germanic variations of this name and it is also used as an anglicization of the Ir. Parthalan. This was the name of a legendary invader of Ireland, supposed to have been the first to arrive after the Flood, whose followers were called 'Partholonians'.

TAMER

DAMIAN (m)
Gk. from 'to tame or subdue'. This is probably another form of DAMON which was a name given to simple country boys. This is said to derive from Gk. daimon – spirit, demon or tormenter. The name of a 4th century saint who was martyred with his brother, Cosmas. They are the patron saints of surgeons and barbers, and their joint feast day is September 27th.

TENDER AFFECTION

HANAN (f)
Arab. hanna – to feel compassion/sympathise.

THANKFUL

HAMID (m)
Arab. hamida – to praise or commend.

SHUKRI (m), SHUKRIYYA (f)
Arab. shakara – to thank.

THANKSGIVING

THANKSGIVING (f/m)
USA. Sometimes given to a child born on the day of Thanksgiving, the fourth Thursday in November (also see **FESTIVALS**).

THOUGHT-COUNSEL

TANCRED (m)
OG. Thancharat (thanc – thought + radi – counsel). There is a Roman Catholic feast of St Tancred on April 9th.

THUNDERBOLT – (see JEWELS – Diamond)

TOLERANT

SAMIH (m), SAMIHA (f)
Arab. samih – generous, tolerant, magnanimous + samuha – to forgive and be tolerant of.

TOWN BORN

URIEN (m)
Wel. from Lat. urbigeniis – born-in-the-town (also see MUSES).

TREES

An Anglo-Saxon fortune teller was called 'Tan-hlyta'. Hlyta means 'lottery' or 'lot' and tan means 'twig'. So twigs were used to tell the 'lot' or fortune of people. Trees held a very important place in Anglo-Saxon culture: every tree was symbolic of some quality or possessed a particular magical property that people, and especially healers and shamans, knew how to employ. The following chant, for example, was used to protect from black magic:

Roan-tree and red thread,
Haud the witches a' in dread.

Among the Celts, the Ogham alphabet was made up of signs which indicated different trees, each indicating a particular quality or attribute.

ALDER

GWERN (m), GWERNFYL (f)
Wel. gwern – alder tree.

VERE (m), VERNA (f), VERNON (m)
this was originally a Norman French baronial surname, from ver(n) – alder. Now used rarely as a first name. VERNON is a place name which became a surname and then a given name. It means 'place of Alders'. VERNA has also been derived from Lat. vernus – spring (the season).

ALMOND

ALMOND (f)
Gk. amygdale. In a Greek legend, a Thracian princess, the lover of Demophon, died while waiting for his return and was transformed into a flowering almond tree.

ASH-TREE

MELIA (f) Gk.

ASHWOOD

ASHLEY (m/f), ASHLIE (f)
OE. aescleah – old wood. A place name which became a surname and then, since the 1860s, a first name.

TREES

BIRCH

BEDAWS (m), BEDWIN (m)
Wel. bedw – birch. The symbol of readiness: acceptance of marriage was indicated by returning a birch branch.

BIRCH HERO

BEDWYR (m)
Wel. bedw – birch + (g)wr – hero. The name of an Arthurian knight, anglicised to Bedevere.

Fair BRANCH

BARENWYN (f) Corn.

HAZEL

To the Celts, the hazel nut was associated with wisdom – the symbol of protection and authority and also of unyielding stubbornness and refusal. In Norse legend the hazel was sacred to Thor. An ancient Catholic legend tells how the Holy Family sheltered from a storm under a hazel tree during their flight to Egypt. In medieval times a forked hazel twig was used to discover witches – hence the name of 'witch hazel'.

EVELYN (f and sometimes m)
Eng. This derives from a surname, which comes from a Norman given name AVELINE.

HAZEL (f)
OE. haesel – hazel nut. This name was coined in the 19th century.

HAZEL GROVE

COLLWYN (m)
Wel. collwyn – hazel grove.

HOLLY

CELYNEN (f)
Wel. celynen – holly. This was the name of a 6th century Welsh saint.

CLYNOG (m)
Wel. celyn – holly + adjectival suffix.

HOLLY (f)
OE. holegn – holly tree. The shiny, dark evergreen leaves and bright red berries are hung up at Christmas time to signify life. The tree was used in divination and as a decoration since ancient times. This was first used as a name at the beginning of this century and is sometimes chosen for girls born around Christmastime.

OAK

ALLON (m) Heb. Old Testament name.

AIKEN (m) AS. oaken.

Iron OAK

MAELDERN (m)
Wel. mael – iron/metal + derw – oak (also see **IRON**).

TREES

OLIVE

AILBHE (f) Ir.

OLIVE (f)
Lat. oliva – olive. One of the most successful plant names coined in the 19th century. In ancient Greece people held olive branches when they were praying, and heralds sometimes held branches of the tree. Brides sometimes carried an olive garland. The tree, because of its slow growth and capacity to live to a great age, became a symbol of stability and peace. This tradition dates back to Old Testament times when the dove returned to Noah in the ark with an olive branch in its mouth, showing that the flood had subsided. Its rich, soothing oil associated it with prosperity (also see **PEACE**).

OLIVER (m)
Ger. introduced by the Normans. It has been associated with Latin Olivarius – olive tree, or may be from Olaf (see **ANCESTOR RELICS**). The name was first used by Olivier, Charlemagne's retainer, and the close companion of Roland in the Chanson de Roland. This is a Frankish name and, although it appears to be Latin in origin, its roots are actually more likely Germanic.

OLIVIA (f)
first coined by Shakespeare for his character in *Twelfth Night* (1599).

PALM (Date)

TAMAR (f), TAMARA (f)
Heb. 'date palm'. This tree is associated with perfection because of its straightness, height and the goodness of its fruits. The name of two women in the Old Testament, one disreputable and the other described as 'a woman of a fair countenance'. Still in use as a modern Jewish name. TAMARA is the Russian feminine version of the name.

Little PLUM

PRUNELLA (f) Lat. prunus – plum tree.

WILLOW

WILLOW (f)
OE. welig – willow tree. This tree is associated with grace and flexibility and also with freedom. The 'weeping willow' is, of course, symbolic of sadness and represents grief at lost love. Another plant that was used in lovers' divinations. The questioner would walk backwards away from a willow tree and throw a wreath over her head until it caught a branch and held. Every time that the wreath failed to catch a branch equalled another year unmarried! The association of the willow tree with mourning goes back to a psalm in which the Jews hung their harps on a willow.

YEW

IVO (m), IVOR (m), YVONNE (f), YVES (m)
Fr. from OG root iv – yew.

TRUE IMAGE – (see **FLOWERS**)

TRUST

COEL (m)

Wel. coel – trust. The name of the 6th century king of Aeron (Ayr). The original 'Old King Cole' of the nursery rhyme.

TRUTH

ALETHEA (f)

Gk. aletheia – truth, from alethes – true (lit. 'not hidden'). This name was coined around the 17th century and may have resulted from the Puritan fashion of using abstract virtues as names.

FARUQ (m)

Arab. faraqa – to make a distinction or separate, i.e. a 'person capable of distinguishing right from wrong, truth from falsehood.' This quality of distinguishing wisdom is considered very important in Islam, and the *Quran* is sometimes known as 'Al-Furqan' because it clearly distinguishes between right and wrong. King Faruq was the last king of Egypt who was deposed and exiled in 1952.

VERENA (f)

may be derived from Latin for 'truth'. It was the name of a Swiss 3rd century saint and martyr, to whom many churches and chapels are dedicated around Lake Lucerne, as she lived as a hermit near Zürich. It is said that she came originally from Thebes in Egypt. Her feast day is September 1st.

VERITY (f)

Lat. veritas – truth. A popular Puritan name, and still sometimes in use today (see **FAITH**).

TWIN

THOMAS (m), THOMASA (f), THOMASINA (f), TAMSIN (f) Corn.

This was the Aramaic nickname for the Greek name Didymos – twin. The name of one of Jesus' disciples who has come to be associated with lack of faith (a 'doubting Thomas') because he did not believe that Jesus had risen from the dead, until he had placed his fingers in the Lord's wounds. It is said that he later became a missionary in India, where he was martyred. His feast day is December 21st. This was the name of many saints. Thomas à Becket was a 12th century saint, martyr and Archbishop of Canterbury, who was a close friend of Henry II, by whose soldiers' hands he was eventually murdered when matters of Church and state began to clash – the subject of T.S. Eliot's play *Murder in the Cathedral*). St Thomas Aquinas (1225-74) wrote *The Imitation of Christ* which became a guidebook for the mystical and contemplative Christian life. St Thomas More (1478-1535) was the author of *Utopia* and eventually imprisoned and beheaded by Henry VIII for refusing to give up his allegiance to the Pope and the Roman church. He was the subject of the play and film *A Man for all Seasons*. There are many versions of this name, including the Russ. FOMA.

UNFADING

AMARANTHA (f)

Gk. unfading. This was also the name of a legendary Abyssinian paradise. In *Paradise Lost,* Milton wrote of the angels:

Their crowns inwove with Amaranth and gold;
Immortal Amaranth, a flower which once
In Paradise, fast by the tree of life,
Began to bloom.

(see **IMMORTAL**)

UNIQUE

FARID (m), FARIDA (f)

Arab. farada – to be unique. Farida also means a precious pearl and indicates incomparable beauty (see **JEWELS**).

UNIQUE CHOICE

ANGUS (m), ANGUSINA (f) Scot.

Gael. Aonghus, meaning 'unique choice' or 'one choice', from aon – one, implying pre-eminence. This used to be a popular name in Ireland, but is now almost exclusively Scottish. In Celtic mythology Angus Og was a chieftain god who used the four magical treasures of a cauldron, spear, sword and stone to maintain the well-being of mankind and to increase prosperity. It

is the name of one of three legendary Irish brothers who invaded Scotland, bringing with them the 'Stone of Scone' (the Stone of Destiny) which is now embedded in the coronation throne in Westminster Abbey. Angus cattle are supposed to have been named after this Irish invader.

UNITED – (see **JOINED**)

UNITY

UNA (f)

Lat. unus – one. This is the meaning sometimes given to this Irish name in its anglicised form (see **LAMB**). In Spenser's *Faerie Queene* (1596) he used the name to mean the 'oneness of truth' (falsity being multiform), and this probably influenced the creation of the name UNITY by the Puritans (see below).

UNITY (f)

Eng. Another 'virtue' name coined by the Puritans.

UNSWAYING

ATALANTA (f)

Gk. feminine form of Atlas – the giant who held the world on his shoulders, and thus has come to be associated with indomitable strength. She was a swift runner and skilled huntress with whom her suitors had to compete; losers were executed! She was eventually outsmarted, (though not outrun) by Hippomenes who dropped three enticing golden apples in her path which she stopped to pick up.

VALLEY

GLEN(N) (m)
Gael. gleann – valley. A placename and then a surname. Most popular in Canada, possibly imported with Scottish settlers.

Little VALLEY

GLYN(N) (m), GLYNIS (f)
Wel. glyn – little valley

Pierce the VALLEY

PERCIVAL (m), PERCY (m)
OF. perce – pierce + val – valley. A reworking of an ancient Celtic name. The name of the only Arthurian knight who was pure and innocent enough to be able to find the Grail (later that honour was attributed to Galahad). PERCY was originally a famous Northumbrian family name which came to England with the Normans, but it has come to be used as a diminutive of Percival.

VALLEY-DWELLER

DEAN (m), DENA (f), DEANNA (f)
OE. denu – valley (Middle English dene). Transferred use of a surname, which indicated someone who lived in a valley, and also used for someone holding the ecclesiastical office of dean.

VENERABLE KING

XERXES (m)
This Greek name comes from an ancient Persian one: KHSHAYARSHA, kshaya – king + arsha – venerable. This became Achashverosh in Hebrew and XERXES in Greek (see also **KING**, and **MAJESTY**).

VICTORY

There are many Old English names, and one or two of Greek origin which contain the word for 'victory' – such was the recognition given to a strong warrior and one who was victorious in battle. Many of these names have now fallen out of use, but I have included some of them below, as well as names which are still popular.

FAWZI (m), FAWZIYYA (f)
Arab. faza – to achieve/win; implies triumph or accomplishment.

VICTORIOUS ONE

BUDDUG (f)
Wel. buddug – victorious one. This is the Celtic form of the name of the famous Iceni queen who is usually known by her Roman name of BOADICEA.

GHALIB (m)
Arab. ghalaba – to subdue or defeat. 'God is the only conqueror' is inscribed at the entrances to mosques.

VICTOR (m), VICTORIA (f)
Lat. from personal name Victorius – 'conqueror'. Early Christians adopted this name with reference

to Jesus' Resurrection and victory over sin. It was also the name of several popes and martyrs. The feast of St Victor is July 28th. The name VICTORIA became known in England as a result of the accession of Queen Victoria (1819-1901) and has been adopted by non-royalty since the 1940s. St Victoria's feast day is December 23rd. VICKY and VICKI are English pet forms which are used as names in their own right.

VINCENT (m)

St Vincent de Paul (1580-1660) founded the Society of St Vincent de Paul and the Sisters of Charity who were committed to caring for the poor and this order is still in existence today. UINSEANN (m) is the Irish form of this name which is not much in use today.

Bringer of VICTORY

BERENICE (f)

Gk. phere – bearer + Nike – goddess of Victory. Implies bringer of victory or good news.

Good VICTORY

EUNICE (f)

Gk. eu – good /well /fine + nike – victory. Adopted by the Puritans, because it was the name of the mother of Timothy, who introduced him to Christianity.

VICTORY-PEACE

SIEGFRIED (m)

OG. sigu – victory + frithu – peace.

VICTORY PEOPLE

NICHOLAS (m), NICOLA (f), NICODEMUS(m)

Gk. nike – victory + laos – people. The name presumably means something like 'people's victory' or 'the people are victorious'. According to legend Nicholas, a 4th century Bishop of Myra in Turkey, supplied three marriage portions to destitute maidens, which he placed in stockings and threw through their windows at night. This gave rise to the tradition of Santa Claus, (from the Dutch, Sinterklaas), better known to us as 'Father Christmas'. The feast of Saint Nicholas is celebrated on December 6th and is a more important children's day in some European countries than is Christmas Day. Another story of St Nicholas tells of the miracle he performed in bringing three murdered children back to life. During a time of famine their bodies had been cut up and placed in a barrel of salt to preserve them! He has thus become the patron saint of children, of brewers, of coopers (presumably because of the barrel in which he found the dismembered children!), as well as of sailors (he saved some people from drowning at sea), merchants, travellers, the poor and pawnbrokers, as well as a patron saint of Greece and Russia, where he is much venerated and where the name is in the form NIKOLAI. An old Russian saying reassures: 'If God dies, we still have St Nicholas.' NICODEMUS in the New Testament was a Pharisee who visited Jesus in secret by night, not wanting to be seen to go by day, as he wanted the Master to clarify a point in his teaching. This led Jesus to explain the cornerstone of his message – that it was not that men had to return to their mothers' wombs to be reborn, but rather 'Unless a man be born again of water and the Holy Spirit he cannot enter into the kingdom of God'. In chapter 7 of the Gospel of St John we read that this same man risked his position in defence of Jesus at his trial, saying 'Doth our law judge *any* man before it hear him and know what he doeth?' How deeply this Pharisee had been affected by his meeting with Jesus is further demonstrated by the fact that St. John also reports that he brought a mixture of myrrh and aloes to prepare the corpse of Jesus for burial after his crucifixion. St. NICO-DEMUS was a Greek monk, scholar and mystic who lived in the 18th century. His *Philokalia* was a collection of spiritual writings which is still in use in the Orthodox Church. His feast day is August 3rd. The term 'Old Nick', which is applied to the devil, derives from Niccolo Macchiavelli, the wily and scheming politician. The malignant water sprites of Norse mythology, or <u>nixies</u>, from <u>necce</u> – to kill, looked like innocent children but haunted streams where they lured travellers to a watery death by singing to them.

COLIN (m)

Eng. diminutive form of medieval name which was a short form of <u>Nicholas</u>. Now used as a name in its own right, and generally not recognised as originally a short form of Nicholas. Gael. It is also the English version of the Gaelic <u>Cailean</u>, a personal Scottish name particularly favoured by the Campbells.

VICTORY-PROTECTION

SIGMUND (m)

OE. <u>sige</u> – victory + <u>mund</u> – protection. Not in use in England after the 14th century.

VICTORY-STRENGTH

SEWAL (m)

OE. from <u>Sigewald</u>; compound of <u>sige</u> – victory + <u>weald</u> – strength. Not found in use after the 16th century.

VICTORY-WORD

SIGURD (m) OE.

VIGOROUS

ARTEMIS (f)

The Greek goddess of the hunt and of the moon, equivalent to the Roman Diana, whose name has been said to mean 'whole, sound, vigorous' (see **MOON** and **GODS & GODDESSES**).

VIGOROUS MAN

FERGUS (m), FERGUSIANA (f) (rare!)

Gael. <u>Fearghas</u> This name is supposed to have come to Scotland from Ireland with the Gaels in the 5th century, under the leadership of <u>Fergus mac Erca</u>, and is recorded as being that of St Columba's grandfather. The rich sometimes anglicised this as Ferdinand and the less wealthy as <u>Fardy</u>. FERGAL is the Irish form of this name.

VIRGIN

VIRGINIA (f)

Lat. from the Roman family name <u>Verginius</u>. It has been associated with <u>ver</u> – the spring, <u>vireo</u> – to flourish and <u>viridis</u> – green; all of which words indicate newness, freshness and youth. In 14th century Italy women were sometimes named VIRIDIS. The name came into favour after the

American province was named by Sir Walter Raleigh after Elizabeth I of England, the 'Virgin Queen'. The first child born to the settlers in America, in August 1587, was named <u>Virginia</u>. It was also the name of a Roman maiden whose father killed her to save her the dishonour of being raped by a corrupt ruler who was trying to claim she was actually his slave.

VIRTUE

ARETHA (f)

Gk. <u>arete</u> – virtue. This name was made popular by the singer, <u>Aretha Franklin</u>. In its older form ARETHUSA it is the name of a Greek nymph who was pursued by a river god from Greece to Sicily and eventually had to turn herself into a spring to escape him!

VIRTUE (f)

Lat. <u>virtutes</u>. This name alludes to the Seven Christian Virtues and is an example of the sort of name favoured by the Puritans. Originally, the root of this word comes from Latin <u>vir</u> – man, implying manly qualities, from which our modern word <u>virile</u> derives. The ancient Sanskrit word for 'energy' is <u>viriya</u>.

VIRTUOUS

FADIL (m)

Arab. <u>fadala</u> – to excell, surpass. Implies virtuousness, generosity and distinction.

Beautiful VOICE – (see **MUSES**)

WARBLING

TAGHRID (f)
Arab. gharada – to sing or warble (see **BIRDS**).

WATCHER

ERYL (m/f)
Wel. eryl – watcher. First used in 1893.

WATCHFUL

GREGORY (m)
Lat. Gregorius, from Gk. gregorein – to watch, be vigilant.A popular early Christian name. The name of several saints and 16 popes, the most famous of which was Pope Gregory the Great (540-604). He founded monasteries in Rome and Sicily, before becoming Pope. He wrote an outline of the duties of the clergy and has given his name to 'Gregorian chant' or plainsong. He reigned for 14 years and was largely responsible for the conversion of the Anglo-Saxons. The feast of St Gregory is March 12th. It was Pope Gregory XIII who gave his name to the 'Gregorian Calendar' which was introduced in 1582. Popular in Scotland (especially in the Middle Ages), in the form of GREGOR.

IRA (m)
Heb. The name of one of king David's priests.

Adopted by the Puritans and now mainly used in America.

Son of the WAVE

DYLAN (m)
Wel. This is the traditional meaning ascribed to this name. Dylan was a legendary sea-god. He plunged into the sea at baptism and swam like a fish. All the waves of Britain and Ireland wept at his death. The name actually probably derives from Wel. dylanwad – influence (see **SEA**).

WEALTH

MATH (m)
Wel. math – treasure/wealth. Math ap Mathonwy was the great legendary Celtic demi-god of increase (see also **PROSPERITY**).

WEALTHY

ALODIE (f) OE.

WEARIED

LEAH (f)
Heb. Although this has also been interpreted as 'languid' and was another Puritan favourite, it is probably *not* a name with which you would wish to endow your hopeful and innocent daughter! She was the first wife of Jacob.

WELCOME

ASPASIA (f)
Gk. This was the name of a priestess of the sun and also a famous 5th century BC Athenian

teacher of eloquence of whom Socrates was a pupil. She was the mistress of Pericles and was known for her wit and cleverness.

Her name's Aspasia, but us calls her Spash.

E.C. Smith[23]

WELL-BEING

SALAMA (m)
Arab. Well-being or safety, from salima – to be unharmed.

WELL BORN

EUGENE (m), EUGENIA (f)
Gk. Eugenios from eu – good/well + genes – born; i.e. 'noble'. This was the name of several early saints, including a 5th century bishop of Carthage, a 7th century bishop of Toledo and 4 popes. EOGHAN is the Irish form of this name, EWAN the popular Scottish form, OWEN the Welsh and YEVGENY the Russian. (This was the name of a popular 4th century missionary who preached in Russia and became the focus of a devoted following, and, in this century, the name of the well-known Georgian poet, YEVGENY YEVTUSHENKO). The feast day is June 2nd. EUGENIA was used in the Middle Ages, but not revived until the 19th century when it was the name of the Empress Eugenie, the wife of Napoleon III of France. In 1870 she fled to England, where she lived until her death. St Eugenia's day is December 15th (also see **NOBLE**).

WHOLE

EMMA (f), IRMA (f)
Ger. irm(en)/erm(en) – whole / entire. Pet form of names such as Irmgard. Came into English use at the end of the 19th century. The feast of St Emma is April 11th.

WHOLESOME – (see FLOWERS – Marshmallow)

WILL-PEACE

WILFRED (m)
OE. will – will/desire + frith – peace. The name of a famous 7th century Northumbrian saint whose feast is April 24th (see **PEACE**).

WINE

DENIS (m), DENNIS (m), DENISE (f)
Gk. from DIONYSUS, the Greek god of wine and ecstasy. Implies great commitment to life, spontaneity, energy and passion (see also **GODS & GODDESSES**).

LAYLA (f)
Arab. pre-Islamic name referring to wine and its intoxicating effects. The name of a heroine, equivalent to the European Juliet, and symbol of romantic love. There is a famous Arabic expression: 'Each mourns or sings for his own Layla', or each follows his own desire.

WING

ALETTE (f)
Fr. diminutive form of Lat. ala – wing (see **BIRDS**).

WINGED GIFT

ALDORA (f) Gk.

WISDOM

ATHENE (f)
Gk. goddess of wisdom. The etymology of this name is old and uncertain. It is not known whether she was named after the city of <u>Athens</u> or vice versa.

HIKMAT (m/f) Arab. <u>hikma</u> – wisdom.

MINERVA (f)
The Roman goddess of wisdom, whose name is said to derive from the Latin <u>men</u> – mind.

SOPHIA (f)

Gk. SOPHY is the traditional English form. Saint Sophia is much venerated in the Eastern Church. Her feast day is September 30th and a famous church in Istanbul is called after her. When the Emperor Justinian built the magnificent church of <u>Santa Sophia</u> he said that he had surpassed Solomon himself. Sometimes Sophy was used to render the Gaelic <u>Beathag</u> – blessed. SONIA is the anglicised form of SONYA – the Russian pet form, which has been a name in its own right since the 1920s.

YESHE (m/f) Tib.

(Also see **GODS & GODDESSES**).

WISE

CREENAN (m) Manx. from Old Irish <u>creen</u> – old/worn out + <u>creeney</u> – wise.

HAKIM (m)
Arab. <u>hakama</u> – to pass judgement.

WISH

AMANI (f)
Arab. <u>mana</u> – to desire, or find by good luck. This name means wishes, aspiration, desires.

'UMNIYA (f)
Arab. <u>wasama</u> – to desire, wish for, find by good luck.

WOMANLY

'ABLA (f)
Arab. lit. 'woman possessing a fine and full figure', from 'abula – to be big or full. An ancient, pre-Islamic Arab name still popular today.

ANDREA (f) Gk.

CAROLINE (f)

Ital. The wife of George II, Caroline of Branden-burg-Anspach introduced this name to Britain in the 18th century and made it instantly popular.

CAROL(E) (f)

Originally this name came from <u>Christmas</u> carols and was not a short form of Caroline. It is now a name in its own right. In fact, a Christmas 'carol' meant originally a round dance.

CHARLENE (f)

CHARLOTTE (f)

This is a diminutive form which has been in use in England since the 17th century (though some say it was here in the 12th) and was the name of the wife of George III, as well as of the famous 19th century novelist, Charlotte Bronte.

These are just some of the many variations of the feminine forms of <u>Charles</u> and these names all share a joint feast day with St Charles, November 4th (see **MANLY**).

Strong WOMAN OF GOD

GABRIELLE (f) Fr.,
GABRIELLA (f) Ital. (See **GOD**)

WONDERFUL – (see **ADMIRABLE**)

WOOD

KEITH (m)

Cel. placename, which became surname (among the Scottish aristocracy) and then a first name. Not generally used in England until this century.

Of the WOODS

SILVIA (f), SILAS (m)

Lat. <u>silva</u> – wood. <u>Rhea Silvia</u> was the mythical mother of Romulus and Remus, the founders of Rome. <u>Silvanus</u> was the Roman god of the woods and his attendants were called <u>Silvanae</u>. He was the protector of husbandmen and crops and he was depicted as an old man holding a cypress tree. SILAS is the short form of Silvanus. It was adopted by Christianity as it was the name of the 6th century sainted mother of Gregory the Great. Her feast day is November 3rd. To call someone 'sylvan' in the Middle Ages meant that they were a forest dweller and barely human. SILVIA was a popular name in the Renaissance and was often given to shepherdesses (see **TREES**).

SILVESTER (m)

St Silvester was the first pope to govern the Church when it was free from persecution (314-35). His feast day is December 31st and coincides with New Year celebrations in some parts of Europe.

WORK

IDA (f)

ON. <u>idh</u> – labour. <u>Idhuna</u> was a Norse goddess of the spring and guardian of the youth-giving apples of the gods. Regained popularity in the 19th century. The Irish version of this name derives from Old Irish <u>itu</u> – thirst. It (in the form of ITA) was the name of the famous Abbess Kileedy whose feast is celebrated on January 15th (see **INDUSTRIOUS**).

WORLD MIGHTY

DONALD (m),
DONALDA (f), DONELDA (f) – both
Scottish Highland forms.
Gael. Domhnall, from Old Celtic dubno – world
+ val – rule. In the 8th and 9th centuries DONAL
was a royal name in Ireland. It is one of the most
ancient Irish names, which is usually anglicised as
Daniel. The Irish surname O'Donnell derives
from this name. Donal of Bangor was an Irish
saint whose feast day is April 26th. In Scotland,
the name is closely associated with the Macdonald clan of the medieval Lords of the Isles.
Although considered a very Scottish name, which
it is, (in the mid 19th century it was the 16th
most frequently used name) it has been more
popular this century in the U.S.A and Canada.

YELLOW – (see COLOURS)

YOUNGEST

IEUAF (m)
Wel. probably from ieuangaf – youngest.

YOUTH

HEBE (f)
Gk. hebos (m) – young. She was a daughter of
Zeus, a minor goddess, the cup-bearer of the
gods and the personification of the freshness of
youth (see CUPBEARER).

MABON (m)
Wel. from maponos – a youth. This was the
name of an ancient Celtic deity, equivalent to
the Greek Apollo.

Help of YOUTH

INGEBIARD (f) Manx. from ON.

In the prime of YOUTH

GHASSAN (m)
Arab. ghassaniyy – 'very beautiful'.

THEIR BODIES ARE
BURIED IN PEACE:
BUT THEIR NAME LIVETH
FOR EVERMORE

Book of Wisdom
Ben Sira (c. 190 BC)

Names of disputed or uncertain meaning

The unworthiness of works on this subject is caused by the fact that one author copies from another, and but few writers would seem to possess more than a superficial acquaintance with two or three languages. Thus it happens that the name **Lambert** is translated 'fair or bright lamb'; **Gilbert,** 'bright helmet'; **Adelaide,** 'noble cheer'... all of which renderings and a thousand more of the like kind, may be forthwith suffocated, and interred with this epitaph – TALIBUS CARDUIS PASCUNTUR ASINI.

Richard Stephen Charnock[24]

This was the rather pompous and judgemental complaint of a scholarly writer of a book about first names in 1882. His Latin epitaph means 'ASSES ARE FED ON SUCH THISTLES'. The poor man would probably turn in his grave today if he could see the plethora of popular naming books which have been published in the last thirty years, some of them making the wildest stabs at meaning or etymology and others simply ignoring the challenge and settling, unconcerned, for the most popular or immediately appealing interpretations. Whilst I certainly would not have been able to compile this book without 'copying' from many others more learned than I, and without the assistance of years of previous research made available to me by the cornucopian shelves of the British Library, and whilst I am not 'acquainted' with more than three languages and only well-acquainted with two of those, I have endeavoured, to the best of my capacity, to be as accurate as possible in the meanings and interpretations I have given, according to the information available to me. Rather than settling for the easiest, most appealing way out in the case of several names, I have decided, due to the discussion, dispute or controversy surrounding their origins and exact meanings, to include them in this separate section. Many of these names are either very popular, very common or very beautiful in sound or appearance. Several of them are also associated with interesting stories or legends.

In this section I have also included some names whose origins are complex or whose meanings do not lend themselves easily to clear classification, as well as some names in common usage which have undesirable meanings, such as **Brendan** (m), which probably means 'stinking hair'.

AARON (m)

This name may be Egyptian and its origin and meaning are doubtful. Various suggestions have been put forward, including 'to enlighten', 'to retard or hinder' and 'the most high'. It is traditionally said to derive from Hebrew har-on – 'mountain of strength', but this is more folklore than etymology. He was the brother of Moses and Miriam and the first High Priest of Israel.

ABELARD (m)

I have seen this name claiming derivation from Germanic sources and meaning 'nobly resolute' or 'noble firmness'. One book claimed that it was from Middle English, meaning 'guardian of the Abbey larder'. Whatever its origin, this name will be linked forever with Heloïse in their tragic story of the love affair between her and Peter Abelard (1079-1142), the French theologian and philosopher. Her family were so outraged that they arranged Abelard's castration. The blighted lovers took Holy Orders and ended their days in monastic confinement.

ADINA (f)

– as well as being a Persian name, also exists in Hebrew, originally as a male name in the Bible. It has been translated as 'delight', 'desire' or as 'slender'.

ALAN (m)

Gaelic scholars have suggested that this name means 'rock' or 'noble'. It was the name of a Welsh and Breton saint and supposed to have come from Brittany to England. ALUN is the Welsh version of this name and ALANA is one of several feminine forms.

ALARIC (m)

– was a traditional name for the kings of the Ostrogoths. It was revived in the 19th century as part of a return of interest in the Gothic. It comes from the Germanic ala – all, or ali – stranger, or possibly adal – noble + ric – ruler / power and has been interpreted as 'noble ruler'. St Alaricus was a 10th century monk who lived in Switzerland. The feast day is September 29th.

ANTONY (m)

Antonius is a Roman clan name of unknown meaning and probably of Etruscan origin. It has been said to mean 'strength', 'praiseworthy', 'of inestimable value', or to imply descent from one of Hercules' sons, Antius. St Antony of Alexandria was a 3rd century saint who lived as a hermit in the desert where he sat atop a T-shaped staff, with his pet pig at his feet, which gave rise to the saying 'As fat as St Antony's pig'. This colourful character is considered to be the founder of monasticism. Charlotte Yonge related how the letter T was considered fortunate and that the ancient hieroglyph of St Antony's cross was a symbol of security of which it was said 'Kill not them upon whom ye shall see the letter Tau' (the Greek letter 'T'). St Antony became the patron saint of swineherds, and another saying, 'He will follow him like St Antony's pig' was used to indicate scorn at obsequious behaviour. 'St Antony's pigs' used to roam the London streets, as the proctors of St Antony's hospital were allowed to let swine feed on public land. St Antony of Padua (who actually came from Lisbon!) was a disciple of St Francis of Assisi. His eloquence and learning are said to have caused the fish to raise their heads from the sea to listen to him. He is the patron saint of lost things. I recall praying to him frequently as a child, usually with considerable success, though the 'reason' for this would take a little more explanation than the scope of this present book allows. His feast is June 13th. ANTONIA and ANTOINETTE (Fr.) are feminine forms of this name. The usual English form of ANTHONY arose in the 16th century from trying (incorrectly) to make the name derive from Greek anthos – flower. ANTON (m) and ANTONINA (f) are Russian forms of this name.

ARAMINTA (f)
– was coined by Sir John Vanbrugh in 1705.

BRENDAN (m)
– has for some reason been interpreted as 'stinking hair' (bren – stinking + find – hair) and also as deriving from the Celtic word, Breanainn – 'prince'! A popular and ancient Irish name, it was the name of several early saints, including the famous St Brendan the Navigator (484-577) who actually sailed his coracle in the Atlantic and, the legend says, landed in America. Mount Brandon in Co. Kerry was named after him. His feast day is May 16th.

CAESAR (m)
Some have claimed that this name means 'long-haired', though the original holder of this name was supposed to be bald. Charnock in 1882 claimed that the name came from the Persian sar – leader, commander or prince; hence its associated meaning in Tsar, Kaiser etc.

CAMILLA (f)
– is from the old Roman family name Camillus whose (probably non-Roman) origins and exact meaning are obscure. It was the name of the Queen of the Volscians, a warrior maiden who fought in the army of Aeneas. She was supposed to have been such a fast runner that she could run over a wheatfield without bending a single blade or over the sea without getting her feet wet! It has been suggested that the name means 'attendant at a religious rite' or at the sacrifices to the gods, because the young male and female attendants were called camilli and camillae. It was also the name of the swift-footed attendant to Diana, the huntress. It was used in Europe in the Middle Ages and revived in the 18th century. The feast of St Camilla is on March 3rd. CAMILLO (m) is uncommon, except in Italy.

CASIMIR (m)
– is a Polish name which until recently was always translated as 'announcement or proclamation of peace'. It has now been suggested that it actually means the opposite – 'great destroyer' or 'destroyer of peace'! This is the name of the 15th century patron saint of Poland (feast day March 4th) whose father had ambitions for him to conquer Hungary, but he retired from the world to pursue his love of theology and the art of peace, and later died of consumption. He is invoked for protection against the plague in the Catholic Church. The name was popular for a while in England in the 19th century.

CASSANDRA (f)
– is probably *not* a name you would want to give to your innocent daughter, as, despite the fact that its meaning is unknown, it has been interpreted as 'entangler of men'! She was the beautiful daughter of the Greek king, Priam. Apollo gave her the gift of prophecy in order to seduce her. She deceived him and he cursed her; and from then on her prophecies were always disbelieved.

CEDRIC (m)

– was coined by Sir Walter Scott for a character in 'Ivanhoe' (1819). It was also the name of the character of Little Lord Fauntleroy in the novel by Frances Hodgson Burnett (1886), which is perhaps the reason it has come to be considered an effeminate name for a boy.

CYRUS (m)

– is a very old name. It comes from Kuru, which is said to be older than Sanskrit and may come from the word <u>Khur</u> meaning 'the Sun'. <u>Kureish</u> was the original Persian form of this name, which became <u>Koreish</u> among the Hebrews, <u>Kyros</u> to the Greeks and <u>Cyrus</u> to the Romans. It was the name of the 500 BC founder of the Persian Empire. St Cyrus was an Alexandrian physician who was persecuted for visiting Christians. He was buried in Egypt and his ashes were transported to Rome. His feast is January 31st.

DEIRDRE (f)

– has been interpreted variously as 'one who rages', 'sorrowful', 'fear', and 'the broken-hearted'. This is the name of a tragic Irish heroine who was betrothed to the King of Ulster, Conchobhar, and eloped with her lover, Naoise. The abandoned king murdered him and his two brothers. The story was sometimes taken to be symbolic of the fate of Ireland under English rule. Yeats and Synge both used this legend in their writings.

DOREEN (f)

– is most likely an Irish name (where it is very popular), from an ancient Irish name <u>Doireann</u>, derived from <u>Dorren</u> – sullen (not a winning choice for a little girl!). Others say it is a diminutive of <u>Dorothy</u> – 'gift of God'. This was a very popular name in the 1920s. Some have said that a novel of this name, published in 1894, resulted in the name's increased popularity.

DRUSILLA (f)

– comes from the old Roman family name <u>Drausus</u> and was taken as a cognomen by a man named Livius who killed a Gaul of that name. It was also the name of Caligula's sister and mistress. It became popular in the 17th century with the Puritans, because of the mention of a Jewish woman of that name whose conversion to Christianity by St Paul is mentioned in the Acts of the Apostles. St Drusilla's day is September 22nd.

DWIGHT (m)

– may derive from the Old English <u>hwit</u> – white / fair or from the French name <u>Diot</u>, which derives from the name of the Greek god of wine and ecstasy, <u>Dionysus</u>. This name is particularly popular in America, because of President <u>Dwight</u> D. Eisenhower, who was apparently named after two well-known New England brothers – one a journalist and member of the House of Representatives and the other a clergyman and teacher who became president of Yale. Here is an example of how thorough one needs to try to be in establishing the correct origin of a name: I have seen this name interpreted in a popular dictionary as meaning 'from the Isle of Wight'!

ELAINE (f)

– may be a Welsh name meaning 'fawn', as it is the name of one of the Arthurian characters (the mother of Galahad), whose names are mostly of Welsh origin. It was once thought to be a form of HELEN but is now considered to be an independent name.

ELEANOR (f)

– is from the Old French ALIENOR, which has been derived from a Greek word, meaning 'pity, mercy', from an Arabic word meaning 'God is my light', from the same root as the name HELEN, and thus meaning 'bright/light' and also from a Germanic root ali meaning 'foreign'. Eleanor of Acquitaine came from the south of France as the queen of Henry II in the 12th century and brought the name to England with her.

EMLYN (m)

– is a Welsh name of uncertain origin. It may have a Latin or a Celtic origin, or it may even be the Latinised form of an ancient Celtic name.

EVADNE (f)

– is of uncertain meaning. The first syllable is probably from Gk. eu – good. It is the name of two women in Greek legend, one of whom came to be regarded as the symbol of wifely devotion, as she threw herself onto her husband's funeral pyre. The name was completely out of use until 'Dr. Evadne Hinge' of the drag comedy/music duo 'Hinge and Bracket' revived it.

FERDINAND (m)

– has been interpreted as meaning 'ready or prepared for a journey', from the Visigothic words farth – a journey and nand – ready/prepared. However, nand has also been given the meaning of 'peace', rendering the name's meaning as something like 'journey of peace'. This name was brought to Spain in the 6th century and became hereditary among Spanish kings.

FRASER (m)

– has been interpreted as meaning 'charcoal burner', but it actually derives from a French place name of unknown meaning, from which came a surname, which has been spelt as Frisselle, Freseliere and Fresel. Those of that surname have claimed that it derives from fraise – strawberry, and the strawberry flower is featured in the coat of arms of that family. This was a Scottish surname, but is now more common elsewhere as a first name.

GEOFFREY

– combines the second element frith – peace with a first element of uncertain meaning. It was probably formed from the combination of several names. The Old German name Gaufrid (gavja – district) was confused with Godafrid (from guda – god + frithu – peace). Walafrid meant 'peaceful traveller' and Gisfrid meant 'vow of peace'. The name was introduced to Britain by the Normans. It was very popular in England and France in the late Middle Ages. Geoffrey Chaucer (c. 1340-1400) was the author of the famous *Canterbury Tales* and Geoffrey of Monmouth (110-54) wrote a *History of the Kings of Britain* which was an important influence on later medieval romance writers. Jeffrey is another usual spelling of this name.

GERVASE (m), GERVAISE (f)

– is an English name which was introduced by the Normans. The first syllable is OG. ger – spear, but the meaning of the second half has not been discovered. The remains of St Gervase were discovered in Milan in 386, after a premonition of St Ambrose. He was declared to be a martyr and his feast is June 19th.

GILDAS (m)

– was the name of the earliest British historian who lived in the 6th century, from 516-570. He was a contemporary of <u>Dewi</u> (St. David) and the meaning of his name is uncertain. It has been suggested that it means 'bright son' from the Welsh <u>gild</u> – brightening (or peace) + <u>gwas</u> – lad / son.

GLADYS (f)

– some say comes from Lat. <u>Claudius</u>, the Roman family name that may have referred to the *lameness* of one of its early members. Others say this is a Welsh name, from <u>gwladus</u> – ruler (<u>gulad</u> meant a 'piece of territory').

GRAINNE (f)

– is an ancient Irish name of uncertain origin. It has been interpreted as 'grain goddess'. The name of a legendary Irish princess, who eventually committed suicide after her lover was killed by the man she had originally deserted.

GRIFFITH (m)

– is a Welsh name whose second element (<u>iud</u>) means 'lord', but, as the first element is uncertain, the exact meaning of the whole name is not known. Gruffydd ap Llewellyn was a famous 11th century Welsh ruler who won many victories over the English, until defeated by King Harold in 1063. GRIFFIN is a derivative form of this name. The mythological griffin had a lion's body with an eagle's head and wings, symbolizing strength, swiftness and intelligence.

GUY (m)

– is of disputed meaning, possibly deriving from Ger. <u>witu</u> – wood or <u>wit</u> – wide. <u>Gui</u> is the French word for mistletoe. <u>Guion</u> was the name given to a Celtic dwarf (perhaps because of some Druidic connection with the mistletoe). In Old French <u>guyer</u> or <u>guier</u> meant to guide or

direct. A <u>guidon</u> was a standard bearer. It was a popular Norman name, perhaps after the hero of the Crusades, Guy of Warwick. Baron Guy de Laval obtained permission from Pope Pascal II for all his descendants to be named after him, in memory of his services in the Holy Land. There is a feast of St Guy on September 12th. He was a 10th century Belgian saint. The name fell into disrepute after the capture (in 1605) of the leader of the 'Gunpowder Plot' – Guy Fawkes, but came back into favour in the 19th century.

HELOISE (f)

– is the French form of ELOISE which was popular in the 18th century. This name may be Germanic in origin, or it may be a form of LOUISE (see **FAMOUS IN BATTLE**) and its meaning is unknown. It was the name of the famous and tragic wife of the 12th century French philosopher and theologian, Peter Abelard. The letters exchanged after their enforced parting are classics of spiritual / romantic literature. She has become a symbol of faithfulness and devotion.

HORACE (m)

– comes from the Lat. family name <u>Horatius</u>. It may originally have been Etruscan and was used by admirers of the first century poet <u>Horace</u> (Quintus Horatius Flaccus). <u>Horatio</u> was the name of the famous admiral Nelson, but is no longer common in England. HORATIA is the feminine version of this name.

IMOGEN (f)

– derives from the name IGNOGE, which first appeared in Geoffrey of Monmouth's 11th century History of the Kings of Britain. She was the wife of Brutus, the mythical first king of Britain. In a contemporary description of

Shakespeare's Cymbeline, his heroine's name is spelt INNOGEN (he took the story from Holinshead) and then as IMOGEN in the first printed version of the play, which was probably the result of an error on the part of the printer. The name is Celtic in origin, probably deriving from Gael. inghean, meaning 'girl or maiden'. It is sometimes interpreted as 'daughter' or 'beloved child'. The name IMAGINA was used in the Middle Ages, but IMOGEN has not been popular in this country until this century.

JESSICA (f)

– apparently coined by Shakespeare for the daughter of Shylock in *The Merchant of Venice*. The first part of the name may well be Hebrew, while the second is Venetian. Attempts have been made to give it a satisfactory Hebrew etymology. 'God is looking' is a plausible suggestion, but the meaning is still uncertain.

JOB (m)

The meaning of this Hebrew name is uncertain. It may mean 'afflicted' or 'persecuted'. In the Alexandrian version of the Old Testament it is noted in the margin that he was originally called JOBAB which means 'shouting'. He has come to be associated with great patience in the face of many trials and hardships. The trials sent by God included the deaths of his family and a plague of boils. His patience was rewarded in the end by being restored to even greater prosperity than before: '...for he had fourteen thousand sheep, and six thousand camels and a thousand yoke of oxen and a thousand she-asses.' He lived to be a hundred and forty years old and his story was a favourite in the Middle Ages. The name, predictably, as a model of unquestioning obedience and forbearance, was popular with

the Puritans. He is mentioned in the Qur'an and Muhammad took his name to mean 'penitent'. He is revered in Arabic tradition and known as Ayoub or Eyub, and a nickname for the long-suffering camel was Ayi Ayub – 'Father of Job'.

JOCELYN (f)

– was originally a man's name but is now used for women. It is from an English surname which derives from a Norman personal name Joscelin which came originally from the name of a Germanic tribe – the Gauts.

JOSS (m)

– is the short form of JOCELYN which is now a name in its own right.

JOYCE (f)

This name was formerly used for both sexes, but now is exclusively feminine. Its origins are disputed, some saying that it comes from a Breton name, JODOCUS, interpreted as meaning 'champion' or 'lord', and others that it derives from the same root as JOY. It returned to use in the 17th and 18th centuries as a female name and was strongly revived in the 19th century.

JULIAN (m)

This name derives from the ancient Roman clan of the Julii who claimed to be descended from Venus, the goddess of love. Her grandson, Ascanius, changed his name to Iulus which means 'the first down on the chin' and it is for this reason that this name has sometimes been interpreted as 'hairy' or 'downy bearded'. This theory is disputed and some scholars say that the name actually derives from deus – god. Julian was the name of various early saints, and a Roman emperor who attempted to return the

Empire from Christianity to paganism. One St Julian was told by a stag when he was hunting that he would kill his parents. Seeking to bypass his fate, he fled the country, but his parents followed. He did not recognise them on re-meeting, and, in a fit of jealousy, he killed them. In recompense he spent the rest of his life ferrying wayfarers over the river and giving them lodging. He has, for this reason, been given the patronage of travellers, along with St Christopher. The feast of St Julian is March 8th. This was a common name for women for centuries, notably of the famous 14th century mystic, Julian of Norwich. JULIANA and JULIA are the modern feminine forms of this name. GILLIAN is an equivalent which was very popular in the 17th century and then became debased to mean 'wench' or 'flirt': a 'Gill-flirt' meant a giddy young girl. JILL, originally a short form of Gillian, is now an independent name in its own right and was already used in the phrase 'Jack and Jill' in the 15th century. JULIET and JULIETTE derive from the French and Italian forms. JULIE is another French diminutive form of Julia, which has become a name in its own right (see **MONTHS OF THE YEAR**).

KAY (m)

As well as being a feminine short form of various names beginning with 'k', this is also the medieval masculine name of one of King Arthur's knights. It is said to be a Celtic form of the Roman name, Gaius, whose origin is uncertain, but which has been interpreted as meaning 'I rejoice'.

LANCELOT (m)

– was the name of the famous right-hand knight of king Arthur whose name was almost certainly of Celtic origin but whose precise meaning is unknown.

LAVINIA (f)

– is the name of the wife of Aeneas, and thus was known as the mother of the Romans. The name came to mean 'woman of Rome'. It has been claimed that she gave her name to the town of Lavinium, but it is much more likely to be the other way round, as her name is almost certainly pre-Roman. This was a popular name in the Renaissance, and again in the 18th century.

MARY (f)

– comes from the Hebrew root M-y-r-m – MIRIAM. Some associate this with marah – bitterness (a strange thing to call a little girl) or 'wished for child' (unlikely, as these were usually male!), or rebel or rebelliousness or the sea, from Old German mar. This latter meaning has led to the interpretation of 'Myrrh of the Sea' and 'Lady of the Sea' as epithets for the Virgin Mary in the Middle Ages. It has been suggested that the possible meaning of 'bitterness' could refer to the pains of childbirth or to the sadness, grief and misfortune that were the lot of the Israelites at the time of the enslavement in Egypt. Moses' sister was called Mary. The Blessed Virgin became a major devotional focus in the Catholic Church and there was an Italian proverb, equivalent to our 'like looking for a needle in a haystack' which was 'Cercar Maria in Ravenna', ('looking for Mary in Ravenna'), referring to the large number of churches dedicated to her name. It was an 18th century habit to Latinise names by adding the feminine ending -a, thus giving us the name MARIA. The name has also been associated with the powers of a seeress, as Moses' sister, Miriam, was a prophetess. Interestingly, the word 'marionette' derives from this name, and it was used to describe puppets of Maid Marion, images of the Blessed Virgin and dolls used in witchcraft. MAIRE is the Irish version of this name, which is very popular now, but was rarely used before the 17th century. MARILYN is a 20th century derivative of Mary. MAUREEN is the anglicised version of a diminutive of Maire. MOIRA is an anglicised form of this and now a name in its own right. In Ireland MAURA is also regarded as an anglicised form of Mary, but it is, in fact, the feminine of Maurus, meaning 'Moor'. MARIOT is a Cornish version of this name. MARYAM is the Arabic version, possibly from the Syriac word for 'elevated'. This is a common name among Muslims as well as Christians.

MERLIN (m)
This is the anglicization of the Welsh name MYRDDIN. Arthur's famous wizard was known as Myrddin Emrys in Welsh and as Merlin Ambrosius in Latin. The derivation of his name is unclear. He is associated with Carmarthen (Caerfyddin in Welsh). This means: caer – fort + myr or mor – sea + ddin – hill and its Latin name was Moridumum.

MERYL (f)
– is a recent coinage, made popular by the actress Meryl Streep who was christened Mary.

MILES (m)
– is an English name of Norman origin, but its derivation and meaning are unknown. It came to be associated, as a pet form of Michael, with the Latin word for 'soldier' – miles, because of the Archangel Michael's link with battling with the forces of evil. MILO was the common medieval form, which is still in use in Ireland.

MORGAN (m/f)
– is a Welsh name, the second part of which comes from Old Celtic cant – circle. The first part of the name may come from mor – sea or mawr – great. It may mean 'great brilliance' or 'sea born', but, ultimately its meaning is not known. It is mainly a masculine name, but is sometimes used as a female name, after King Arthur's sorceress-sister, Morgan le Fey.

MOSES (m)
This name may come from an Egyptian phrase meaning 'drawn out of the water', from the Coptic mo – water + usha – saved. The Hebrew word masah means 'The Great Law-Giver'. Mousa is the Arabic version of this name and Magsheesh is an Irish version.

NEIL (m)
– is the anglicised version of the Gaelic name Niall. Very popular in Scotland. It may mean 'cloud', 'passionate' or 'champion'.

NOAH (m)
– is a biblical name of unknown meaning. The name of the famous builder of the ark who rescued his family and a pair of every animal from the Flood, it has been interpreted as meaning 'rest' and also 'comfort'. A popular name in the 17th century and the name of the man who wrote *Webster's Dictionary* and who introduced spelling changes into American-English.

PENELOPE (f)
The name of the faithful wife of Odysseus who sat spinning as she waited for her wandering husband's return. It is of obscure meaning. Some say it derives from the Greek word for 'duck' and others, 'bobbin' – perhaps because of her association with spinning. The gypsy name, PENELI, may be a version of this. It is some-

times given as an English version of the Irish FIONNGHUALA, (FENELLA), which actually means 'white shoulder'.

ROSALIND (f)

– some say that the name comes from the Old German roots (h)ros – horse + lindi – serpent, and that the name was carried by the Goths to Spain. Others say that lindi means 'weak, tender or soft'. The Germans called the snake the lind-wurm – supple worm. Litheness was considered to be beautiful and the snake was associated with wisdom and flexibility. More recently philologists (people who study the origin and development of languages) are saying that it is composed of words meaning 'fame' + 'shield'. More poetically, it has been assumed that the name derives from Latin and means 'beautiful rose'. Linda in Spanish means 'beautiful' (see **ANIMALS – Serpent**)

Rosalind / Linda – serpent

REBECCA (f)

– translated by some as 'captivating' or 'flattering'. Said to derive from heb. rabak – to bind, referring to the firmness of the marriage bond which united the biblical Rebecca and her husband Isaac. Others have said that this name means 'cow', from Heb. marbek – cattle stall. The name may, in fact, derive from an earlier Aramaic word of unknown meaning.

ROSAMUND (f)

– has a similar controversy surrounding it to that of Rosalind. It derives from the Old German compound of (h)ros – horse + munda – protection. In the Middle Ages, it was attributed to coming from Latin rosa – rose + munda – pure, or rosa + mundi – of the world. (see **ANIMALS – Horse**).

RUTH (f)

– has been said to mean 'friend/companion' or 'vision/appearance'. The archaic word ruth means pity or remorse (as in the modern word 'ruthless'), but this is not connected with the name. Because of the loyalty of the biblical Ruth, the name has come to be associated with that quality and with compassion, though the actual origin and meaning of the name are uncertain. It is probably not even a Hebrew name, because it is said in the Bible that she was a 'Moabitess'. Her feast day is September 1st.

SABRINA (f)

– was the daughter of the mythological second king of Britain, after whom the River Severn is supposed to have been named, after her tyrannical stepmother took over the kingdom, had her killed and her body thrown into the river. In fact, it is more likely that she was named after the river, the origins of whose name are very old and lost in the mists of time.

SELWYN (m)

– is a surname used widely in the Middle Ages as a first name. It is probably a compound of either <u>sele</u> – prosperity or hall + <u>wine</u> – friend. Or it may derive from the Old French <u>Seluein</u>, from Latin <u>Silvanus</u> – 'of the woods' (from which the name <u>Silvia</u> derives).

SHIRLEY (f)

OE. This is a place name which became a surname and then a man's name and is now exclusively a female name! Some say it means 'shire meadow' (<u>scir</u> – county/shire + <u>leah</u> – meadow/clearing), and others suggest it might mean 'bright wood' (or meadow): <u>scir</u> meaning 'bright' and <u>leah</u>, 'wood'. It was Charlotte Bronte's novel, 'Shirley' (1849) which fixed the name firmly as a female first name.

TATIANA (f)

– is a Russian name and was the name of several early Christian saints. It derives from the Roman family name <u>Tatius</u> whose meaning is unknown, though some have said that the feminine <u>Tatiana</u> means 'silver'. It has also been suggested that the name derives from Latin baby talk for 'daddy'. St Tatiana's feast day is celebrated on January 12th. TANIA is another Russian form of this name.

TERENCE (m)

– is from the Roman clan name <u>Terentius</u> which is of uncertain origin and unknown meaning. It was the name of a 2nd century Roman comic playwright, who came a slave to Rome from Carthage and was freed by his owner, from whom he inherited his name. It was also the name of an early saint whose feast day is August 29th.

TERESA / THERESA (f)

This lovely name was first recorded in Spain and, though it has been associated with the Greek word for 'reaper' (Charlotte Yonge called it a 'harvest' name) and the Greek island Thera, there is no foundation for either of these. St Teresa of Avila, the 16th century nun and mystic made the name more popular. She was said to be a combination of 'the eagle and the dove' and there are stories of her forthright, fiery temperament. One tells how she was riding one day on a wet and muddy road when her horse threw her. As she hauled herself to her feet to remount, she raised her head heavenwards and shook her fists, railing at her beloved Lord. It is said that she heard a voice telling her 'Teresa, this is how I treat my friends'. 'Then no wonder you haven't got many!' the nun replied. She was one of the first women to be declared an official Doctor of the Church, in 1970. St Thérèse of Lisieux, known as 'the Little Flower' is also highly venerated. TREASA is the Irish version of this name.

THADDEUS (m)

– may be from the Aramaic meaning 'praise' or 'desired' or it may be a variation of <u>Theodore</u> – gift of God (see **GOD**). It was the name given to Judas, the Apostle, to distinguish him from Judas Iscariot. The feast of St Thaddeus is October 28th. In Ireland it was used to translate *tadgh* – poet (see **POET**). <u>Faddei</u> is a Russian form of this name.

THELMA (f)

– was invented in 1887 by Marie Corelli for the Norwegian heroine of her novel, 'Thelma'. It is believed to derive from Greek <u>thelema</u> – wish, i.e. 'act of will'.

TITUS (m)

– was a Roman family name which was possibly of Etruscan origin and is of unknown meaning.

TRACEY (f)

– is the transferred use of a surname from the name of a French village which came originally from a Gallo-Roman personal name meaning 'an inhabitant of Thrace'. It was formerly a masculine name and later used as a pet form of Teresa (see above).

VANESSA (f)

– was invented by Jonathan Swift (1667-1745) for a poem called 'Cadenus and Vanessa' (1726).

WANDA (f)

Some say this comes from Vandal, meaning a member of a wandering Germanic tribe. Others say it comes from vand – stem. It is a Slavic name, found in Poland in the 19th century and introduced into English speaking countries by a novel in 1883.

YOLANDE (f)

– found in this form in Old French, but may be originally Germanic. There was a 13th century daughter of the King of Hungary called St. Jolenta. Some say the name is from Latin and means 'modest' or 'violet'. There are many variations, including Iolanthe.

The Tao that can be told
is not the eternal Tao.
The name that can be named
is not the eternal name

Lao Tzu: *Tao Te Ching*

Names index from *Aaron* to *Zona*

'Who are *you?*' said the caterpillar. This was not an
encouraging opening for a conversation. **ALICE** replied,
rather shyly, 'I – I hardly know, sir, just at present – at least
I know who I *was* when I got up this morning, but I think I
must have changed several times since then.'

> Lewis Carroll: *Alice's Adventures
> in Wonderland*

And out of the ground the Lord God formed every beast of
the field, and every fowl of the air; and brought them unto
ADAM to see what he would call them.

> *Genesis II 19*

Aaron (m) – mountain (and see
DISPUTED NAMES)
Abbas (m) – sullen
Abd'ul/Abd'allah (m) – servant of **God**
Abel (m) – breath
Abelard (m) – noble firmness
Abiah (m) – God is my father
Abiathar (m) – father of abundance
Abigail (f) – 'my father rejoices'
Abir (m) – fragrance
'Abla (f) – womanly
Abner (m) – father of light
Abraham (m) – father of the multitude
Abram (m) – high **father**
Absalom (m) – father of peace
Ada (f) – happy/prosperous
Adah (f) – ornament
Adam (m) }
Adamina (f) } red earth (see COLOURS)

Adela (f) – noble
Adelaide (f) – noble kind
Adelbern (m) – noble bear
Adele (f) – noble
Aderyn (m) – bird (see BIRDS)
Adil (m) – just
Adina (f) – desire (see DISPUTED
NAMES and DAYS OF THE WEEK)
Adolf (m) – noble **wolf** (see ANIMALS)
Adonis (m) – lord
Adrian (m) }
Adriana (f) } of the Adriatic
Aegle (f) – brightness
Aelhaearn (m) – iron brow
Aelwyn (m) – fair brow
Aeneas (m) – praiseworthy
Affrica (f) – pleasant
Agatha (f) – good
Aglaia (f) – brightness (see GRACES)

Agnes (f) – lamb & pure
Ahlam (m) – dream
Ahmad (m) – most **praised**
Aidan (m) – fire
Aiken (m) – oak ⎤ (see TREES)
Ailbhe (f) – olive ⎦
Aina (f) – always
Aine (f) – brightness
A'isha (f) – alive and well
Aisling (f) – dream
Alan (m) ⎤ (see DISPUTED NAMES)
Alana (f) ⎦
Alaric (m) – (see DISPUTED NAMES)
Alasdair (m) – see Alexander
Alaw (m) – melody
Alban (m) ⎤ white (see COLOURS)
Albinia (f) ⎦
Albert (m) ⎤ noble bright
Alberta (f) ⎦
Albion (m) ⎤ rock/mountain
Albina (f) ⎦
Albreda (f) – elf-counsel
Alcyone (f) – calm
Aldora (f) – winged gift
Aldous (m) – old
Aldwyn (m) – old **friend**
Alethea (f) – truth
Alette (f) – wing
Alexander (m) ⎤ defender of men
Alexandra (f) ⎦
Alexandr (m) – see Alexander
Alexei (m) – see Alexis
Alexis (m/f) – defender
Alfred (m) ⎤ elf-counsel
Alfreda (f) ⎦
Algar (m) – elf-spear
Algernon (m) – moustached
Ali (m) – elevated
Alice (f) – noble

Alice

Alisa (f) ⎤ noble
Alison (f) ⎦
Alisdair (m) ⎤ see Alexander
Alistair (m) ⎦
Aliza (f) – happy
Alla (f) – scarlet (see COLOURS)
Allegra (f) – lively
Allon (m) – oak (see TREES)
Allow (m) – see ELF
Alma (f) – nurturing
Almeta (f) – ambitious
Almond (f) – see TREES
Alodie (f) – wealthy
Aloysius (m) – see Louis
Alpha (f/m) – the beginning & first (see
    NUMBERS)
Alpheus (m) – successor
Alphonse (m) – noble eagerness
Alphonso (m) – battle ready
Alphonsus (m) – noble eagerness
Althea (f) – marshmallow (see
    FLOWERS)
Aluric (m) – elf-counsel
Alva (m) – height
Alvar (m) – elf-army
Alverdine (f) – elf-counsel (see ELF)
Alvin (m) – elf-friend

Alvina (f) – elf-friend

Alvita (f) – animated

Amabel (f) – loveable

Amadeus (m) ⎫
Amadea (f) ⎭ beloved of **God**

Amal (f) – hope

Amalia (f) – industrious

Amalthea (f) – God-nourishing

Amanda (f) – loveable

Amani (f) – wish

Amarantha (f) – unfading

Amariah (m) ⎫
Amaris (f) ⎭ God speaks

Amaryllis (f) – rippling stream (see
    FLOWERS)

Amaziah (m) – God is strong

Amber (f) – yellow (see JEWELS)

Ambrose (m) – immortal

Ambrosine (f) – immortal (also see
    JEWELS)

Amelia (f) – industrious

Amethyst (f) – (see JEWELS)

Amica (f) – friend

Amin (m) – honest

Amina (f) – peaceful

Aminta (f) – 'I protect'

Amir (m) – prince & prosperous

Amittai (m) – honest

Amjad (m) – more **glorious**

'Ammar – long **life**

Amnon (m) – faithful

Amos (m) – bearer

Amy (f) – loved

Anadil (f) – nightingales (see BIRDS)

Anaiah (m) – God answers

Ananiah (m) – God has shown himself

Anarawd (f) – eloquent

Anastasia (f) – resurrection

Anatole (m) – sunrise

Anatoli (m) – sunrise

Anchor (m) – anchor (see also SEA)

Andrea (f) – womanly

Andrei (m) ⎫
Andrew (m) ⎭ manly

Anemone (f) – breath (see FLOWERS)

Aneurin (m) – golden

Angarona (f) – release from **grief**

Angel (m) ⎫
Angela (f) ⎬ messenger
Angelet (f) ⎭

Angelica (f) – messenger (also see
    FLOWERS)

Angelina (f) – messenger

Angharad (f) – much **loved**

Angus (m) ⎫
Angusina (f) ⎭ unique choice

Anhun (f) – selfless

Anita (f) – see Ann

Ann (f) – favour

Annabel (f) – loveable

Annette (f) – see Ann

Annice (f) – fulfilment

Anona (f) – fruitful

Anselm (m) – divine **helmet**

Anthea (f) – flowery (see FLOWERS)

Anthony (m) – (see DISPUTED
    NAMES)

Antigone (f) – contrary birth

Antoinette (f) ⎫
Anton (m) ⎬
Antonia (f) ⎬ (see DISPUTED
Antonina (f) ⎬   NAMES)
Antony (m) ⎭

Anushka (f) – see Ann

Anwar (m) – clearer

Anwen (f) – very **beautiful**

Anwyl (f) – dear

Aodhfin (m) – white fire

Aoife (f) – beauty

Aphrodite (f) – sea-born

Apollonia (f) – sun

Apollonius (m) – sun

April (f) – (see MONTHS OF YEAR)

Aquila (m) – eagle (see BIRDS)

Arabella (f) – moved by **prayer**

Araminta (f) – (see DISPUTED
    NAMES)

Archibald (m) – truly bold

Aretha (f) – virtue

Ariane (f)/Ariadne (f) – (see HOLY)

Arianrod (f) – silver disc (see COLOURS)

Arianwen (f) – silver-white (see
    COLOURS)

Ariel (m) – (see Lion of GOD)

Arkadi (m) – Arcadia

Armaghan (m) – gift

Arnold (m) – eagle power (see BIRDS)

Artemas (m) – devotee of Artemis (see
    GODS & GODDESSES)

Artemis (f) – (see MOON and
    VIGOROUS)

Artemisia (f) – devotee of Artemis (see
    FLOWERS)

Arthek (m) } bear hero
Arthene (f)

Arthgen (m) – son of the **bear** (see
    ANIMALS)

Arthur (m) – bear hero

Arthyen (m) – see Arthur

Asa (m) – healer

As'ad (m) – happiest

Asher (m) – happy

Ashley (m/f) } ashwood (see TREES)
Ashlie (f)

Ashraf (m) – more **honourable**

Asia (f) – East

Asim (m) – protector

Askell (m) sacred cauldron of the gods

Asma (f) – prestige

Aspasia (f) – welcome

Asthore (f) – loved one

Astra (f) – (see STARS)

Astrid (f) – divinely beautiful

Asumari (f) – sky

'Ata Allah (m) – gift of **God**

Atalanta (f) – unswaying

Atarah (f) – crown

Athanasius (m) – immortal

Athelstan (m) – noble stone

Athene (f) – wisdom

Atif (m) – compassion

Auberon (m) – noble **bearlike** (see
    ANIMALS)

Aubrey (m) – elf-power

Auburn (f) – auburn (see COLOURS)

Audrey (f) – noble strength

August (m/f)
Augusta (f)   } majesty
Augustine (m)
Augustus (m)

Aulay (m) } ancestor relics
Auliffe (m)

Aurddolen (f) – golden link (see
    COLOURS)

Aurelia (f) } golden
Auriel (f)

Aurora (f) – dawn

Austin (m) – see August

Autumn (f) – (see SEASONS)

Aveline (f) – pleasantness

Averil (f) – boar battle (see ANIMALS)

Avgust (m) – majesty

Avis (f/m) – (see BIRDS)

Avital (f) – dew

Aviva (f) – spring (see SEASONS)

Avril (f) – April (see MONTHS OF
    THE YEAR)

Awel (f) – breeze
Awen (f) – the Muse
Awena (f) – poetry
Ayala (f) – deer (see ANIMALS)
Aylmer (m) – noble famous
Aylward (m) – guardian
Ayman (m) – blessed
Aymelek (f) – moon angel
'Ayn al-hayat (f) – fountain of life
Ayperi (f) – moon fairy

Ayteri (f) – moon body
Azalea (f) – (see FLOWERS)
Azaniah (m) – God has heard
Azariah (m) – God has helped
Azhar (f) – flower (see FLOWERS)
Aziz (m) } beloved
Aziza (f) }
Azriel (m) – God is my help
Azure (f) – skylike

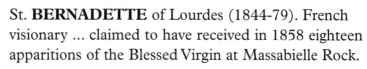

St. **BERNADETTE** of Lourdes (1844-79). French visionary ... claimed to have received in 1858 eighteen apparitions of the Blessed Virgin at Massabielle Rock.

Chambers Biographical Dictionary

In search of complete solitude **BENEDICT** started forth once more, alone, and climbed further among the hills ... In this wild and rocky country he came upon a monk called Romanus, explaining his intention of leading the life of a hermit.

Butler: *Lives of the Saints*

Badr (f/m) – moon
Baethan (m) – little **foolish** one
Bahija (f) } joy
Bahjat (m) }
Bairbre (f) – see Barbara
Baldwin (m) – bold friend (also see FRIEND)
Balthasar (m) – 'Baal protect the king'
Banan (m) – white (see COLOURS)
Banba (f) – Ireland
Baptist (m) } baptist
Baptiste (f) }

Barak (m) – lightning
Barbara (f) – foreigner
Barenwyn (f) – fair branch (see TREES)
Barnabas (m) – son of **consolation**
Barry (m) – spear
Bartholomew (m) – son of Talmai
Baruch (m) – blessed
Barzillai (m) – of iron
Basil (m) – king
Basim (m) – smiling
Bathsheba (f) – daughter of the **oath**
Beata (f) – blessed

Beathag (f) ⎱ life
Beathan (m) ⎰

Beatrice (f) – blessed (see also She who makes HAPPY)

Beatrix (f) – (see Beatrice)

Bedaws (m) – birch (see TREES)

Bede (m) – prayer

Bedwin (m) ⎱ birch (see TREES)
Bedwyr (m) ⎰

Beli (m) – bright

Belinda (f) – serpent (see ANIMALS)

Benedict (m) – blessed

Beraiah (m) – God has created

Berechaiah (m) – God blesses

Berenice (f) – (see VICTORY)

Bernal (m) – bear power (see ANIMALS)

Bernard (m) ⎱ bear brave (see
Bernadette (f) ⎰   ANIMALS)

Bertha (f) – bright

Berthold (m) – bright power

Bertram (m) – bright raven (see BIRDS)

Bertrand (m) – bright shield

Beryl (f) – brilliant (see JEWELS)

Berwyn (m) – bear friend

Bethel (m) – house of **God**

Beulah (f) – married

Beverley (m/f) – beaver stream (see ANIMALS)

Bianca (f) – white (see COLOURS)

Blaise (m) – lisping

Blanche (f) – white (see COLOURS)

Blanchefleur (f) – flower fair (see FLOWERS)

Bleddyn (m) – little wolf ⎱
Bledig (m) – wolf   ⎰ (see
Bledri (m) – wolf ruler   ANIMALS)
Bleiddud (m) – wolf land

Blodyn (f) – blossom   ⎱ (see
Blodeuwedd (f) – flowerlike ⎰ FLOWERS)

Blodwen (f) – flowerfair / white flowers (see FLOWERS)

Blossom (f) ⎱ (see FLOWERS)
Bluebell (f) ⎰

Boaz (m) – strength

Bonaventure (m) ⎱ lucky
Boniface (m)   ⎰

Bonnie (f) – pretty

Boris (m) – battle glory

Boyd (m) – yellow hair (see COLOURS)

Branwen (f) – darkly **beautiful**

Brenda (f) – flaming sword (see SWORD)

Brendan (m) – (see DISPUTED NAMES)

Briallen (f) – first rose (see FLOWERS)

Brian (m) ⎱ hill
Briana (f) ⎰

Bridget (f) – high

Bronwen (f) – white breast (see COLOURS)

Bruno (m) – brown (see COLOURS)

Buddug (f) – victorious one

*Easy, breezy **CAROLINE***
With thy locks all raven-shaded,
From thy merry brow upbraided,
And thine eyes of laughter fill.

Old English Ballad

*Thursday of **COLUMBA** benign,*
Day to send sheep on prosperity,
Day to send cow on calf,
Day to put the web in the warp.

Carmina Gadelica, Vol I

Cadmus (m) – man from the East (see DIRECTIONS)

Caesar (m) – (see DISPUTED NAMES)

Caitlín (f) – pure

Camilla (f) – (see DISPUTED NAMES)

Calliope (f) – (see MUSES)

Calvin (m) – bald

Camelia (f) – (see FLOWERS)

Candida (f) – white (see COLOURS)

Cara (f) – dear

Caradoc (m) – love

Carbry (m) – charioteer

Carmel (f) – orchard

Carmen (f) – song

Carol (f) }
Caroline (f) } womanly

Carwyn (m) – blessed love

Carys (f) – love

Casimir (m) – (see DISPUTED NAMES)

Cassandra (f) – (see DISPUTED NAMES)

Catherine (f) }
Catriona (f) } pure

Cecil (m) – blind

Cecilia (f) }
Cecily (f) } blind

Cedric (m) – (see DISPUTED NAMES)

Cedrych (m) – bounty pattern

Ceinwen (f) – beautiful and blessed

Celandine (f) – (see FLOWERS)

Celeste (f) – heaven

Celynen (f) – holly (see TREES)

Ceneu (m) – cub

Ceridwen (f) – poetry

Chantal (f) – stone

Charis (f) }
Charissa (f) } grace

Charity (f) – charity

Charlene (f) – womanly

Charles (m) – manly

Charlotte (f) – womanly

Charmian (f) – joy

Chere (f) – dear

Cherry (f) }
Cheryl (f) } charity

Chlöe (f) – young green shoot (see FLOWERS)

Chloris (f) – blooming (see FLOWERS)

Chögyam (m) – ocean of truth

Christabel (f) ⎫
Christian (m) ⎬ Christian
Christine (f) ⎭

Christopher (m) – bearer of **Christ**

Claire (f) ⎫
Clara (f) ⎬ bright
Clarissa (f) ⎭

Clarence (m) ⎫ illustrious
Clarice (f) ⎭

Claudia (f) ⎫ lame
Claude (m) ⎭

Cledwyn (m) – (see SWORD)

Clematis (f) – (see FLOWERS)

Clemence (f) ⎫
Clement (m) ⎬ merciful
Clementine (f) ⎭

Cleo, Cleopatra (f) – father's glory

Clotilda (f) – famous **battle**

Clover (f) – (see FLOWERS)

Clydai (m) – fame

Clydno (m) – fame devourer

Clydog (m) – renowned

Clydri (m) – fame-ruler

Clynog (m) – holly (see TREES)

Coel (m) – trust

Coinneach (m) – handsome

Colin (m) – see Nicholas

Colleen (f) – girl

Collwyn (m) – hazel grove (see TREES)

Columbine (f) – (see FLOWERS)

Conan (m) – small hound (see ANIMALS)

Conn (m) – high

Connor (m) – lover of hounds (see
    ANIMALS)

Conrad (m) – brave

Constance (f) ⎫ constant
Constantine (m) ⎭

Cora (f) – maiden

Coral (f) – (see JEWELS)

Corcan (m) ⎫ heart
Cordelia (f) ⎭

Corinna (f) – maiden

Cornelia (f) ⎫ horn
Cornelius (m) ⎭

Coronella (f) – little crown (see
    FLOWERS)

Cosima (f) – order

Colm (m) ⎫
Colman (m) ⎬ dove (see BIRDS)
Columba (m) ⎭

Cosmo (m) – order

Craig (m) – rock

Cranog (m) – like the stork or heron
    (see BIRDS)

Creenan (m) – wise

Crispin (m) – curly

Crocus (f) – (see FLOWERS)

Crystal (f) – (see JEWELS)

Cunedda (m) – goodness

Cuthbert (m) – bright/famous

Cyndeyrn (m) – chief monarch

Cynfael (m) – iron **chief**

Cynfarch (m) – horse **chief**

Cynferth (m) – first perfection (see
    NUMBERS)

Cynfor (m) – chief sea

Cynfran (m) – chief raven (see BIRDS)

Cynfrig (m) – offshoot of a chief

Cyngen (m) – son of a **chief**

Cynhafal (m) ⎫ chieflike
Cynog (m) ⎭

Cynidr (m) – chief snake

Cynthia (f) – moon

Cynwrig (m) ⎫ chief hero
Cynyr (m) ⎭

Cyrene (m) – mistress of the **bridle**

Cyril (m) – lord

Cyrus (m) – (see DISPUTED NAMES)

DIANA, Italian goddess of woodland and wild nature, protector of women ... may have been thought of as a moon-goddess.

Chambers Biographical Dictionary

When he came near he called anxiously, '**DANIEL**, servant of the living God, has your God whom you serve continually been able to save you from the lions?'

Book of Daniel, 6:20
Revised New English Bible

Daffodil (f) – (see FLOWERS)

Dafydd (m) – beloved

Dahlia (f) – (see FLOWERS)

Daisy (f) – the day's eye (see FLOWERS)

Damaspia (f) – horse tamer (see ANIMALS)

Damian (m) – tamer

Daniel (m)
Danielle (f)
Daniella (f)   } God is my judge
Danil (m)

Dante (m) – enduring

Daphne (f) – laurel (see FLOWERS)

Daria (f)
Darius (m) } protector

David (m)
Davina (f) } beloved

Dawa (f/m) – moon & Monday (see DAYS OF THE WEEK)

Dean (m)
Deanna (f) } valley dweller
Dena (f)

Deborah (f) – bee

Dedwydd (m) – happy

Deiniol (m) – attractive (also see Daniel)

Deirdre (f) – (see DISPUTED NAMES)

Delfine (f)
Delfinia (f) } dolphin (see ANIMALS)

Delia (f) – moon

Delicia (f) – delight

Delphinia (f) – larkspur (see FLOWERS)

Delwen (f) – neat and fair

Demeter (f) – Earth mother

Demetrios (m) – of the **Earth** mother

Denise (f)
Dennis (m) } (see WINE)

Derek (m) – ruler of the people

Derfel (m) – (see IRON)

Dermot (m) – envy free

Desiree (f) – desired

Desmond (m) – (see MUNSTER)

Diamond (f) – (see JEWELS)

Diana (f) – moon

Dilys (f) – genuine

Dinah (f) – judgement

Dionissij (m) – (see WINE)

Diya (m) – brightness

Dmitri (m) – of the **Earth** mother

Dolphin (m) – dolphin (see ANIMALS)

Dominic (m)
Dominique (f) } of the Lord

Donald (m) ⎱
Donalda (f) ⎰ world mighty
Donelda (f)

Dora (f) ⎱ gift
Dorinda (f) ⎰

Dorcas (f) – gazelle (see ANIMALS)
Doreen (f) – (see DISPUTED NAMES)
Dorian (m) – Dorian man
Doris (f) – Dorian woman
Dorje (m) – diamondlike (see JEWELS)
Dorothy (f) – gift of God
Dougal (m) – dark stranger
Douglas (m) – black water
Drusilla (f) – (see DISPUTED NAMES)
Dudley (m) – Dudda's clearing

Dulcie (f) – sweet
Duncan (m) – brown warrior (see COLOURS)
Dunstan (m) – dark stone
Durand (m) – enduring
Dustin (m) – Thor's stone (see GODS & GODDESSES)
Dwight (m) – (see DISPUTED NAMES)
Dyddgu (f) – love day
Dyfan (m) ⎱
Dyfnog (m) ⎰ ruler of a tribe
Dyfnwal (m)
Dylan (m) – son of the **wave**
Dynawd (m) – given

As names go, **EVE** seems to fulfil every possible requirement, being easy to say and spell, clearly indicating its sex, and having an impeccable biblical background.

Leslie Dunkling: *First Names First*

Here is **EDWARD** Bear coming downstairs now, bump, bump, bump, on the back of his head, behind Christopher Robin. It is, as far as he knows, the only way of coming downstairs, but sometimes he feels that there really is another way, if only he could stop bumping for a moment and think of it.

A.A. Milne: *Winnie-the-Pooh*

Eamon(n) (m) – prosperity
Eartha (f) – Earth
Eavan (f) – beautiful
Ebenezer (m) – stone of help
Edana (f) – little **fire**
Eden (m) – fortunate **bearcub** (see ANIMALS)

Edern (m) – monarch
Edgar (m) – spear of good fortune
Edith (f) – fortunate **battle**
Edmund (m) – prosperity guardian
Edna (f) – pleasure
Ednyfed (m) – bold bird (see BIRDS)
Edryd (m) – restoration

Edward (m) – prosperity guardian

Edwin (m)
Edwina (f) } fortunate **friend**

Egan (m) – fire

Egbert (m) – bright sword

Egidia (f) – goat (see ANIMALS)

Eglantine (f) – (see FLOWERS)

Eibhlin (f) – bright

Eiddwen (f) – fond fair

Eileen (f)
Eilidh (f) } bright

Eilir (m) – butterfly (see ANIMALS)

Eiluned (f) – idol

Einion (m) – anvil

Eira (f) – snow

Eirian (f) – silver (see COLOURS)

Eirig (m) – splendid

Eiriol (f) – snowdrop (see FLOWERS)

Eirlys (f) – gold-sweet
Eiros (m) – flame-colour } (see COLOURS)

Eirwen (f) – white **snow**

Eithne (f) – little **fire**

Ekaterina (f) – pure

Elaeth (m) – spiritual being

Elain (f) – fawn (see ANIMALS)

Elaine (f) – (see DISPUTED NAMES)

Eleanor (f) – (see DISPUTED NAMES)

Electra (f) – amber (see JEWELS)

Elen (f) – angel/nymph (see ANGEL)

Elfid (m) – Autumn (see SEASONS)

Elfod (m) – intellectual

Elfreda (f) – elf strength

Elgan (m) – bright circle

Elihu (m) – 'He is my **God**'

Eli (m) – high

Elias (m)
Elijah (m) } the Lord is **God**

Ella (f) – all

Ellis (m) – the Lord is **God**

Elisaveta (f)
Elizabeth (f) } God is my oath

Elisha (m) – God has helped

Elkanah (m) – God has created

Elmer (m) – noble-famous

Eloise (f) – (see Heloise in DISPUTED NAMES)

Elroy (m) – king

Elvira (f) – blonde (see COLOURS)

Elwyn (m) – white brow (see COLOURS)

Emerald (f) – richly green (see JEWELS)

Emily (f) – rival

Emlyn (m) – (see DISPUTED NAMES)

Emma (f) – whole

Emmanuel (m) – God is with us

Emrys (m) – immortal

Emyr (m) – honour

Enda (m) – bird

Enddwyn (f) – great **bliss**

Enfys (f) – rainbow

Engelbert (m) – bright **angel**

Enid (f) – soul

Enoch (m) – experienced

Enos (m) – man

Eoghan (m) – well born

Ephraim (m) – fruitful

Erasmus (m) – beloved

Erensa (f) – love

Eric (m) – eternal **ruler**

Erica (f) – eternal ruler and heather (see FLOWERS)

Ermin (m) – lordly

Ermolai (m) – messenger

Ernait (f)
Ernan (m) } knowing

Ernest (m)
Ernestine (f) } earnestness

Ersa (f) – dew

Eryl (m/f) – watcher

Esmée (f) – esteemed
Esmond (m) – grace protection
Estelle (f) – star
Esther (f) – myrtle and Venus (see FLOWERS and GODS & GODDESSES)
Eswen (f) – strength
Ethan (m) – ancient
Ethel (f) – noble
Eugene (m) }
Eugenia (f) } well born
Eulalia (f) – sweet speech
Eunice (f) – (see VICTORY)
Eunys (f) – pleasure
Euphemia (f) – eloquent

Euphrosyne (f) – cheerfulness (see GRACES)
Eurliw (f) – golden }
Eurwen (f) – gold-fair } (see COLOURS)
Eusebius (m) – pious
Eustace (m) }
Eustacia (f) } fruitful
Evadne (f) – (see DISPUTED NAMES)
Evangeline (f) – good news
Eve (f) – life
Evelyn (f) – hazel (see TREES)
Ewan (m) – well born
Ewig (m) – deer (see ANIMALS)
Ezekiel (m) – God strengthens
Ezra (m) – help

It was something new to call a girl **FLORENCE**. Within fifty years there would be thousands of girls all over the world christened FLORENCE in honour of this baby, but in the summer of 1820, when Fanny Nightingale fixed on the name for her daughter, it was new.

Cecil Woodham Smith: *Florence Nightingale*

From the very first, the highly sensitive nature of St. **FRANCIS** was intensely alive to the beauty of Nature.

Canon Knox Little, 1897: *St. Francis of Assisi*

Fabian (m) – beangrower
Fadi (m) }
Fadia (f) } saviour
Fadil (m) – virtuous
Fahd (m) – panther (see ANIMALS)
Faith (f) – faith

Faraj (m) – remedy
Farid (m) }
Farida (f) } unique
Faruq (m) – truth
Fatima (f) – 'the **lady** who weans her children'

Fatin (f) – charming

Fausta (f) }
Faustus (m) } lucky & fortunate

Fawzi (m) }
Fawziyya (f) } victory

Fay (f) – faith

Fayruz (f) – turquoise (see JEWELS)

Faysal (m) – judge

Felicia (f) }
Felicity (f) } happy
Felix (m) }

Fenella (f) – white shoulder (see COLOURS)

Feodor (m) – gift of **God**

Ferdinand (m) – (see DISPUTED NAMES)

Fergal (m) }
Fergus (m) } vigorous man

Fergusiana (f) – vigorous woman

Fern (f) – fern }
Ffion (f) – foxglove } (see FLOWERS)
Fflur (f) – flower }

Fiachra (m) – raven (see BIRDS)

Fidda (f) – silent one

Fikri (m) }
Fikriyya (f) } meditative

Fingal (m) – fair valour

Finlo (m) – light

Finn (m) – fair

Fiona (f) – white (see COLOURS)

Firishta (m/f) – angel

Fitz (m) – son

Flannan (m) – red }
Flavia (f) – yellow } (see COLOURS)

Fleur (f) }
Flora (f) } flower (see FLOWERS)

Florence (f) – flowering (see FLOWERS)

Fortunata (f) – lucky

Frances (f) }
Francesca (f) } freewoman

Francis (m) – freeman

Frederica (f) }
Frederick (m) } peaceful ruler

Frank (m) – (see FREEMAN)

Franklin (m) – freeman

Fraser (m) – (see DISPUTED NAMES)

Freya (f) – noble lady

GLADYS was frequently disowned as the type of name associated with that slightly giggling girl of fiction, fond of cheap scent, high heels and whispering in corners.

G.B. Stern: *A Name to Conjure With*

GEORGE III was a peace-loving man who built up a magnificent library (now in the British Museum) and a great collection of pictures. One of his worst faults was his obstinacy. He was fond of music and farming and gained the nickname 'Farmer George'.

Children's Britannica Vol 8

Gabriel (m) – strong man of **God**

Gabriella (f), Gabrielle (f) – strong woman of **God**

Gad (m) – fortunate

Gaia (f) – Earth

Gail (f) – see Abigail

Galahad (m) – hawk (see BIRDS)

Galen (m) – calm

Galina (f) – jackdaw (see BIRDS)

Gamaliel (m) – God is my reward

Gareth (m) – gentle

Gavin (m) } hawk (see BIRDS)
Gawain (m) }

Gaynor (f) – white and soft (see COLOURS)

Genesius (m) – creation

Geoffrey (m) – (see DISPUTED NAMES

George (m) – earth worker

Georgi (m) ⎫
Georgette (f) ⎬ see George
Georgia (f) ⎪
Georgina (f) ⎭

Geraint (m) – old

Gerald (m) } ruling **spear**
Geraldine (f) }

Gerard (m) – strong **spear**

Gerda (f) – protection

Gershom (m) – bell

Gethin (m) – dusky

Gertrude (f) – strong **spear**

Gervaise (f) } (see DISPUTED
Gervase (m) } NAMES)

Ghada (f) – graceful

Ghadir (f) – stream

Ghalib (m) – victorious one

Ghassan (m) – in the prime of **youth**

Ghayth (m) – rain

Ghufran (m) – forgiveness

Gideon (m) – hewer

Gilbert (m) – bright **pledge**

Gildas (m) – (see DISPUTED NAMES)

Giles (m) – goat (see ANIMALS)

Gillian (f) – (see Julian in DISPUTED NAMES)

Gilmere (m) – merry youth

Giselle (f) – pledge

Gladys (f) – (see DISPUTED NAMES)

Glenda (f) – holy and good

Glen(n) (m) – valley

Glenys (f) – holy and fair

Gloria (f) – glory

Gloukera (f) – sweet

Glykera (f) – sweet

Glyn(n) (m) ⎱ little **valley**
Glynis (f) ⎰

Glywys (m) – governor

Goewin (f) – sprightly

Gofannon (m) – smith

Gordon (m) – dweller at the triangular hill estate

Grace (f) – grace

Grainne (f) – (see DISPUTED NAMES)

Gregory (m) – watchful

Greta (f) – see Margaret

Griffin (m) ⎱ (see DISPUTED NAMES)
Griffith (m) ⎰

Griselda (f) – grey battle maiden (see COLOURS)

Grugwyn (f) – white heather (see FLOWERS)

Guinevere (f) – fair and yielding

Guy (m) – (see DISPUTED NAMES)

Gwaednerth (m) – blood strength

Gwalchmai (m) – hawk (see BIRDS)

Gwarthen (m) – shelter

Gwen (f) ⎱ blessed & fair
Gwenda (f) ⎰

Gwendolen (f) – blessed/fair ring

Gwendydd (f) – morning **star**

Gwenfair (f) – Blessed Mary

Gwenfrewi (f) – blessed reconciliation

Gwenhwyfar (f) – see Guinevere

Gwenllian (f) – white & flaxen (see COLOURS)

Gwennol (f) – swallow (see BIRDS)

Gwenog (f) – smiling

Gwenonwy (f) – lily of the valley (see FLOWERS)

Gwern (m) – alder (see TREES)

Gwernfyl (f) – (see TREES)

Gwesyn (m) – little lad

Gwilym (m) – will-**helmet**

Gwion (m) – elf

Gwlithyn (f) – dewdrop

Gwrgan (m) – hero-bright

Gwrnerth (m) – hero-strong

Gwyddon (m) – seer

Gwyeira (f) – white **snow**

Gwylfai (f/m) – May day (see MONTHS OF THE YEAR)

Gwyneth (f) – bliss

St. **HILDEGARD**, Abbess of Rupertsberg, called in her own day the 'Sibyl of the Rhine', was one of the great figures of the 12th century and one of the most remarkable of women. She was the first of the great German mystics, a poet and a prophet, a physician and a political moralist, who rebuked popes and princes, bishops and lay-folk, with complete fearlessness and unerring justice.

Butler: *Lives of the Saints*

*Then he sang of **HIAWATHA**,*
Sang the song of Hiawatha,
Sang his wondrous birth and being,
How he prayed and how he fasted,
How he lived and toiled and suffered,
That the tribes of men might prosper.

H.W. Longfellow: *The Song of HIAWATHA*

Habakkuk (m) – embrace
Habib (m) ⎫ beloved
Habiba (f) ⎬
Hadassah (f) – myrtle (see FLOWERS)
Hadi (m) ⎫ guide
Hadiyya (f) ⎬
Hadil (f) – cooing of pigeons (see BIRDS)
Haf (m) ⎫ summer fullness (see
Hafwen (f) ⎬ SEASONS)
Hafiz (m) – guardian
Hakim (m) – wise
Hala (f) – halo
Hamelen (m) – home
Hamid (m) – thankful
Hana (f) – bliss
Hanan (f) – tender affection
Hani (m) ⎫ happy
Haniya (f) ⎬
Hannah (f) – favour
Harith (m) – good provider

Harold (m) – army power
Harriet (f) – home rule
Harvey (m) – battle worthy
Hasan (m) – good
Hasim (m) – decisive
Havelock (m) – ancestor relics
Hayley (f) – hay meadow
Haytham (m) – eagle (see BIRDS)
Hazel (f) – hazel (see TREES)
Heather (f) – heather (see FLOWERS)
Hebe (f) – youth
Hector (m) – holding fast
Heddwen (f) ⎫ blessed peace
Heddwyn (m) ⎬
Heilyn (m) – cupbearer
Helen (f) – bright
Helga (f) – holy
Heloise (f) – (see DISPUTED NAMES)
Henrietta (f) ⎫ home rule
Henry (m) ⎬

Hepzibah (f) – 'my **delight** is in her'

Hereward (m) – army defence

Herbert (m) – army bright

Herman (m) – soldier

Hermia (f) – (see MESSENGER)

Hermione (f) – messenger

Heulwen (f) – sunshine

Hiba (f) – gift

Hikmat (m/f) – wisdom

Hilary (f) – cheerful

Hilda (f) – battle

Hildegarde (f) – battle stronghold

Hippolyta (f) } setting **horses** free
Hippolytus (m) } (see ANIMALS)

Hisham (m) – generous

Holly (f) – holly (see TREES)

Honey (f) – honey

Honoria (f) } honour
Honour (f) }

Horace (m) } (see DISPUTED NAMES)
Horatia (f) }

Howard (m) – high guardian

Hubert (m) – bright mind

Hugh (m) } heart
Hughina (f) }

Humbert (m) – bright warrior

Humphrey (m) – peaceful & strong

Huw (m) – heart

Hyacinth (f) – hyacinth (see FLOWERS)

Hywel (m) – eminent

IPHIGENIA is not only an epic heroine; she was once a Mycenean goddess, whose name appears on the tablets recording offerings.

Peter Levi: *Pelican History of Greek Literature*

'The name **IVOR** Novello is euphonious'

Noel Coward

Iaian (m) } God is gracious
Ian (m) }

Ianthe (f) – violet (see FLOWERS)

Ibtisam (f) – smiling

Ida (f) – work

Idnerth (m) – strong lord

Idris (m) – ardent lord

Ieuaf (m) – youngest

Ieuan (m) – God is gracious

Ignatius (m) – fiery

Iman (m) – faith

Imogen (f) – (see DISPUTED NAMES)

India (f) – India

Iney (f) – kernel

Ingebiard (f) – help of **youth**

Ingram (m) – raven (see BIRDS)

Ingrid (f) – (see GODS & GODDESSES)

Innes (m/f) – island

Iolanthe (m) – (see Yolande in DISPUTED NAMES)

Iphigenia (f) – serpent-born (see
  ANIMALS)
Ira (m) – watchful
Iris (f) – rainbow (see FLOWERS)
Irma (f) – whole
Isaac (m) – laughter
Isabel(le) (f) – see Elizabeth
Isaiah (m) – God is salvation
Isidora (f) ⎱ gift of Isis (see GODS
Isidore (m) ⎰   & GODDESSES)

Ismail (m) – God hears
Isolde (f) – fair
Ithel (m) – generous lord
Ithiel (m) – God is with me
Ivan (m) – God is gracious
Ivar (m) – young **spring**
Ivo (m) – yew (see TREES)
Ivor (m) – lord and yew (see TREES)
Ivy (f) – ivy (see FLOWERS)

'I have no name:
  I am but two days old.'
'What shall I call thee?'
JOY *is my name.'*
'Sweet joy befall thee'
                William Blake: *Infant Joy*

JOHN is often called 'a good old English name' (John Bull was the typical Englishman), but in Scotland it is Ian, in Ireland Sean, Hans in Germany, Juan in Spain and Giovanni in Italy.

                James Glennon: *4001 Babies' Names*
                              and their Meanings

Jabir (m) – restorer
Jack (m) – see John
Jacob (m) ⎱ supplanter
Jacqueline (f) ⎰
Jael (m) – goat (see ANIMALS)
Jalal (m) ⎱ glory
Jalila (f) ⎰
Jamal (m) ⎱
Jamil (m) ⎬ beautiful
Jamila (f) ⎰

James (m) – supplanter
Jane (f) ⎱
Janet (f) ⎬ God is gracious
Janice (f) ⎰
Japheth (m) – 'may he **expand**'
Jared (m) – rose (see FLOWERS)
Jasmine (f) – jasmine (see FLOWERS)
Jason (m) – healer
Jasper (m) – master of the treasure (see
  JEWELS)

Jawahir (f) – jewel (see JEWELS)

Jeanette (f) } God is gracious
Jeannine (f) }

Jeffrey (m) – (see Geoffrey in DISPUTED NAMES)

Jemima (f) – dove (see BIRDS)

Jennifer (f) – fair and yielding

Jeremy (m) – appointed by **God**

Jerome (m) – sacred name

Jesse (m) – gift

Jessica (f) – (see DISPUTED NAMES)

Jethro (m) – excellence

Jewel(l) (f) – see JEWELS

Jig-me (m) – fearless

Jill (m) – see Julian in DISPUTED NAMES

Jinan (m/f) – paradise

Joan (f) } God is gracious
Joanna (f) }

Job (m) – (see DISPUTED NAMES)

Jocelyn (f) – (see DISPUTED NAMES)

Joel (m) } only Yahweh is **God**
Joelle (f) }

John (m) – God is gracious

Jole (m) – Yule

Jonah (m) – dove (see BIRDS)

Jonquil (f) – reed (see FLOWERS)

Jordan (m) – River **Jordan**

Joseph (m) } God shall add
Josephina (f) }

Joss (m) – (see DISPUTED NAMES)

Joy (f) } joy (see DISPUTED
Joyce (f) } NAMES)

Jude (m) – praise

Judith (f) – jewess

Julian (m) – (see DISPUTED NAMES)

Julia (f)
Juliana (f)
Julie (f) } (see Julian)
Juliet (f)
Juliette (f)

July (f) – (see Julian and MONTHS OF THE YEAR)

Jum'a (m/f) – Friday (see DAYS OF THE WEEK)

June (f) – June (see MONTHS OF THE YEAR)

Juno (f) – see June

Juniper (f) – juniper (see FLOWERS)

Jupiter (m) – father sky

Justin (m) } just
Justine (f) }

> Petruchio: *Good morrow, Kate, for that's your name, I hear.*
>
> Kate: *Well have you heard, but something hard of hearing;*
> *They call me **KATHERINE** that do talk of me.*
>
> William Shakespeare:
> *The Taming of the Shrew*

At one Lenten season, St **KEVIN** ... fled from the company of men to a certain solitude ... as he knelt in his accustomed fashion, with his hand outstretched through the window and lifted up to heaven, a blackbird settled on it, and busying herself as in her nest, laid in it an egg. And so moved was the saint that in all patience and gentleness he remained, neither closing nor withdrawing his hand: but until the young ones were fully hatched he held it out unwearied, shaping it for the purpose.

A.M. Allchin & Esther de Waal:
from *Threshold of Light*

Kamal (m) – perfection
Karam (m) – generosity
Karen (f) – pure
Karl (m) – manly
Kate (f) ⎫
Katherine (f) ⎬ pure
Kathleen (f) ⎭
Kay (m) – (see DISPUTED NAMES)
Keir (m) – swarthy
Keith (m) – wood
Kenelm (m) – helmet
Kenna (f) ⎫
Kenneth (m) ⎬ handsome
Keren (f) ⎫
Kerena (f) ⎬ horn of eye-paint

Kerenhappuch (f) – horn of eye-paint
Kerron (m) – black (see COLOURS)
Keturah (f) – fragrance
Kevin (m) – comely
Kezia (f) – cassia (see FLOWERS)
Khadija (f) – premature child
Khalid (m) ⎫
Khalida (f) ⎬ immortal
Khalil (m) – friend
Khamis (m) ⎫ Thursday (see DAYS
Khemisse (f) ⎬ OF THE WEEK)
Kieran (m) – little **dark** one
Kirill (m) – lord

It is as though **LILITH**, as God's dark avenging anima, and the flame of the revolving sword, retains much of the ancient Goddess power over childbirth, life and death.

Barbara Black Kultov: *The Book of Lilith*

And when he thus had spoken, he cried with a loud voice, '**LAZARUS** come forth'. And he that was dead came forth, bound hand and foot with graveclothes: and his face was bound about with a napkin.

St John's Gospel 11:43

Laban (m) – white (see COLOURS)

Labhrainn (m) ⎫
Labhras (m) ⎭ laurel (see FLOWERS)

Laetitia (f) – delight

Lambert (m) – land bright

Lancelot (m) – (see DISPUTED NAMES)

Lara (f) – seagull (see BIRDS)

Laura (f) – (see Laurel)

Laurel (f) – laurel (see FLOWERS)

Lauren (f) – (see Laurel)

Lavinia (f) – (see DISPUTED NAMES)

Lawrence (m) – laurel (see FLOWERS)

Layla (f) – wine

Lazarus (m) – God is my help

Leah (f) – wearied

Leanda (f) – lion woman ⎫ (see
Leander (m) – lion man ⎭ ANIMALS)

Lee (m) – meadow

Lemuel (m) – belonging to **God**

Leo (m) ⎫
Leon (m) ⎬ lion (see ANIMALS)
Leona (f) ⎭

Leonard (m) – strong as a lion (see ANIMALS)

Leonie (f) – lion (see ANIMALS)

Leopold (m) – people's leader

Leroy (m) – king

Levi (m) – joined

Lewis (m) – famous in battle

Lhakpa (f) – Wednesday (see DAYS OF THE WEEK)

Lhamo (f) – goddess (see GOD)

Liam (m) – will helmet

Lilian (f) – lily (see FLOWERS)

Lilith (f) – screech owl (see BIRDS)

Lily (f) – lily (see FLOWERS)

Linda (f) – serpent (see ANIMALS)

Linus (m) – flax (see FLOWERS)

Lionel (m) – little lion (see ANIMALS)

Llawdden (m) – pleasant

Lleufer (m) – splendid

Llew (m) – shining

Llewellyn (m) – lion likeness (see ANIMALS)

Llian (f) – linen

Llinos (f) – linnet (see BIRDS)

Lloyd (m) – grey-haired (see COLOURS)

Lodes (f) – damsel

Lorraine (f) – from Lorraine

Louis (m) ⎫
Louisa (f) ⎬ famous in battle
Louise (f) ⎭
Loveday (f) – loveday (see LOVE)
Lucille (f) ⎫
Lucinda (f) ⎬ light
Lucius (m) ⎪
Lucy (f) ⎭

Ludmila (f) – loved by the people
Lugh (m) – sun
Lujaya (f) – silent one
Luke (m) – man from **Lucania**
Luna (f) – moon
Lydia (f) – woman of **Lydia**
Lynette (f) – idol

*Are you asleep, **MIRIAM**, my child?*
We are like rivers, now calm, and now wild,
And deep within us an ancestor's seed,
Their pride and their pain, their vision, their deed,
Their past now returning to children and heirs.
You are not alone, and your life is theirs.
MIRIAM, my life – my child, good night!

Richard Beer-Hofmann (trans. Karl Darmstadter):
Lullaby for Miriam

MICHAEL is the prince of the heavenly hosts ... Michael is the commander-in-chief of the celestial army. His name means 'Looks Like God' or 'Who Is As God'. He is strong and young and handsome, and in Renaissance paintings is depicted as wearing armour. He is the protector of the Roman Catholic Church, as well as the patron saint of the Hebrew nation ... Michael can appear in three of the seven heavens simultaneously ... Michael is made of snow.

Sophy Burnham: *A Book of Angels*

Mabel (f) – loveable
Mabon (m) – youth
Machonna (m) – intelligence
Madeleine (f) – magnificent
Madiha (f) – praise
Madog (m) – fortunate
Maeldern (m) – iron oak (see TREES)

Maelrys (m) – ardent metal
Maelwas (m) – iron lad
Maeve (f) – intoxicating
Magdalen (f) – magnificent
Magnolia (f) – magnolia (see FLOWERS)
Maha (f) – eyes
Mahasin (f) – charms

Mahir (m) – skilful

Mahmud (m) – praiseworthy

Maia (f) – May (see MONTHS OF THE YEAR)

Maire (f) – see Mary

Malachi (m) ⎫
Malachy (m) ⎭ messenger

Malcolm (m) – servant of St **Columba**

Malise (m) – servant of **Jesus**

Malvina (f) – smooth brow

Manar (m/f) – lighthouse

Manfred (m) – man of **peace**

Marcella (f) ⎫
Marcelline (f) ⎬ of Mars
Marcia (f) ⎭

Margaret (f) – pearl (see JEWELS)

Margery (f) ⎫
Margo (f) ⎭ see Margaret

Marguerite (f) – daisy & pearl (see FLOWERS & JEWELS)

Marigold (f) – gold flower of Queen Mary (see FLOWERS)

Marilyn (f) – see Mary

Marina (f) ⎫
Mariot (f) ⎭ of the sea (see Mary)

Marius (m) – of Mars

Marjoram (f) – marjoram (see FLOWERS)

Mark (m) – of Mars

Marmaduke (m) – devotee of St **Maedoc**

Martha (f) – lady

Martin (m) ⎫
Martina (f) ⎬ of Mars
Martine (f) ⎭

Maruna (f) – seal

Mary (f) – (see DISPUTED NAMES)

Maryam (f) – see Mary

Matfei (m) – gift of **God**

Math (m) – wealth

Mathias (m) ⎫
Matthew (m) ⎭ gift of **God**

Maura (f) ⎫
Maureen (f) ⎭ see Mary

Maurice (m) – Moor

Mavis (f) – songthrush (see BIRDS)

May (f) – May (see FLOWERS and MONTHS OF THE YEAR)

Maynard (m) – strong

Maysa (f) – graceful

Megan (f) – see Margaret

Mehetabel (f) – God makes happy

Meinwen (f) – slender fair

Meirion (m) – dairyman

Melangel (f) – sweet **angel**

Melanie (f) – black (see COLOURS)

Melchior (m) – king

Melek (m) – king

Melia (f) – ashtree (see TREES)

Melinda (f) – honey

Melissa (f) – bee

Melita (f) – honey

Melody (f) – melody

Melony (f) – black (see COLOURS)

Mercedes (f) – mercy

Mercy (f) – mercy

Meredith (m) ⎫
Meredydd (m) ⎭ magnificent **chief**

Merend (f) ⎫
Mererid (f) ⎭ see Margaret

Merle (f) – blackbird (see BIRDS)

Merlin (m) – (see DISPUTED NAMES)

Meryl (f) – (see DISPUTED NAMES)

Michael (m) ⎫
Michaela (f) ⎪
Michele (f) ⎬ who is like **God**
Michelle (f) ⎭

Migmar (m/f) – Tuesday (see DAYS OF THE WEEK)

Mikhail (m) – see Michael

Mildred (f) – mild power

Miles (m) – (see DISPUTED NAMES)

Millicent (f) – strong worker

Mimosa (f) – mimosa (see FLOWERS)

Minerva (f) – wisdom

Mirabelle (f) ⎱ admirable
Miranda (f) ⎰

Miriam (f) – (see DISPUTED NAMES)

Modest (f) – modesty

Modron (f) – earth goddess

Moelwyn (f) – fair head

Moira (f) – see Mary

Mona (f) – noble

Mordeyrn (m) – great **monarch**

Morfael (m) – great **iron**

Morgan (m) – (see DISPUTED
   NAMES)

Morien (m) – sea-born

Morris (m) – Moor

Morwenna (f) – maiden

Moses (m) – (see DISPUTED NAMES)

Mubarak (m) – blessed

Muhammad (m) – praiseworthy

Muhsin (m) ⎱ beneficent
Muhsina (f) ⎰

Mungo (m) – amiable

Munir (m) ⎱ shining
Munira (f) ⎰

Munya (f) – hope

Murcard (m) – sea expert

Murdina (f)) ⎱ mariner
Murdoch (m) ⎰

Muriel (f) – sea-bright

Musidora (f) – (see MUSES)

Mustafa (m) – chosen

Mwynwen (f) – mild and fair

Myfanwy (f) – my **rare** one

Myghin (f) – mercy

Myrna (f) – beloved

Myrtle (f) – myrtle (see FLOWERS)

And she said unto them, 'Call me not **NAOMI**, call me Mara, for the Almighty hath dealt very bitterly with me. I went out full and the Lord hath brought me home again empty.'

The Book of Ruth II:20

And the Lord said unto **NOAH**, 'Come thou and all thy house into the ark, for these have I seen righteous before me in this generation.'

Genesis VII:1

Nabil (m) ⎫ noble
Nabila (f) ⎭

Nada (f) – generosity

Nadia (f) ⎫ hope
Nadine (f) ⎭

Nadir (m) ⎫ precious
Nadira (f) ⎭

Nadya (f) – dew

Naim (m) ⎫ carefree
Naima (f) ⎭

Najib (m) ⎫ noble
Najiba (f) ⎭

Najla (f) – eyes

Nancy (f) – favour

Naomi (f) – pleasantness

Narcissus (m) ⎫ daffodil (see FLOWERS)
Narkiss (m) ⎭

Natalie (f) ⎫
Natalya (f) ⎬ birth
Natasha (f) ⎭

Nawal (f) – gift

Neil (m) – (see DISPUTED NAMES)

Nerissa (f) – sea nymph

Nerys (f) – lady

Nesta (f) – pure

Nestor (m) – homecoming

Niamh (f) – bright

Nicodemus (m) ⎫
Nicholas (m) ⎬ victory people
Nicola (f) ⎭

Nigel (m) – black (see COLOURS)

Nilufar (f) – lotus (see FLOWERS)

Nina (f) – praiseworthy

Noah (m) – (see DISPUTED NAMES)

Noble (m) – noble

Nolan (m) – champion

Nona (f) – ninth (see NUMBERS)

Nora (f) – honour

Norbert (m) – famous in the North

Norbu (m) – jewel (see JEWELS)

Norma (f) – Northwoman (see DIRECTIONS)

Norman (m) – Northman (see DIRECTIONS)

Nova (f) – new

Nur (m/f) – light

Nyima (m) – sun & Sunday (see DAYS OF THE WEEK)

*... poor **OPHELIA***
Divided from herself and her fair judgement,
Without the which we are pictures or mere beasts.

Hamlet, Act IV Sc 5

OMAR's Epicurean Audacity of Thought and Speech caused him to be regarded askance in his own Time and Country. He is said to have been especially hated and dreaded by the Sufis, whose Practice he ridiculed, and whose Faith amounts to little more than his own, when stript of the Mysticism and formal recognition of Islamism under which OMAR would not hide.

Edward Fitzgerald:
Omar Khayyam, The Astronomer-Poet of Persia

Ocean (f) – ocean
Obadiah (m) – servant of **God**
Octavia (f) – eighth (see NUMBERS)
Odette (f) ⎫
Odile (f) ⎭ prosperity
Olaf (m) – ancestor relics
Olga (f) – holy
Olivia (f) ⎫
Olive (f) ⎭ olive (see TREES and PEACE)
Oliver (m) – ancestor relics
Olwen (f) – white track (see COLOURS)
Omar (m) – flourishing
Onyx (f) – nail (see JEWELS)

Opal (f) – precious stone (see JEWELS)
Ophelia (f) – help
Oran (m) – green
Oriana (f) – golden (see COLOURS and MORNING SUN)
Orla (f) – golden lady (see COLOURS)
Orlando (m) – famous in the land
Orson (m) – little **bear** (see ANIMALS)
Osbert (m) – bright god
Ösel (m) – radiance
Osip (m) – God shall add
Otto (m) – prosperity
Owen (m) – well born

PERSEPHONE herself plucked dainty crocuses and white lilies. Intent on gathering, she little by little strayed far ... Her father's brother saw her, and no sooner did he see her than he swiftly carried her off and bore her on his dusky steed into his own realm.

Ovid (trans. Sir J G Frazer): *Fasti IV*

And Simon **PETER** answered and said, 'Thou art the Christ, the Son of the Living God.' And Jesus answered and said unto him: 'Blessed art thou, Simon bar-Jona for flesh and blood hath not revealed it unto thee, but my Father which is in heaven. And I say also unto thee, that thou art PETER, and upon this rock I will build my church.'

St Matthew's Gospel XVI 16-18

Padarn (m) – fatherly

Pamela (f) – honey (see also BEE)

Pan (m) ⎫ all
Pandora (f) ⎭

Pansy (f) – thoughtful (see FLOWERS)

Parthenope (f) – maiden

Pasang (m/f) – Friday (see DAYS OF THE WEEK)

Pascal (m) ⎫
Pascale (f) ⎬ Easter (see FESTIVALS)
Pascow (m) ⎭

Patience (f) – patience

Patricia (f) – noblewoman

Patrick (m) – nobleman

Paul (m) ⎫
Paula (f) ⎪
Paulette (f) ⎬ small
Pauline (f) ⎪
Pavel (m) ⎭

Peace (f) – peace

Pearl (f) – pearl (see JEWELS)

Pema (f) – lotus (see FLOWERS)

Penba (m/f) – Saturday (see DAYS OF THE WEEK)

Pencast (m/f) – Whitsuntide (see FESTIVALS)

Penelope (f) – (see DISPUTED NAMES)

Pentecost (m/f) – Whitsuntide (see FESTIVALS)

Penwyn (m) – fair head

Percival (m) ⎫ (see VALLEY)
Percy (m) ⎭

Perdita (f) – lost

Peregrine (m) – pilgrim

Perpetua (f) – perpetual

Peter (m) ⎫
Petra (f) ⎬ rock
Petronella (f) ⎭

Philana (f) ⎫ lover of mankind
Philander (m) ⎭

Philemon (m) – kiss

Philip (m) ⎫ lover of horses
Philippa (f) ⎭ (see ANIMALS)

Philomela (f) – singing

Philomena (f) – beloved

Phineas (m) – oracle

Phoebe (f) – bright

Phuntsog (m/f) – good luck

Phurbu (m/f) – Thursday (see DAYS OF THE WEEK)

Phyllida (f) }
Phyllis (f) } leafy (see FLOWERS)

Piers (m) – rock

Polymnia (f) – (see MUSES)

Pomona (f) – apple

Poppy (f) – poppy (see FLOWERS)

Prima (f) }
Primus (m) } first (see NUMBERS)

Primrose (f) – first rose (see FLOWERS)

Primula (f) – (see FLOWERS)

Priscilla (f) – ancient

Prunella (f) – little plum (see TREES)

Pryderi (m) – carefulness

Pwyll (m) – discretion

The passion of St **QUINTINUS** (or Quentin) is a worthless recital of tortures and marvels. It says that his limbs were stretched with pulleys on the rack till his joints were dislocated, his body torn with iron wire, boiled pitch and oil were poured on his back and lighted torches applied to his sides. By the ministry of an angel he escaped from prison but was taken again while preaching in the market place. Rictiovarus ordered him to be tortured anew, and at last his head to be cut off, whereupon a dove issued from the gaping neck and flew away into the heavens.

Butler: *Lives of the Saints*

Quentin (m) – fifth (see NUMBERS)

RACHEL was beautiful and well-favoured.

Genesis XXIX:17

When **RICHARD**'s contemporaries called him 'Coeur de Lion' they paid a lasting compliment to the king of beasts. Little did the English people owe him for his services, and heavily did they pay for his adventures.

Winston S Churchill:
A History of the English Speaking Peoples

Rachel (f) – ewe (see ANIMALS)
Rafaela (f) } God heals
Rafaella (f) }
Rafat (m) – merciful
Raina (f) – queen
Raja (m) } hope
Rajya (f) }
Rajab (m) – revered
Ralph (m) } wolf counsel (see
Ralphina (f) } ANIMALS)
Ramadan (f) – Ramadan
Ramona (f) – wise **protectress**
Rana (m) } eye-catching
Ran(y)a (f) }
Randal (m) } wolf shield (see
Randolph (m) } ANIMALS)
Ranulf (m) – wolf counsel (see
    ANIMALS)
Raphael (m) – God heals
Rashad (m) }
Rashid (m) } rightly **guided**
Rashida (f) }
Raymond (m) – wise **protector**
Rayner (m) – counsel-warrior
Rebecca (f) – (see DISPUTED NAMES)
Regina (f) – queen
Reginald (m) – mighty

Renata (f) }
René (m) } reborn
Renée (f) }
Renfred (m) – counsel peace
Renowden (m) – mighty
Reuben (m) 'Behold! a son.'
Reynard (m) – decision strong
Reynold (m) – mighty
Rex (m) – king
Rhain (m) – spear
Rhea (f) – Earth
Rhedyn (f) – fern (see FLOWERS)
Rhiangar (f) – (see MAIDEN)
Rhiannon (f) – goddess
Rhianwen (f) – fair **maiden**
Rhoda (f) – rose (see FLOWERS)
Rhodri (m) – circle
Rhona (f) – (see ISLAND)
Rhonwen (f) – fair lance
Rhun (m) – awesome / awful
Rhydderch (m) – exalted ruler
Rhys (m) – ardent
Richard (m) – strong **ruler**
Rida (f) – contentment
Ridwana (f) – paradise
Rigdzin (m) – awareness

Rita (f) – see Margaret

Robert (m)
Roberta (f)
Robin (m) } fame-bright
Robina (f)

Roderick (m) – fame-ruler

Roger (m) – fame-spear

Roisin (f) – rose (see FLOWERS)

Roland (m) – famous in the land

Rolf (m) – famous **wolf** (see ANIMALS)

Romeo (m) – pilgrim to **Rome**

Ronald (m) – mighty

Ronan (m) – seal (see ANIMALS)

Rory (m) – red (see COLOURS)

Rosalie (f) – rose (see FLOWERS)

Rosalind (f) – (see DISPUTED NAMES)

Rosamund (f) – (see ANIMALS – Horse and DISPUTED NAMES)

Rose (f) – rose (see FLOWERS)

Rosemary (f) – dew of the sea (see FLOWERS)

Rosen (f) – rose (see FLOWERS)

Rosenwyn (f) – fair rose (see FLOWERS)

Rowan (m) – (see TREES)

Rowena (f) – tall and fair

Roxana (f) – dawn

Roy (m) – red (see COLOURS)

Rudolf (m) – famous **wolf** (see ANIMALS)

Rufus (m) – red (see COLOURS)

Rupert (m) – fame-bright

Rurik (m) – fame-ruler

Russell (m) – red (see COLOURS)

Ruth (f) – (see DISPUTED NAMES)

*What light is light, if **SILVIA** be not seen?*
What joy is joy, if SILVIA be not by?

William Shakespeare:
Two Gentlemen of Verona, Act III, Sc. 4

And, behold, there was a man in Jerusalem, whose name was **SIMEON** ... And it was revealed unto him by the Holy Ghost that he should not see death before he had seen the lord's Christ.

St Luke's Gospel II:25/26

Sabah (f) – morning

Sabbati (f) – Saturday (see DAYS OF THE WEEK)

Sabina (f) – Sabine woman

Sabir (m) – patient

Sabrina (f) – (see DISPUTED NAMES)

Sacha (m) – see Alexander

Sacheverell (m) – roebuck leap

Sadhbh (f) – sweet

Sadie (f) – princess

Saffron (f) – saffron (see FLOWERS)

Safiyya (f) – confidante

Sahar (f) – dawn
Salah (m) – goodness
Salana (f) – well being
Salathiel (m) – requested from **God**
Sally (f) – princess
Salome (f) ⎫
Salomea (f) ⎬ woman of **peace**
Salwa (f) – consolation
Sami (m) ⎫ elevated
Samya (f) ⎭
Samih (f) ⎫ tolerant
Samiha (f) ⎭
Samson (m) – sun child
Samuel (m) ⎫ name of **God**
Samuil (m) ⎭
Sana (f) – radiance
Sanchia (f) ⎫
Sancho (m) ⎬ holy
Sanctan (m) ⎭
Sangye (m) – Buddha
Sarab (f) – mirage
Sarah (f) – princess
Saraid (f) – excellent
Saul (m) – asked for from God
Sawsun (f) – lily of the valley (see
    FLOWERS)
Sawyl (m) – name of **God**
Sayyid (m) – master
Scholastica (f) – scholar
Sean (m) – God is gracious
Sebastian (m) – man from SEBASTIA
Sebti (m) – Saturday (see DAYS OF
    THE WEEK)
Secunda (f) ⎫ second (see
Secundus (m) ⎭ NUMBERS)
Seirian (f) – sparkling
Seiriol (f) – cheerful
Selene (f) – moon
Selina (f) – heaven

Selwyn (m) – ardorous fair one (also see
    DISPUTED NAMES)
Semyon (m) – hearkening
Septima (f) ⎫ seventh (see
Septimus (m) ⎭ NUMBERS)
Seraphima (f) ⎫ burning one
Seraphina (f) ⎭
Serena (f) – calm
Serle (m) – armour
Seth (m) – compensation
Sewal (m) – victory-strength
Sextus (m) – sixth (see NUMBERS)
Shadi (m) ⎫ singer
Shadya (f) ⎭
Shahira (f) – renowned
Shakir (m) – grateful
Sharif (m) ⎫ distinguished
Sharifa (f) ⎭
Sharon (f) – plain
Sheila (f) – blind
Shirley (f) – (see DISPUTED NAMES)
Sholto (m) – sower
Shukri (m) ⎫ thankful
Shukriyya (f) ⎭
Sidney (m) ⎫ of St **Denis**
Sidony (f) ⎭
Siegfried (m) – victory-peace
Sigmund (m) – victory-protection
Sigurd (m) – victory-word
Silas (m) ⎫
Silvester (m) ⎬ of the **woods**
Silvia (f) ⎭
Simeon (m) ⎫
Simidh (m) ⎬ hearkening
Simon (m) ⎪
Simone (f) ⎭
Sinead (f) ⎫ God is gracious
Siobhan (f) ⎭
Siomon (m) – hearkening

Sive (f) – goodness
Sixtus (m) – polished
Solomon (m) – man of **peace**
Somerled (m) – summer wanderer (see
    SEASONS)
Sonia (f)
Sonya (f)
Sophia (f)   } wisdom
Sophy (f)
Sorcha (f) – brightness
Sorley (m) – summer wanderer (see
    SEASONS)
Stacey (f) – resurrection
Stacy (f) – fruitful
Stanislas (m) – glory

Stanley (m) – clearing
Stella (f) – star
Stephen (m) – crown
Sterling (m) – excellent
Stuart (m) – steward
Suha (f)
Suhayl (m) } star
Suleima (f) – woman of **peace**
Sulien (m) – sun born
Sulwyn (f) – sun fair
Susan (f) – lily (see FLOWERS)
Svetlana (f) – lightbearer
Swithin (m) – strong
Sybil (f) – oracle

At dinner, a dish of roast partridges had been served, and she was eating with great gusto and enjoyment. Someone reproached her that it was unseemly for a bride of Christ to have such zest for a participation in the mundane aspects of the world. St **TERESA** replied, 'When it's prayer time, pray; when it's partridge time, partridge!'

Lawrence Le Shan: *Clairvoyant Reality*

Then saith he to **THOMAS**, 'Reach hither thy finger, and behold my hands; and reach hither thy hand and thrust it into my side: and be not faithless but believing'... Jesus saith unto him 'Thomas, because thou hast seen me thou hast believed: blessed are they that have not seen and yet have believed.'

St John's Gospel, 20: 27/29

Tabitha (f) – gazelle (see ANIMALS)
Tace (f) – silent
Tadgh (m) – poet
Taghrid (f) – warbling
Tahir (m) – pure

Tahiyya (f) – salutation
Talal (m) – joy
Taliesin (m) – radiant brow
Tamar (m)
Tamara (f) } date palm (see TREES)

Tamir (m) – rich

Tancred (m) – thought counsel

Tangwyn (m) – peace-blessed

Tania (f) – (see Tatiana)

Tansy (f) – tansy (see FLOWERS)

Tara (f) – hill

Tariq (m) – one who comes by **night**

Tarub (f) – enraptured

Tashi (m) – good luck

Tatiana (f) – (see DISPUTED NAMES)

Taufiq (m) – success

Tegan (f) } beautiful
Tegid (m)

Tegwen (f) – beautiful and fair

Terence (m) – (see DISPUTED NAMES)

Teresa (f) – (see DISPUTED NAMES)

Tertia (f) – third child (see NUMBERS)

Tewdwr (m) – gift of **God**

Thaddeus (m) – (see DISPUTED NAMES)

Thalia (f) – bloom (see FLOWERS and GRACES)

Thana (f) – praise

Thanksgiving (m) – Thanksgiving

Thekla (f) – glory of **God**

Thelma (f) – (see DISPUTED NAMES)

Theodora (f) } gift of **God**
Theodore (m)

Theobald (m) – people's leader

Theodoric (m) – ruler of the people

Theodosia (f) – God-giving

Theophania (f) – Epiphany (see FESTIVALS)

Theophilus (m) – loved by **God**

Theresa (f) – (see DISPUTED NAMES)

Thirza (f) – delight

Thomas (m) }
Thomasa (f) } twin
Thomasina (f)

Thora (f) – (see Thor in GODS & GODDESSES)

Thorold (m) – Thor's strength (see GODS & GODDESSES)

Thubten (m/f) – possessor of **strength**

Thurayya (f) – star

Thurstan (m) – Thor's stone (see GODS & GODDESSES)

Timothea (f) } hidden by **God**
Timothy (m)

Tiobaid (m) } people's leader
Tioboid (m)

Titus (m) – (see DISPUTED NAMES)

Toby (m) – God is good

Topaz (f) – topaz (see JEWELS)

Torquil (m) – Thor's cauldron (see GODS & GODDESSES)

Tracey (m) – (see DISPUTED NAMES)

Trahaiarn (m) – ironlike

Treasa (f) – see Teresa

Trevor (m) – large **homestead**

Tristram (m) – sad

Tryphena (f) – daintiness

Tsering (m/f) – long life

Tudor (m) – gift of **God**

Turlough (m) – (see Thor in GODS & GODDESSES)

 **URSULA**, the daughter of a Christian king in Britain, was asked in marriage by the son of a pagan king. She, desiring to remain unwed, got a delay of three years, which time she spent on shipboard, sailing about the seas...

Butler: *Lives of the Saints*

'I am well aware that I am the "umblest person going,"' said **URIAH** Heep, modestly.

Charles Dickens: *David Copperfield*

Ulric (m) ⎫ wolf power (see
Ulrica (f) ⎬ ANIMALS)
Ultima (f) ⎫ last child (see
Ultimus (m) ⎬ NUMBERS)
'Umayma (f) – mother
'Umniya (f) – wish
Una (f) ⎫ unity
Unity (f) ⎬

Urania (f) – sky
Uriah (m) – light of **God**
Uriel (m) – God is light
Urien (f) – (see MUSES)
Urien (m) – privileged birth
Ursula (f) – little **bear** (see
        ANIMALS)

The Latin <u>verus</u> (true), and the Greek <u>iconica</u> (an image), were strangely jumbled together by the popular tongue in the name of a crucifix at Lucca, which was called the Veraiconica, or **VERONICA** ... Another VERONICA is the same countenance upon a piece of linen, shown at St Peter's. Superstition, forgetting the meaning of the name, called the relic St VERONICA'S handkerchief, accounting for it by inventing a woman who had lent our Blessed Saviour a handkerchief to wipe His face during the passage of the *Via dolorosa*, and had found the likeness imprinted upon it.

Charlotte M. Yonge:
A History of Christian Names

VINCENT de Paul, having been once recognised as philanthropist and social reformer, becomes responsible for all the good works undertaken; anything that was accomplished outside the range of his influence has either been attributed to him or else ignored as unworthy of serious attention...

E. K. Saunders: *Vincent de Paul, Priest and Philanthropist*

Valda (f) – power
Valentine (m) – healthy and strong
Valerie (f) ⎫ healthy
Valery (m) ⎭
Vanessa (f) – (see DISPUTED NAMES)
Vanya (m) – God is gracious
Varvara (f) – foreigner
Vasilii (m) – king
Vaughan (m) – little
Venetia (f) – of Venus (see GODS & GODDESSES)
Vera (f) – faith
Vere (m) – alder (see TREES)
Verena (f) ⎫ truth
Verity (f) ⎭
Verna (f) – spring and alder (see SEASONS and TREES)

Vernon (m) – alder (see TREES)
Veronica (f) – true icon (see FLOWERS)
Vesta (f) – hearth
Victor (m) ⎫ victorious one
Victoria (f) ⎭
Vida (f) – life
Vincent (m) – victorious one
Viola (f) ⎫ violet (see FLOWERS)
Violet (f) ⎭
Virginia (f) – virgin
Virtue (f) – virtue
Vitalis (m) – life
Vivian (m) ⎫ lively and animated
Vivien (f) ⎭
Vladimir (m) – will **helmet**
Vorgell (f) – sea-bright
Vyvyan (m) – animated

'I thought all the fairies were dead,' Mrs Darling said. 'There are always a lot of young ones,' explained **WENDY**, who was now quite an authority, 'because you see when a new baby laughs for the first time a new fairy is born, and as there are always new babies, there are always new fairies.'

J.M. Barrie: *Peter Pan*

WILLIAM next invented a system according to which everyone had to belong to somebody else, and everybody else to the King. This was called the Feutile System, and in order to prove that it was true he wrote a book called the Doomsday Book.

W.C. Sellar & R.C. Yeatman: *1066 & All That*

Wahib (m) ⎫
Wahiba (f) ⎬ generous

Waldo (m) – power

Wallace (m) – Celtic

Walter (m) – ruler of armies

Wanda (f) – (see DISPUTED NAMES)

Wangmo (f/m) – power

Warren (m) – game park keeper

Wasim (m) – handsome

Wilfred (m) – will peace

Wilhelmina (f) ⎫
William (m) ⎬ will **helmet**

Willow (f) – willow (see TREES)

Wilma (f) ⎫
Wilmot (f) ⎬ will **helmet**

Winifred (f) – blessed reconciliation

Winston (m) – joystone

Woodrow (m) – house by the wood

Wystan (m) – battle stone

Rather late in life he (Socrates) married the reputedly shrewish **XANTHIPPE**.

Chambers Biographical Dictionary

Except within the context of his wars with the Greeks our sources tell us little of **XERXES** in his reign. As a result, this Great King, the trusted son of a dynamic father, and, in a sense, the very model of the Near Eastern emperor, remains something of an enigma.

Cambridge Ancient History Vol IV 2nd Ed.

Xanthe (f) – yellow (see COLOURS)
Xanthippe (f) – yellow horse (see ANIMALS)
Xavier (m) – the **new** house

Xaviera (f) – the **new** house
Xenia (f) – hospitable
Xerxes (m) – venerable king

She who delights the Buddhas past, present and future with her metamorphic dance
She to whom the great Orgyen entrusted his divine authority,
She of infallible memory, matrix of profound hidden treasure,
She who attained supreme power, a rainbow body, a vajra body,
*Her name is **YESHE** Tsogyelma...*

Keith Dowman:
from *Sky Dancer, the Secret Life and Songs of the Lady Yeshe Tsogyel*

On April 22, 1916, a boy was born to the Menuhins, whom they named **YEHUDI**, which in Hebrew means 'the Jew'.

Robert Magidoff & Henry Raynor: *Yehudi Menuhin*

Yahya (m) – God is gracious
Yang-dron (f) – lamp of auspicious energy
Yang-chen (f) – sweet speech

Yarrow (f) – yarrow (see FLOWERS)
Yasir (m) – ease
Yelena (f) – bright
Yeshe (m/f) – wisdom

Yevgeny (m) – well born
Yolande (f) – violet (see FLOWERS)
Yorick (m) ⎫
Yuri (m) ⎭ earth worker

Yusra (f) – ease
Yves (m) ⎫
Yvonne (f) ⎭ yew (see TREES)

The first **ZAYNAB** in his [Muhammad's] life was his daughter by Khadija. The second was ZAYNAB-bint-Khuzayma, who married the Prophet in 625 but died a few months later ... The third was ZAYNAB-bint-Jahst, cousin of the Prophet. Muhammad married her after his adopted son agreed to divorce her. The last ZAYNAB in Muhammad's life, and the most revered by Muslims, was his granddaughter...

Patrick Hanks & Flavia Hodges:
A Dictionary of First Names

ZEUS; in Greek myth and religion, the supreme god ... His name indicates an Indo-European origin, being found in the Indic sky-god Dyaus pita, the Roman Jupiter, the German Tues-day, Latin <u>deus</u>, 'god', <u>dies</u>, 'day', and Greek <u>eudia</u>, 'fine weather'.

M.C. Howatson: *Oxford Companion to Classical Literature*

Zaccheus (m) – pure
Zachary (m) – God has remembered
Zadok (m) – righteous
Zahra (f) – blossom (see FLOWERS)
Zaki (m) ⎫
Zakiyya (f) ⎭ pure
Zaynab (f) – zaynab (see FLOWERS)
Zedekiah (m) – God is righteous
Zeev (m) – wolf
Zenaida (f) – daughter of **Zeus** (see GODS & GODDESSES)
Zenia (f) – hospitable

Zeno (m) – gift of **Zeus** (see GODS & GODDESSES)
Zenobia (f) – Zeus-life (see GODS & GODDESSES)
Zepaniah (m) – hidden by **God**
Zephyrine (f) – west wind (see DIRECTIONS
Zillah (f) – shade/shadow
Zinnia (f) – zinnia (see FLOWERS)
Zoe (f) – life
Zona (f) – girdle

PART THREE

NAMING CEREMONIES

Sun-goddess of the Earth ...
various evils may you seize!
And further ... you shall not let them loose again!
But for the child, life, fitness and long years continually give!

Hittite Birth Incantation
Performed by midwife as priestess and spokesperson for newborn
C. 3000 BC

Creating a Naming Ceremony

We are not getting what we need. Look at the walking wounded in your neighbourhood, your family, your mirror. Support for the crucial tasks of each stage in the life cycle, common in so-called primitive tribes and peasant village life, is much more difficult and unappreciated in modern society. We no longer honour life's whole sacred journey. Our rituals are empty; they mean nothing, they no longer empower us for the psychic tasks we need to undertake. What are our rituals for birth, for childhood, for puberty, for maturity, for death? Do we have any that are really transforming? I think not. That's why we need to practise a creative contemporary shamanism suited to our turbulent, tenuous times.

G. Roth and J. Loudon[1]

The meaning and purpose of ceremony

For a ceremony to be effective the facilitator has to have the power to effect a change in consciousness of the participants, and they also have to be willing themselves. Indigenous shamanic traditions such as the Native American, Tibetan and Hawaiian have many effective performers of ritual, who include exorcists, rainmakers, healers and teachers.

When life is lived with an awareness of the sacred in every moment, ritual may no longer be necessary. All of life can then be recognised as sacred ceremony.

When I speak of power I mean a way of working and using all your energy – including your spiritual energy – in a direction that allows you to become a whole person, capable of fulfilling whatever visions the Creator gives to you.

Sun Bear[2]

But in our materialistic culture there is so much working against us, enticing us away from awareness of the sacred. The purpose of ceremony is to focus awareness and invoke presence, and it can be a very creative way of re-charging our batteries, re-affirming our commitment and raising extra energy for a specific function, such as naming a newborn infant. Ceremony can invoke, inspire and unite. The collective power of a gathering is greater than the sum of its parts.

In this section of the book I will first examine various existing traditions of naming ceremony, then look at how one can form one's own.

Christian baptism

Although a child has usually already been named informally, at baptism he or she is *formally* addressed by the name for the first time. Though name-giving is not the prime purpose of baptism, it also serves as this in many cases.

In the last two sentences of St Matthew's Gospel (Matt. 28: 19 & 20), Jesus says: 'Go ye, therefore, and teach all nations, baptizing them in the name of the Father, and of the Son and of the Holy Ghost, teaching them to observe all things whatsoever I have commanded you: and lo, I am with you always, even unto the end of the world.' In the New Testament, according to the Greek syntax, the phrase reads: baptism into the *name* of Christ.

As Michael Green says in his lucid book[3] about baptism, 'Christian baptism is a thorny subject.' It means different things to different Christians. One thing is certain, it is central to Christian belief and has been practised in common (in different forms) since the beginning of Christianity. Whenever God made a covenant with His people, it was marked by a physical sign – Noah saw the rainbow, Moses was given the Passover and Abraham was commanded to introduce circumcision. Circumcision was the sign of the Old Law, while baptism is the sign of the New. Whilst some advocate infant baptism, which brings the child into the family of Christian people, others are utterly opposed to it and favour adult baptism with full immersion. This second kind of baptism indicates repentance and faith – the washing away of the old life and the taking on of the new. Yet others speak of the necessity of baptism 'in the Holy Spirit' to come to the fullness of Christian life, a baptism which represents spiritual transformation, and the inspiration to live an entirely new and different quality of life. Some Christian groups even say that baptism is not necessary. Many people, on the other hand, have conformed to tradition and convention by 'having the baby done' as a mere social gesture. The sacrament of baptism is summarised as follows by Michael Green:

> It is the rite of entry into the Christian church. It is ineffective until there is repentance and faith, but it stresses the initiative of God. It offers to us all the blessings of the covenant between God's grace and our response. It binds us into a unity of life not only with Jesus Christ, but with all baptised believers the world over. And it plunges us into that most profound of mysteries, the dying and rising of Jesus Christ our Lord.

Godparents

Godparents, sometimes known as sponsors, go back to the days when adult converts did not have Christian parents. The Godparent spoke for the new convert and helped him or her to live the Christian life. Today Christian Godparents have to have been baptised and confirmed. Usually parents choose three (with two of the same sex as the child) but two is the minimum number allowed. Parents are advised to choose very carefully; they *may* if they wish be godparents to their own child. They need to consider if the Godparents will befriend the child, it they will help him or her to know Jesus and to be part of the Church. They are meant to be able to help the growing child pray – both in church and at home, and to help him or her on the way to confirmation and communion.

The signs of baptism

The 'outward signs' of baptism are: Water, the Sign of the Cross and Light. At the beginning of the service of infant baptism the parents are asked if they are willing to help and encourage the child to 'learn to be faithful in public worship and private prayer, to live by trust in God, and come to confirmation.' The parents and God-parents are asked to respond to the following questions:

- DO YOU TURN TO CHRIST?

  – I TURN TO CHRIST.

- DO YOU REPENT OF YOUR SINS?

  – I REPENT OF MY SINS.

- DO YOU RENOUNCE EVIL?

  – I RENOUNCE EVIL.

The baby is then blessed with the Sign of the Cross on the forehead. This is often done with oil which has been blessed by the bishop on Maundy Thursday. Oil has long been a sign of spiritual strengthening (see TIBETAN Section, page 263). Water is a sign of washing away sin, of wiping the slate clean. This benefit is not supposed to have been earned, but rather is a gift of grace. The priest blesses the water, saying:[4]

Almighty God, whose Son Jesus Christ was baptised in the river Jordan; we thank you for the gift of water to cleanse us and revive us; we thank you that through the waters of the Red Sea, you led your people out of slavery to freedom in the promised land; we thank you that through the deep waters of death you brought your Son, and raised him to life in triumph. Bless this water, that your servants who are washed in it may be made one with Christ in his death and in his resurrection, to be cleansed and delivered from all sin.

Send your Holy Spirit upon them to bring them to new birth in the family of your church, and raise them with Christ to full and eternal life.

For all might, majesty, authority and power are yours, now and for ever.

Then the parents and Godparents attest to their faith in the Holy Trinity: Father, Son and Holy Spirit. The priest then baptises the baby, addressing him or her by name: '...I BAPTISE YOU IN THE NAME OF THE FATHER, AND OF THE SON AND OF THE HOLY SPIRIT.'

After this, parents and Godparents are sometimes given a lighted candle by the priest. This symbolises sharing the light of new spiritual life. People are encouraged to keep the candle and light it every year on the anniversary of the baptism to encourage them in their faith and to renew their promises.

The last two aspects of the baptism service are *worshipping*, whereby the child is now recognised as being in a new relationship to Christ and fellow Christians, and *witnessing*. It is usual in the Church of England that baptisms take place during the Sunday service. It is not seen as a private affair, but rather a public celebration when the whole Church welcomes a new member.

The 'Christian Community'

The Christian Community is a church which grew out of the work and Christ awareness of Rudolf Steiner. It has its own rites and ceremonies, including a baptism ceremony. It would lead us too far afield to go into the background of this 'movement for religious renewal', but it has some interesting things to say about naming and baptism:

> If a name were needed only to indicate which person was meant, a number would be much more efficient. In instances where this was indeed the situation, as with registration numbers of soldiers or prisoners, this ... led to their mistreatment, and in some cases to loss of personality. Through these and countless other examples (most of them negative) it becomes obvious that *our given name, our Christian name, is sacred, because it is united with the kernel of our being, of our essence.* (My italics.)
>
> Maarten Udo de Haes[5]

This same book makes the interesting recommendation that parents keep to themselves the name they have chosen for their child, and not voice it before the baptism ceremony: 'Then, when the name is spoken over the child at baptism, it will have an even greater intensity and reality.'

The baptism ritual in the Christian Community uses the elements of water, salt and ash to symbolise the three powers of the soul: *water* represents thinking and is inscribed as a triangle on the forehead. This endows movement, life and growth, and refers to the first seven years of childhood (as well as the first third of the child's entire life). *Salt* is traced on the chin in a square, representing the will and the preserving, crystallizing functions of the earth. This blesses the years between 7 and 14 (and the second part of life up to the age of 40). Finally *ash* is marked in a cross on the child's chest – signifying fire and the qualities of love and sacrifice, and blessing the final years of childhood from 14 to 21, as well as the final third of life.

Naming babies in the Russian Orthodox tradition

In the Orthodox Church a blessing is given to the mother on the day after the birth of her child, and again forty days later (this was the first time that the mother and baby appeared in public and in pagan times the child was believed to be vulnerable to the influence of devils until that time); and babies are named on the eighth day after birth, which symbolises the Kingdom of God beyond this world, to which the child is ritually admitted by the power of his naming. In earlier days the naming and baptism would take place at home if the child was sick – in any room except the birthing room, which was considered to be unclean.

In the Russian Church the Naming Rite has an established liturgical form which is laid down. By naming the child, the Church is not only acknowledging that he is a unique human being, but also sanctifying him by linking his name to that of Christ, and laying the way for a person to person relationship between that individual and God. The naming service is concluded with the remembrance of the Presentation of the Infant Jesus in the Temple to the old sage, Simeon, to which it is likened. (See box below for the Slavonic Rite).

Russian Orthodox baptism, though in essence akin to other Christian baptism, differs from it in several features of emphasis. The washing away of original sin is the least emphasised part of the ritual. Instead, the acceptance of the candidate into the Kingdom of Heaven on Earth and into the living Body of Christ is the cause for celebration and the centre of the ritual. The one to be baptised is anointed with chrism (holy oil), as one would anoint the body of a king or queen, reminiscent of the crowning of the bride and groom in the Orthodox marriage ceremony. Not only

AT THE NAMING OF A CHILD,
WHEN HE RECEIVETH HIS NAME, ON THE
EIGHTH DAY AFTER HIS BIRTH

The priest maketh the sign of the cross upon the forehead, lips and breast of the Infant and saith this Prayer:

Let us pray to the Lord.

O Lord our God, we pray unto thee, and we beseech thee, that the light of thy countenance may be shown upon this thy servant ...(name); and that the cross of thy Only-begotten Son may be graven in his (her) heart, and in his (her) thought: that he (she) may flee from the vanity of the world and from every evil snare of the enemy, and may follow after thy commandments. And grant, O Lord, that thy holy name may remain unrejected by him (her); and that he (she) may be united, in due time, to thy holy Church; and the dread Sacraments of thy Christ may be administered unto him (her): That, having lived according to thy commandments, and preserved without flaw the seal, he (she) may receive the bliss of the elect in thy kingdom; through the grace and love towards mankind of thine Only-begotten Son, with whom also thou art blessed, together with thine all-holy, and good, and life-giving Spirit, now, and ever, and unto ages of ages. Amen.

Then taking the Infant in his arms, he standeth before the door of the Temple, or before the holy image of the most holy Birth-giver of God, and maketh the sign of the cross, saying:

Hail, O Virgin Birth-giver of God, thou who art full of grace! For from thee hath shone forth the Sun of Righteousness, Christ our God, who giveth light to them that are in darkness. And rejoice, thou aged, righteous man, that didst receive in thine arms the Redeemer of our souls, who giveth unto us resurrection!

Translation from the Slavonic rite, from the Orthodox service book, USA

is the head anointed, but also the ears, the hands, the heart, between the shoulders, and the knees and feet – symbolizing the sealing of the person with the sign of the cross and the anointing and protection of the whole body. People are also baptised with full immersion and this rite is far more elaborate than in the Western Church. It is poetic and majestic, and includes three exorcisms to expel evil as well as the baptism itself.

Islamic naming practices

The best names in the sight of God are Abdu'llah – servant of God; Abdu'r Rahman – servant of the Merciful One.

Traditional sayings of Muhammed

Do not defame one another, nor call one another by nicknames. It is an evil thing to be called by a bad name after embracing the true Faith.

The Koran[6]

There are 99 names of Allah in the Qur'an (Koran) and one hidden one – *Ism Allah al-a'zam* – the Greatest Name of Allah. This has been concealed to encourage people to read the entire Qur'an. People are encouraged to memorise all these 99 names, which are attributes of God and, above all, to find the One who is Named. These names are connected with all aspects of life and it is common, and encouraged, to combine *Abd* (slave, servant of) with one of the 99 attributes of Allah; such as 'Servant of the All-Seeing' or 'Slave of the Compassionate One'.

Arabic is the chief language in 18 countries and the sixth most common language in the world. The Arabic word for name is *'alam* which comes from the root *alima* – to know. Islam means *surrender:* surrender to Allah and to the guidance of Muhammed, his Prophet. Central to the religion is faith in the rightness of living according to Islamic Law, and to the Sayings *(Hadith)* of the Prophet, both of which are set out in the Qur'an (that which is read, recited or rehearsed). Islam offers guidance on every aspect of family life and for important rites of passage, and the naming of babies is no exception. The traditional way in which infants were blessed, named and initiated into Islamic society is still practised today, with slight regional variations which are more cultural than religious in origin.

Allah was originally known to the pagans of the area (Mecca) as an ancient god who embraced both the feminine and masculine aspects of the deity. 'Al' or 'El' refers to the male principle... 'La' or 'lah' represents the feminine.

Peter Moon[7]

Introducing the child to prayer

Immediately after birth the baby is washed and called to prayer, thus initiating him or her without delay into the Islamic community. This is done by reciting the two calls to Prayer: the *Adhan,* which calls true Muslims to their obligatory prayers five times daily and is recited into the baby's right ear; then the *Iqamah,* announcing that prayer is about to begin, which is spoken into the left ear of the infant. Realizing the importance of early impressions, this is intended to remind the child that the very purpose of life itself is to worship Allah. This may be done by anyone, but it is preferred that it is done by a religious person or elderly family member.

Blessing and gift giving

Even before the newborn is introduced to the breast, a small portion of date is mashed to a liquid by chewing it with saliva, and this is placed in the baby's mouth. This is often done by an older member of the family and is a re-enactment of one of the deeds of the Prophet. It is strongly emphasised in Islam that, whether the practitioner understand the reason for it or not, it is a test of faith simply to follow the prescribed codes of conduct laid down by tradition. From a modern perspective, it could be observed that the sweetness of the date is beneficial to the baby and that, with the placing of adult saliva in the baby's mouth, protective intestinal flora are introduced into the infant's digestive tract. Sometimes a finger is simply placed in the baby's mouth and moved from side to side to stimulate the muscles of the mouth and prepare them for suckling.

The child is named seven days after birth and this is accompanied by several other ceremonies. Boys are circumcised at this time and it is also required by Islamic law that the baby's head (whether male or female) be completely shaved. This has a cleansing effect and also stimulates the hair follicles to produce a new and thicker hair growth. The shaved hair is then weighed and a sum of money equal to the weight of the hair is given away in charity. In some countries olive oil and saffron are rubbed into the baby's head. The *Aquiqa* also takes place at this time. This is the killing of a sheep or lamb (two for a boy, one for a girl). The meat is cooked to provide a meal for the relatives and guests and also further gifts for the poor.

Presents are brought for the baby and, if it is a girl, these consist mainly of gold. She can gather quite a heap by the end of the day! The husband often presents the new mother with a gift.

Other naming customs

There were other Arabic customs associated with the naming of children which are not part of the Islamic religious tradition. In Egypt the baby would sometimes be placed in a sieve and have flowers thrown upon him or her and be shaken up and down, while the guests sang songs. In Iraq infants were sometimes wrapped in tight swaddling clothes for three to five months, to give their small bodies something to grow strong against, and in Northern Iraq the Kurdish people sometimes placed a short plank of wood between the legs of the baby to straighten them before they wrapped the baby up.

Naming a Jewish baby

Man has three names: one by which his fond parents call him, another by which he is known in the outside world and a third, the most important of all, the name which his own deeds have procured for him.

Hebrew saying

Yad Vashem, a memorial for the Holocaust, is in Jerusalem. It has a whole library that catalogues the names of the six million martyrs. Not only did the library have their names, it also had where they lived, were born, anything that could be found out about them. These people existed and they mattered. 'Yad Vashem', as a matter of fact, actually means 'memorial to the name'.

N. Goldberg[8]

The *Torah* provides the foundation of Jewish law and its interpretation. It consists of history, morality and ethical teachings and covers the five biblical books: Genesis, Exodus, Leviticus, Numbers and Deuteronomy.

The *Talmud* explains the laws in the *Torah*. It is in two parts: the *Mishnah*, which was completed in the third century AD, and the *Gemorah* which was completed about 500 AD and which expands on the explanations in the *Mishnah* to encompass all situations in life. The *Talmud* contains the great debates of the Rabbis, the decisions they came to, and collected Jewish lore, sayings and stories. To make this extensive information more accessible, the Rabbis began to codify it by topic, to create what are now called *The Codes*. Rabbi Moses ben Maimon (1135-1204), now known as Maimonides, wrote the *Mishne Torah* in which he arranged the Talmudic laws methodically.

In 1567 Rabbi Joseph Caro published the *Shulchan Aruch* ('the Prepared Table'), which related Jewish laws and practice to daily life, and this has become the standard reference work on Jewish observance and law.

Although Jewish life is governed by many laws, there are none which relate to the naming of children. Rather, what is commonly practised belongs to the realm of custom, deriving from tradition, folklore or superstition. Over the years laws have become embellished by local custom; some modern, some from Eastern Europe Jewish communities; some from the United States. These days most Jewish parents choose a name from their country of residence and a separate Hebrew name as well, maybe in honour of a deceased relative.

Girls receive a name in the synagogue when the father is being called to an *Aliyah* (the reading of the *Torah*). This usually takes place on the first Sabbath after birth, but a girl may be named whenever the *Torah* is read. A baby girl is named with the prayer:

> *He who blessed Sarah, Rebbekah, Leah and Rachel, Miriam the Prophetess and Esther the queen, may He bless this dear girl. Let her be called ... (girl's and father's names) ... in a lucky hour. May she grow up in health and peace, and may her parents live to celebrate her wedding.*

Boys are named at their Bris (circumcision), eight days after birth, the day of birth being counted as the first day. On the Friday evening before the celebration, the 'Welcome to the Son' *(Shalom Zachar)* is held. This consists of feasting and study in the home of the newborn, and a Rabbi addresses the guests and blesses the child. Circumcision (Os Ha Bris – the sign of the covenant) is one of the oldest Jewish rites – symbolizing the covenant God made with the 'chosen people', which is recounted in Genesis 17: 10-12. So important is this initiation to the Jewish people that when the Emperor Hadrian issued an edict in 135 AD, prohibiting mutilation of the body, Jews persisted in the practice of circumcision, even under pain of death. During the ceremony prayers are said that the boy will have:

- a life crowned with the study of Torah
- a fruitful marriage (to pass on Judaism)
- good deeds and a good life

The baby is named:

> *Our God and God of our fathers, preserve this child to his father and mother, and may his name be called in Israel (first name) the son of (name of father).*

At the end of the ceremony a few drops of wine, blessed by the Mohel or the Rabbi, are given to the baby. Wine symbolises life, joy, the Torah, Israel and Jerusalem.[9]

A modern Druid naming ceremony

This ceremony was performed on the Isle of Iona in 1990. Before it began, the three-month-old baby was taken from the parents and held by another person. The participants stood in a circle and the baby was brought in and presented to each in turn as they gave her a gift. These gifts were placed in a box and kept for the child. As the little girl reached her parents, she was given back to them with the words of blessing:[10]

Who seeks entry
into our world?

One who has
travelled the Great
wheel of death and
Rebirth many times
and who's time
has come to return
to the physical world:-

From the West out of
the womb of the Great
Mother we welcome you:-
little one

We greet you and thank
those who guide you for
your safe return into
this world :-

I give you the blessing of
the Solar Father who
seeded you:-
the blessing of the Great
Mother who gave you form:-
the blessing of Iona may her
strength and tranquility
be allways with you:-

I give you the name
that will be with you
throughout your
journey

There are others also who
wish to welcome you:-

(signatures of the guests)

We hand you over to the
safe-keeping of those who
brought you to birth in the
physical world:- May the
Great Ones guide and
bless them:-

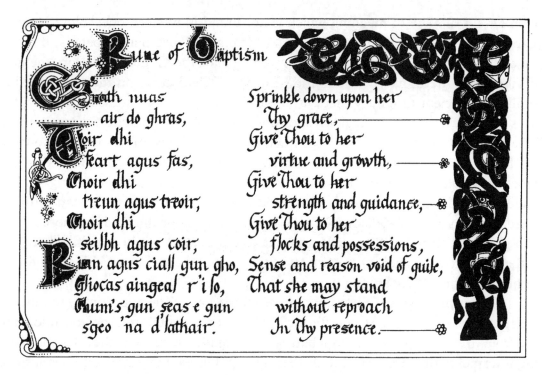

Rune of Baptism

The calligraphic panel reads:

Rune of Baptism

Sprinkle down upon her
Thy grace, ———
Give Thou to her
virtue and growth, ———
Give Thou to her
strength and guidance, ———
Give Thou to her
flocks and possessions,
Sense and reason void of guile,
That she may stand
without reproach
In Thy presence. ———

Naming Tibetan babies

Joyful to have such a human birth
Difficult to find; free and well-favoured.
But death is real, comes without warning –
This body will be a corpse.
Recognizng this, may my mind turn
towards the Practice.[11]

I was eight when His Holiness, Tenzin Gyatso, the 14th Dalai Lama of Tibet was forced into exile by the Chinese invasion. I do not remember being aware even of the existence of Tibet much before I was 21, let alone feeling any interest in it. In 1973 I visited my first Tibetan meditation centre in Scotland[12] and a few months later in England was introduced to my first Tibetan lama (spiritual teacher). This was to herald a connection with a tradition which lasted in one form or another for 20 years. It is because of the warmth and gratitude I feel for the Tibetans and what I have received from their sacred tradition, that I am including this section. Also, and most importantly to this book's purpose, Tibetan names carry real spiritual power and often have a subtlety of meaning which is not found in western ones. Now, after 30 years of genocide, there are more Chinese living in Tibet than Tibetans, but this tragedy contains an ironic blessing. If it were not for the Chinese invasion, the gifts of Tibet might never have come to the West. The Dalai Lama and the Tibetan exiles fulfilled an ancient prophecy made in the eighth century by Padmasambhava ('the lotus born') who was principally responsible for establishing Buddhist teachings in Tibet. Guru Rinpoche ('precious spiritual teacher') as he is affectionately known to the Tibetans, foresaw that 'when the iron bird flies and horses run on wheels' the Tibetans would be 'scattered like ants' across the earth and the teachings of the Buddha would settle 'in the land of the Red Man'. Whether one understands this to mean the land of the native 'redskins' of North America or the lands of those whose skin is of pinkish rather than yellowish hue, the prophecy has been fulfilled and we in the West are the richer for the arrival of the Tibetans and their wealth of profound and ancient knowledge among us.

The auspiciousness of human birth as offering a unique opportunity to practise the Teachings which lead from suffering to liberation is central to Tibetan Buddhism. So, from the very start, Tibetan babies are eligible to receive the blessings and empowerments that are available to their elders. Unless there are complications or inauspicious signs or circumstances surrounding the birth (in which case a special ceremony to neutralise demonic and other negative influences would be performed), no special ceremonies are reserved exclusively for childbirth or the naming of children. However, sometimes prebirth or womb-names are sought from high lamas by anxious parents. In the case of an aristocratic child or special baby, a *tru-sol* purification (lit. washing ritual) would be performed. Most parents would want to have their baby blessed and named by a lama and would seek his advice (and probably also that of an astrologer) in the choosing of a suitable name. Names are chosen carefully with the aim of endowing the child with appropriate and auspicious energies. However, if no spiritual adviser is available, then babies might be named after the day of their birth (see **Days of the Week** in the *Meanings Index)*, or after a natural omen that was present at the birth.

As in all cultures, the birth of a baby is an occasion for celebration, and a Tibetan family would invite their relatives and friends to a party at which *chang* (barley beer) and buttered tea are drunk and *khatas* (ceremonial white scarves) are presented. Sometimes *tsampa* (a sort of barley porridge and the Tibetan staple food) would be offered to the heavens and the baby would be smeared all over with butter – always a symbol of health and prosperity.

Many of the old rituals and customs are less practised today, but in Bhutan they still sometimes take a dab of soot from the bottom of a pan and smear it on the baby's nose – to hide and protect it from demons and negative forces. Traditionally, a purification ceremony was held on the third day after birth (for a boy) and on the fourth (for a girl), and before this had taken place no one would visit the house. This was to cleanse the baby from the 'impurity' of the delivery. The mother would wash her face and hair in warm water and put on clean clothes. In former times the baby would go on its first outing or *go-don* (exit) three days after birth or on an auspicious day, then not go out again for at least a month, but this does not happen these days.

from 'Sky Dancer: The secret life and songs of the Lady Yeshe Tsogyel' [13]

In his book on Tibetan folk culture, Norbu Chopel[14] writes: 'Tibet is not a miracle-filled land as many still think, nor are Tibetans miracle performers. Tibet is a very normal land and the Tibetans are as any other human beings.' In my experience, the Tibetans are some of the most down-to-earth people you could meet, who combine their earthiness with a respect for the non-physical dimensions of existence. There are various ancient customs and ideas associated with childbirth which reflect this. Most of what is done is for the dual reason of protecting the child from harmful influences (non-physical as well as physical) and building a strong and healthy life force. *Lung-ta* is a difficult word to translate. Literally it means 'wind horse' but it refers to the strength of life energy which determines the good fortune or luck potentiality of the individual – and this is what Tibetan parents seek to strengthen in their newborns. This is reflected in the potency of names such as *Rig-dzin* ('holder of awareness') or *Jig-me* ('fearless'). It is said that if a baby smiles when it first meets you, your life will be long. Also, that the grip of a baby is so tight because it does not want to let go of the wish-fulfilling gem that it holds!

Nicknames are very popular among Tibetans and are often more enduring than names given at birth. Examples of these are *Abo* ('brother' – an affectionate nickname from East Tibet) and, more humorously, *phag-ge* ('good pig'), *chig-ge* ('good dog') and *tag-ge* ('virtuous hawk'). Sometimes names poke fun at physical characteristics, such as *na-chen* ('long nose'). The early kings of Tibet were named according to character and attributes and many of these names carry great power and authority.

I would like to conclude this section as it began – with His Holiness, the Dalai Lama who is the spiritual and political leader of the Tibetans and winner of the 1989 Nobel Peace Prize. Like kings, high lamas bear very majestic names. The full name of the Dalai Lama is *Nga-Wang Lo-sang Ye-she Ten-zin Gya-tso*. This breaks down into: *nga* ('speech'), *wang* ('the lord of'), *lo* ('mind'), *sang* ('auspicious'), *ye-she* ('wisdom'), *Ten* ('teachings'), *zin* ('holder of'), *gya-tso* ('ocean'). It could perhaps be rendered as: *Great Oceanic Holder of the Teachings, who is the Master of True Speech and who possesses Auspicious Mind and Wisdom.* Anyone who has met the Dalai Lama or heard him teach will confirm the appropriateness of his name.

Humanist naming ceremonies

Humanism represents an approach to life that is based on reason and our common humanity. The British Humanist Association's[15] introductory leaflet says:

> The defining characteristics of a humanist are freedom from belief in gods, afterlife and the supernatural; the belief that we should try to live full and happy lives ourselves, and, as part of this, help to make it easier for other people to do the same; the belief that all situations and people deserve to be judged on their own merits by standards of reason and humanity; the belief that individuality and social co-operation are both important.

As part of their service to these values, the Association gives advice on naming ceremonies, and can if required provide trained and accredited celebrants for your ceremony. They also operate a helpline and publish a booklet from which the following helpful passage is quoted:

> For humanists the birth of a child is not an act of God. Ideally it is a planned event by parents who are prepared to give that child a secure and loving home ... A ceremony held shortly after birth will provide an opportunity to celebrate the baby's safe arrival and, at the same time, for the parents and others to state their commitment to the child's welfare ... Like all Humanist ceremonies a child's naming or welcoming ceremony is specially composed for the occasion, and the form it takes will vary considerably ... A Humanist naming ceremony is unlike a christening, where parents are making promises before God. Humanist parents state their aspirations, namely their firm intentions and hopes for their child and for themselves, and they make this statement among fellow human beings ... The commitment that Humanist parents like to express will probably include the following resolutions:
>
> - to take joint responsibility for the welfare of the child;
> - to provide continuing love and support, and help the child grow to independence;
> - to respect the child as an individual;
> - to help the child develop physically and intellectually, by encouragement rather than pressure;
> - to influence the child's moral development by good example rather than precept;
> - to help the child develop his or her own opinions, beliefs and values.

(See next page for an excerpt from a Humanist naming ceremony.)

The Baby Naming Society

The Baby Naming Society helps families put together a ceremony entirely tailor-made to suit their circumstances. The society is independent of any movement or philosophy, so is happy to design religious or non-religious occasions. Their booklets guide families through all the necessary preparations for such an event, and provide a range of suggestions on what might be said and done on the day itself.
(See appendix)

DAVID'S WELCOMING DAY

Parents: *We are glad that you are able to be here this afternoon to make this a special day for us. A special time when we can all celebrate the safe arrival of a new member of our family into the world. And although our baby will have no direct memory of this occasion, we hope you will help us to provide a small memento of today by writing a dedication to him in our welcoming book before you leave. Your words may be as brief or as lengthy as you wish. We are inviting first relatives and then close friends to sign the book, symbolizing the importance we attach to the support of our family and friends.*

Our baby was born on the fifth of October. By a nice coincidence his birthday falls in the same month as his parents'. The full names we have given him are:

David Jonathan Max.

*You may have wondered why we have chosen those particular names. We chose **David** as being a name we felt to be simple and unpretentious; and as there is no immediate relation with the same name, as being we hope symbolic of his own individual identity. **Jonathan** we chose from his father's side of the family – his great, great grandfather's name. **Max** was the name of his great grandfather on his mother's side of the family – an artist of great talent and sensitivity, and a person of great courage.*

In honour of our child, David Jonathan Max, we shall proceed to light a candle. The light of the candle is a symbol of a new life, and the hopes which we have for our child. The warmth of the flame represents the warmth of human love and friendship. (The candle is lit.)

> 'Love, all alike, no season knows, nor clime,
>   Nor hours, days, months, which are the rags of time.' – John Donne

We as parents to David, commit ourselves to endeavour, as best we are able, to provide him with a loving, caring home, and to help him determine his true potential in life.

We hope he will acquire the basic human values of kindness, tolerance of others, and honesty. We hope he will take his place as a useful, caring member of society, and that he will appreciate all that is good in the world. We wish him good health and a happy, fulfilled and contented life...

(After further readings, including the reading of a poem which David's father wrote shortly after his birth, the ceremony ends with a toast, the cutting of the cake, and the signing of dedications in the book.)

Excerpt from a Humanist naming ceremony

How to design your own ceremony

Creating a naming ceremony is as individual a matter as planning your own birthday party or deciding how to decorate the table for Christmas dinner. We tend to rely on tradition or precedent in the execution of our ceremonies and festivals, either passed on by our culture and family or handed over to the accepted authority of a professional, such as a midwife, priest or undertaker. Over the years I have participated in, and sometimes led, rituals and ceremonies which do not form part of my Anglo-Saxon/Roman Catholic/20th century materialist inheritance. I have attended two naming ceremonies which were not conventional christenings or baptisms, and I had a hand in the design and planning of one of them. This is described in the section about Peter Francis' Naming Ceremony.

The ceremony

Make sure that everyone can participate or feel involved in some way. Do your best to set it up so that your baby's guests do not feel left out or like mere spectators. The mood is of actively witnessing and accompanying a rite of passage. Perhaps you could ask people to do, bring, say or sing something. Be original! You do not need to rely on inherited vision nor to do anything which does not feel natural, right and easy.

The purpose of a naming ceremony:
- to welcome and incorporate
- to bless
- to name
- to offer gifts
- to make commitments

It will probably be the child's first public appearance and so is a significant occasion. Bear in mind that the baby is still very sensitive (psychologically as well as physically) and needs to be protected from too much sound, light and from over-stimulation in general. Harsh and shocking sensory input (such as photo flashes) should be avoided and an atmosphere of stillness and simplicity generated around the baby. I favour naming the child in or as near as possible to the home.

I don't want to stifle the creativity of all you parents and prospective godparents nor to muscle in as priestess at your ceremony by telling you what to do, but I will share briefly a checklist of what we took into account when planning the ceremony – a few points which might help get you started, keep you going or fire your inspiration:

- Who do you want to involve in the planning?
- Who do you want to invite to witness and/or participate?
- What time of year is it? How will this influence what you do?
- What time of day do you want it to be?
- Will it be formal or informal?
- Will the ceremony take place indoors or outside?
- What sort of room? How will you prepare/decorate it?
- Refreshments? Who will provide them?
- Will you send out invitations/a programme?
- If a programme, what do you want to say, who will design it?
- Do you want to have readings – where from, who will read?
- Do you want music? Live or recorded?
- A simple ritual of your own design can involve everyone.
- What articles will you need to perform this?
- If you want godparents (or equivalent) who is suitable?
- What will their function be at the ceremony and later?

The naming of Peter Francis

Peter Francis' naming ceremony took place on 16 February 1991 at 3 pm, in the room in which he had been born several weeks previously. Over the spot where he had first entered this existence a table was placed. On the table, on a white linen cloth and in each of the four cardinal directions was placed a representation of one of the four elements.

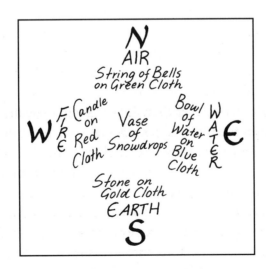

The water was from St Aldhelm's Well in Doulting in Somerset. This well water, to which healing properties have been attributed, was always used for christenings in former days. In the opposite corner of the room, in place of the usual bed, a portable electric organ stood. Peter's Godfather, Julian, who is a musician and composer, provided music for the beginning of the ceremony and accompaniment to the songs that we sang. Along another wall a table was placed to receive the gifts to be presented to the baby.

As the small group of relatives and close friends (some of whom had been present at the birth) gathered in the main living room clutching their programmes, there was a palpable mood of nervousness, anticipation, curiosity and interest. A naming ceremony, as opposed to a baptism or christening, was something that few of us had attended. The contrast between how we related to each other before the ceremony (cautiously, quietly, somewhat stiffly) and afterwards (warmly, fluently, more intimately) was very noticeable. Everyone who came was asked to bring teatime food to share and gradually the table began to fill up with plates of goodies.

As the moment for the ceremony approached, Peter was brought in by his mother, Joanna, dressed in a long, white christening gown and looking very peaceful and contented. Everyone gathered in the small bedroom which had been transformed into a sacred space. Although very different from each other in background and lifestyle, a feeling of unity came upon us as we lined the walls and sat on the floor.

Peter's father, Bob, opened the ceremony by welcoming everyone and explaining why he and Joanna had chosen to welcome, name and bless their son in this way, rather than in a more usual or conventional form. I then read from the Tao Te Ching of the great Nameless out of which flow the many names and the 'ten thousand things'. I explained that the Chinese pictogram for Tao means 'gateway' and indicates the essential nature of reality – the way things really are. Joanna led the welcoming ceremony by formally accepting Peter into her family and she read from *The Prophet* by Kahlil Gibran about the nature of children and parenthood:

> Your children are not your children. They are the sons and daughters of
> Life's longing for itself. They come through you but not from you, and
> though they are with you yet they belong not to you...

He was welcomed into the extended family and his heritage by his maternal grandmother, Susan, and finally into the wider human family by a friend, Sean, who spoke on behalf of all the participants at the ceremony. Next, Bryony, as the eldest child and Peter's only sibling, welcomed her brother by crowning him with a golden gem-studded crown which she had made herself and which winked with sequins.

The songs that we sang were simple and easy to sing. Both were chosen by Bryony, who was five at the time, and who enthusiastically contributed much to the planning of the ceremony and played an active part in its performance. The songs were an adaptation of a children's Christmas carol and another traditional song, this time a Native American medicine chant.

The naming section of the ceremony was introduced by Bob who explained how Joanna and he had come to choose their baby's names and the meaning of each (Peter from the Greek meaning 'rock' and Francis meaning 'a free man' and also 'a Frenchman'). Each of the five elements of which our bodies and planet are composed (earth, water, fire, air and space), as well as being represented symbolically on the table was also represented by a person whose task it was to invoke the blessings of their particular element on behalf of Peter Francis. I carried him in my arms around the table, symbolically out of the element of space from which he had come and through the other elements through which he had journeyed to weave his earthly body. At each resting place, in each of the four directions, he received the blessing and empowering qualities of that element. From space, he moved through air, to fire, to water and finally to earth, where he was given the name of PETER FRANCIS by his father.

Peter's Godfather, Julian, led us in the giving of gifts by publicly stating his commitment to Peter – addressed spontaneously and aloud to the baby, as he lay in his mother's arms at the other side of the room – and presenting him with a cassette recording of music composed especially for the occasion. I followed with my vows and gifts and one by one, clockwise (sunwise) round the room, people stated to Peter and all present the personal significance of his birth and offered their gifts. Some were sung and spoken and some (from family heirlooms to newmade gifts, to cuddly knitted critters) were placed upon the table at the side. It was a very moving moment for me to see and hear and feel so many people speaking spontaneously from the heart with great simplicity, in this society where so few of us are used to being, or being able to be, responsible for our own rites of passage. Peter's parents felt it very important that time be set aside for personal expression and for commitment, as well as for the traditional giving of gifts.

Peter slept quietly through most of his ceremony, gurgling and smiling once or twice in seeming approval. The formal ceremony closed with a song, to be followed by the informal ceremony of eating the tea we had all contributed, complete with a beautiful cake baked by Peter's aunt and uncle, Juliet and Michael; and we drank our tea from elegant china which grandmother had lent for the occasion.

Element Blessing for a naming ceremony

– based on the Tibetan Buddhist mandala of the 'Peaceful Buddhas'[16] and the Native American 'Medicine Wheel'.

I wanted the ceremony for my Godson to be complete and my intention was that, through our words and actions we would consciously and publicly connect the realm of absolute reality and truth to the relative realm of daily life in our modern world. I wanted what we did to be authentic and to tap into, focus and distribute real power.

The Tibetan Buddhist mandala of the Peaceful Buddhas and the Native American Medicine Wheel presented themselves to me as forms which, combined, contained all of our physical, emotional, mental and spiritual energies and the daily, seasonal and lifetime cycles through which we all pass. So, working with the symbols of the five directions (including the centre) and the five elements (including space), I wrote this blessing:

From the Primordial Space of the Unborn, the radiant Emptiness of pure potential, you have journeyed through the intermediate state of becoming, and, through this man and this woman, you have woven the elements into form to come and live among us.

WE WELCOME YOU
WE WELCOME YOU INTO OUR FAMILY
WE WELCOME YOU INTO THE FAMILY OF HUMANKIND
This beautiful Earth is now your home and you are her son.
You come with a gift and a need.
May the circumstances of your life always be auspicious,
that your need may be nourished and your gift expressed and received.

We endow you with the gifts of the five elements
and the ten directions
that your life may be blessed and protected.

In the North, the direction of your birth,
you receive the Winter's gifts of purity and renewal.
Through the purified element of Air,
may you be endowed with
the Wisdom of All-Accomplishing-Action.
May envy be transformed to skilful means.
May your action be unencumbered by thought,
and your wise efforts unimpeded.
May the vibration of your speech meet its mark.

In the East, from the dawn and the Spring,
receive the gifts of Illumination and Inspiration.
May the element of Water
endow you with the Mirror-Like Wisdom of Clarity.
May you see and know all things
for what they truly are.
May fear and anger be transformed in you.

In the South, the Summer's gifts
are Innocence, Trust and easy Growth.
Through the enlightened power of the element of Earth,
may generosity and wealth be yours –
of spirit as well as body.
May poverty and miserliness be healed.
May you be endowed with the Wisdom of Equality –
the gifts of justice, equanimity and balanced view.

And, in the West, may you be endowed with the Autumn's qualities
of Maturity and Introspection.
May you gather and assess the harvest of your actions wisely.
Through the essential power of the Fire element,
may Discriminating Wisdom and the fiery warmth of Compassion be yours.
May the loneliness of separation be healed,
and the folly of greed and grasping be consumed.

In the stillness of Space,
may you rest and simply be;
all things accomplished.
In Original Space,
which is without centre or periphery,
nowhere and everywhere –
always here and now –
is found the seed of freedom.
In the stillness of this timeless, silent vastness
may you realise
the All-Encompassing Wisdom
of your Original Nature.

Taking a *new* name

The close link between name, identity and function means that people can change their names (in our culture usually only the surname) to reflect a change in status or as part of a rite of passage from one stage of life to another. Many of the earth's sacred books give specific advice about this. In the *Satapatha-Brahmana*, a Soma ritual of the late Vedic period, it is said: *Wherefore let a Brahman, if he prosper not, take a second name, for verily he prospers, whosoever knowing this, takes a second name.'* So in keeping with tradition, Mahavira (the founder of Jainism) was given three names: *Vardhamana* – which rendered him free from attack and was the name by which he was known to his parents; *Sramana,* his second name, which meant 'ascetic' because of his ability to courageously pass through great fear and danger and because he went naked and endured severe austerities; and *Mahavira,* his last name, which was given to him by the gods.

From baby name to adult name

If you are having trouble deciding on the right name for your baby, you do not need to rush. One option is to give the newborn a temporary 'baby' name by which he or she will be known until s/he begins to indicate what name would be appropriate. You could have a private name by which the baby is known among family and friends and wait to name the child officially until the more permanent name has been chosen.

Spiritual names

Most religious and spiritual traditions have name-changing rituals associated with being born anew into a new way of life, or clothing oneself in a new spiritual identity.

The term 'Christian name' itself derives from the days of the early Christians, who, when they welcomed a new friend into their company through baptism, gave him or her a 'Christ-ened' name. Christians take on a new additional name at confirmation, confirming the person's transition to adulthood within the Church.

Monks and nuns in most traditions take spiritual names, often of saints or qualities they seek to emulate. The new name usually indicates latent spiritual qualities which can be developed, or endows the person with helpful attributes.

Changes of fortune or status

People sometimes change their name in order to facilitate a change of identity (such as marriage), role or function. Islamic cultures also practised name changing to *bring about* a change in fortune, or if a name was considered too 'heavy'. Muhammad changed the names of several of his followers and those families became known as *Banu Muhawwala* – 'the sons of the one who was changed'.

A new stage in life

Passing into a new time of life, for instance from childhood to adulthood, into middle age, etc could be an occasion when it would be beneficial and appropriate to change one's name.

Among the Native Americans, who practised elaborate naming customs, the speakers of the Muskhogean languages (the Choctaws, the Chickasaws, the Muskokis and the Seminoles) received a series of names at different stages of life:

- secret birth names;
- infancy and early childhood names e.g. 'Walking in Sunshine' or 'Mother gone' (the name of an orphan);
- nicknames of later childhood;
- puberty names, such as 'Snapping Turtle', 'Snake Halooer' and 'Red Rock Iron';
- civil titles, such as 'Crazy Red Arrow' and 'Beloved Individual' (the name of a Chickasaw chief in 1820);
- war titles, such as 'Creeping in Ambush'

All name-changing ceremonies were preceded by a day of solitude, fasting and the performance of rites to avert evil.[17]

Concealment, disguise and protection

Several cultures used naming and its associated powers to protect newborn children or to disguise the identity of the sick or dying in order to avert death. In ancient India it was commonplace to give a child an unpleasant name, such as 'Flies', 'Worms', 'Dusty', 'Dungheap', 'Rat', 'Old Shoe', 'Pepper', 'Old Rag' or 'Radish' in order to scare death away and to protect the child from evil. Sometimes a baby would be placed in the lap of a woman, all of whose children had survived, to be given such unpleasant names. In another custom a stone would be named after the child and given into the care of the village deity. It was recovered with thanks and offerings when the child grew to adulthood.

Turkish midwives would sometimes give the baby a religious 'umbilical name' *(gobek adi)* while cutting the umbilical cord. As many children died young, names were sometimes chosen to bind the baby to earth, such as *Yahya* from *hayya* – to live, or *Ya'mur,* from *'amara* – to flourish. Or the adults would try to cheat the spirits or frighten the jinn by calling the baby by a negative name, or the name of death, such as *Zibalah* (Egyptian) – 'garbage' or *Yamut* – 'he dies'.

The following account, related by Frances Densmore,[18] tells of the renaming of a Chippewa boy by an old man:

> When the child was about 10 years old he became so ill that the parents were afraid that he would die. So they sent tobacco to the old man and asked him to name the child. The old man came, looked at the child, and said he would name it the next day. He told the child's parents not to be afraid that the child would die before the next day. Most of the people assembled there did not believe that the child would live until night, but the man 'talked and prayed' so the child would live until the next day. He gave tobacco to each of those present and told them to return the next day. He told the people that when he named the child they would hear a sharp sound of thunder. The child was alive when the old man came next day, and he named the child *Ce'nawickun* ('He who produces a rattling sound with the movement of his being'). As soon as he had named the child they heard the sound as of sharp thunder, though there were no clouds in the sky and no sign of a storm. Many people talk of this event until this day. The child recovered and lived to an old age.

The Kwakiutl tribe would also wash away sickness by 'washing' a name. The Yokuts gave their children two names in case one of their namesakes died. If both died, the child was called 'No-name'.

In Hebrew tradition a change of name was considered to be one of the four things which could avert evil, and a seriously ill person would sometimes be renamed to include the new name *Hayyim* – life, or *Joshua* – salvation; in order to 'mislead the angel of Death'. The Yiddish name *Altman* – old man, was traditionally given to protect the newborn child from the angel of death, who was supposed to be confused by the name; or else it was conferred to ensure long life. When God changed a person's name in the Bible it signified investing his life with new meaning: such as Abram to Abraham, Sarai to Sarah and Jacob to Israel. If a child died, one born later might be called *Zeda* – 'grandfather', to imply and encourage longevity. Russian Jews in Idaho are recorded as re-naming a sick girl *Ida* – 'life'.

With this Book of the Law containing the thirteen attributes of mercy, we pray and ask for compassion from the Creator of the Heavens and Earth. As it is written 'Oh Lord, oh Lord, mighty, merciful and gracious, long suffering and abundant in love and truth, keeping troth to thousands, forgiving iniquity and transgression and sin.' The Mighty King who sits upon the Throne of mercy, who rules the world with pity and compassion and bestows loving kindness, he who heals the sick of Israel his people, may he grant swift and complete recovery and good life to... who will be named... May he enjoy his name and may the blessing of his name be fulfilled, as it is written '...and I will bless and make thy name great.'

Hebrew name change prayer from 16th century Prayer Book (Mahazor) [19]

The changing of names is also common in Tibet, particularly to denote a new stage of life, such as the taking of religious vows. In this case the new monk will include the name of his initiating lama as one of his. The custom of name changing is also applied to babies if they are ill. Also, it is said that if people talk too much about a person, whether to praise or criticise, that this draws a curse (*mi-kha* – literally 'human mouth') to that person which causes sickness or misfortune. Many children were believed to have died from these curses, so sometimes the baby would be given an ugly or uncommon name to discourage people from using it. Similarly, if a family had suffered difficulties with their babies' births or the death of several children, the next-born might be named something unpleasant, such as 'dog-shit' to divert attention from it, and ward off further misfortune.

Is name changing for us?[20]

We don't generally have any name-changing ceremonies or customs in our culture, nor do we usually change our first names – except perhaps when people undergo a change of sex, in which case they usually just modify their old name (the writer Jan Morris, for instance, used to be James). But is it possible that this lack is a sign that we are out of touch with the power of naming? That we no longer know how to invoke the healing, transformative realities which names can embody? I am not suggesting that we all change our names at the drop of a hat, or as often as we feel like it. In fact, Ted Andrews, in his excellent book *The Sacred Power in Your Name* [21] cautions against this. He points out that we have an intimate connection with the name we attracted to us at birth, and 'changing your name should be a last resort'. But it might be that giving ourselves a new or additional name at certain significant points in our lives might help support the inner changes we are trying to make – and all the more so if we could develop rituals and ceremonies to give an outer, visible form to such transition times.

A name is, as I have tried to show throughout this book, not just an arbitrary appendage, but a kind of bridge between our ordinary everyday existence and other more impalpable realms. When chosen with sensitivity and intuition a name can bind us more deeply to realities which, though essentially nameless, are the source from which all being and naming arises.

> *Here lies One*
>
> *Whose name*
>
> *Was writ*
>
> *In water*

John Keats: the inscription he requested for his gravestone

APPENDIX

The Baby Naming Society

The Baby Naming Society produces a useful guide in two parts.

Part 1 contains sections on:

>The Need for Rites of Passage
>Why is Commitment the Heart of these Ceremonies?
>Why Have a Naming Ceremony?
>Adopted Children
>The Purposes of a Ceremony
>Choosing Someone to Lead the Ceremony
>Where?
>When?
>Appointing the Godparents
>Invitations
>Food and Drink
>Decorations
>Gifts, Mementos and Recording the Event
>Preparing for the Day Itself
>Writing a Will
>Appointing Legal Guardians
>Pensions & Life Insurance
>Joint Parental Responsibility Agreements

Part 2 of the guide presents a whole 'menu' of ideas, all broken down into elements which could be included in a typical ceremony:

>Opening Words
>Naming Your Baby
>Parents' Vows to the Baby
>Parents' Vows to Each Other
>Appointing Godparents
>Appointing Guardians

Including Grandparents and All the Guests
Absent Friends and Relations
Symbolic Actions (e.g. lighting candle, planting a tree)
Signing the Certificate and Recording the Occasion (writing a message for the baby)
Closing Words (toasts and blessings)
Music
Readings and Prayers

Each section offers a wide choice of possibilities, including enabling parents to write their own words. The guide helps families to create their own unique celebration. The BNS takes instructions from each family and then scripts the event, provides a programme to guide guests through the ceremony, and a certificate to record the occasion.

Baby Naming Society
Yeoman's Cottage, Kerswell Green, Kempsey, Worcester, WR5 3PF
Tel: (01905) 371070

The Kabalarians

Personalised Name Reports and *Balanced Name Recommendation Reports* (when changing or choosing a name) can be obtained from:

The Society of Kabalarians of Canada
5912 Oak Street, Vancouver, BC V6M 2W2
Tel: (604) 263 9551
Email: admin@kabalarians.com
Web site: http://www.kabalarians.com

www.babynames.com

Babynames.com is a useful website 'where you will find the most extensive, ethnically diverse names database online'. Search by name or meaning, or go to one of the name lists (Most popular US names, Shakespeare names, African-American names, and Names from the Soaps).

REFERENCES

PART ONE

1   Chögyam Trungpa, *Journey Without Goal*, Prajna Press, 1981.
2   Cf section in this book on 'Naming and Healing' (page 5.)
3   Sophy Moody, *What is Your Name?* London, 1863.
4   In *The Religious Significance of Semitic Proper Names* (John Bolen lectures, 1910), C. H. W. Johns writes: 'It is very probable that the Babylonian imagined that the verb *shamu* – to fix, settle, decide – was the root of *shimu* – a name. Hence, he may have argued, the name (shumu) fixes the thing, confers on it its "fate", makes it definite, defines it. And though he has not found words to say so, he evidently thought that the name made the thing be what it was...'
5   Ka means 'light body' – the energy body which the Egyptians recognised survived death and which was capable of non-physical travel during life.
6   For more information, see: Murry Hope, *The Sirius Connection*, Element Books, 1996.
7   In his research into the geometries underlying the Hebrew alphabet, Stan Tenen has taken the study of the origins of language deeper into the *meaning* behind the form of the *letters* themselves. For more information, contact: The Meru Foundation, PO Box 503, Sharon, MA 02067, USA. (Website: www.meru.org)
8   Trans. J. Eggeling, *Sacred Books of the East.* Vol. 41, 1894.
9   See section on 'Name Changing' in Part 3.
10 *The Koran,* translated by N. J. Danwood, Penguin 1998.
11 *Chippewa Customs,* F. Densmore, Smithsonian Institution, Bureau of American Ethnology, Bulletin no 86, 1929.
12 Carmina Gadelica, Alexander Carmichael, Norman Macleod, Edinburgh, 1900.
13 *Anglo-Saxon Magic*, Dr G. Storms, Martinus Nijhoff, The Hague, 1948.
14 Bishop Kallistos Ware, *The Power of the Name*, the Jesus prayer in Orthodox Spirituality; Marshal Pickering, 1974.
15 Fortunate for me, as it turns out, as my name means womanly which I take as not only descriptive of the fact, but also indicative of what has shown itself to be a major theme for my life – to discover, own and express the depth of my femaleness.
16 V. Mackenzie, *Reincarnation: The Boy Lama,* Bloomsbury, 1988.
17 Sun Bear, *The Path of Power,* Simon and Schuster, 1987.
18 It is a good idea to give someone the task of recording the birth time.
19 *Hales's 2001 Unusual Baby Names,* 1973, reprint 1979; and see also: J. Glennon, *4001 Babies' Names and Their Meanings,* Robert Hale, 1989.

20 It is common practice for Vedic astrologers to advise on appropriate names for infants. Conversely, many can tell you something about your natal astrological chart by referring to your name. (I am indebted to Nick Campion of the Astrological Association for this information.)

21 You can also consult books about mythological figures for inspiring names. An excellent book for girls' names is by P. Monaghan, *The Book of Goddesses and Heroines,* Llewellyn Publications, Minnesota, 1990.

22 Cf E. Harold, *Master Your Vibration,* Grail Publications, NSW Australia, 1995. This is a useful book to help you convert name to number and understand their relationship to destiny.

23 Vibramentology chart, from *Name and Number,* W. Smith.

24 Leslie Alan Dunkling, *First Names First,* Dent, London, 1977.

25 Winthrop Ames, *What Shall We Name the Baby?* Hutchison & Co, 1936.

26 *Newsweek,* 9 July 1973.

27 U. K. Le Guin, *A Wizard of Earthsea,* Harmondsworth Penguin, 1971.

28 In *The Coronet,* September 1959.

29 T. M. Pearce in: *New Mexico Quarterly* (Autumn/Winter 1962-3).

30 W. G. Gaffney, 'A potential influence of given names on character and occupation', in: *Chicago Sun Times,* 30 December 1959.

31 Thich Nhat Hanh from *Being Peace,* Parallax Press, Berkeley, California, 1987.

PART TWO

1 Evidence is coming to light that we need to look to 'non-terrestrial' sources for the origin of Hebrew. Please see the writings of Geoff Boltwood, Murry Hope, Sheldon Nidle and Zecharia Sitchin.

2 A. Norman, *A World of Baby Names,* Perigree, NY 1996. Includes a native American section.

3 C. M. Yonge, *History of Christian Names,* 1884.

4 C. Bamford and W. P. Marsh, *Celtic Christianity,* Floris Books, Edinburgh, 1986.

5 Barbara Koltuv, *The Book of Lilith,* Nicholas Hays Inc, 1986.

6 S. Moody, *What Is Your Name?* London, 1863.

7 see note 3.

8 *The Lacnunga* (Anglo-Saxon medical MS).

9 From the *Eadwine Psalter* at Trinity College Library, Cambridge.

10 *Anglo-Saxon Magic,* Dr G. Storms, Martinus Nijhoff, The Hague, 1948.

11 S. Moody, *What Is Your Name?* London, 1863.

12 For comprehensive information about the healing properties of flowers, contact the International Flower Essence Repertoire, The Living Tree, Milland, Liphook, GU30 7JS. Tel: 01428-741572.

13 Rev. H. Friend: *Flowers and Flower Lore,* George Allen, 1883.

14 In her book, *The Woman with the Alabaster Jar,* Bear & Co., Santa Fe, 1993. Margaret Starbird draws a parallel between the figures of St. Barbara and Mary Magdalene.

15 M. F. Müller, *The Sacred Books of the East.*

16 J. Hastings, *Encyclopedia of Religion and Ethics,* Vol. IX, 1908.

17 Nicholas R. Mann, *Keltic Power Symbols,* Triskele.

18 For information about the healing properties of gems and minerals, contact the International Flower Essence Repertoire. (See under Flowers). The book *Love is in the Earth: a Kaleidoscope of Crystals,* Earth-Love publishing house, Colorado 1995, gives definitive information about every gem and mineral. This book also offers guidance on the relationship between minerals and astrological signs.

19 L. Picknett and C. Prince, *The Templar Revelation: Secret Guardians of the True Identitiy of Christ,* Corgi, 1998.

20 J. M. Robinson (Ed), *The Nag Hammadi Library,* Harper Collins, 1978, 1988, 1990.

21 M. Starbird, *The Woman with the Alabaster Jar,* Bear and Company, 1993. *The Goddess in the Gospels,* Bear and Company, 1998.

22 see note 15.

23 E. C. Smith, *The Story of Our Names,* Harper and Row, New York, 1950.

24 R. S. Charnock, *Praenomina,* Trubner & Co, 1882.

PART THREE

1 G. Roth and J. Loudon, *Maps to Ecstasy, teachings of an urban shaman,* Thorsons, 1997.

2 Sun Bear, *The Path of Power,* Simon & Schuster, 1987.

3 M. Green, *Baptism, its purpose, practice and power,* Hodder and Stoughton, 1987/1991.

4 From the *Alternative Service Book,* 1980.

5 Maarten Udo de Haes, *Baptism in the Christian Community,* Floris Books, 1985.

6 *The Koran,* translated by N.J. Danwood, Penguin, 1998.

7 Peter Moon, *The Black Sun,* Sky Books, 1997

8 N. Goldberg, *Writing Down the Bones,* Shambhala, 1986.

9 B. M. Edidin, *Jewish Customs,* 1941.

10 This naming ceremony was designed and written by Chris and Bill Worthington, and is reprinted here by kind permission of Philip Carr-Gomm.

11 Part of a Tibetan Buddhist preparatory practice known as The Four Thoughts. It is recited daily by Tantric practitioners.

12 Samye Ling in Eskdalemuir.

13 Keith Dowman, *Sky Dancer: The secret life and songs of the Lady Yeshe Tsogyel*, Arkana, 1989. Illustrations copyright Eva van Dam, 1984.

14 N. Chopel, *Folk Culture of Tibet*, Library of Tibetan Works and Archives, Dharamsala, India.

15 The British Humanist Association, 47 Theobald's Rd, London WC1X 8SP. Helpline: 0990-168-122

16 The mandala of the Peaceful Buddhas derives from Tibetan Buddhist teachings on death, dying and the afterdeath state, which ascribe a Buddha to each of the four directions (and the centre). Each Buddha is associated with one of the five elements and with an aspect of enlightened consciousness. The basic idea is that all neurotic emotions are linked to an enlightened state, as they are essentially only *energy* which can be transformed into its *flipside* enlightened quality.

17 N. Toomy, *Proper Names from the Muskhogean Languages*, Hervas Laboratories of American Linguistics, Bulletin 3, 1917.

18 F. Densmore, *Chippewa Customs*, Smithsonian Institution, Bureau of American Ethnology: Bulletin 30, 1910.

19 Translation kindly provided by Ilana Tahan.

20 See Nasreen Pearce, *Name-Changing: A Practical Guide*, Fourmat Publishing, 1990. This book gives legal and practical information on changing your name.

21 T. Andrews, *The Sacred Power in Your Name*, Llewellyn Publications, St Paul, Minnesota, 1998. This is the author's absolutely favourite naming book. It explains how to use the sounds in your name to develop your potential.

BIBLIOGRAPHY

The books listed below are only some of over 100 books which were used in researching this volume.

Bibliographies

Lawson, Edwin D. *Personal Names and Naming: an annotated bibliography,* Greenwood, 1923 and 1987.

Smith, Elsdon C. *Books in English on Personal Names,* Vol. 1, no. 3, University of California Press, 1953.

The power and history of naming

Andrews, T. *The Sacred Power in Your Name,* Llewellyn Publications, St.Paul Minnesota, 1998.

Belden, A. D. *What is Your Name?* Allenson & Co., 1956. (Short biographies of a selection of famous people to illustrate first names.)

Clodd, E. *Magic in Names and Other Things,* Chapman and Hall, 1920.

Dunkling, L. A. *First Names First* , Dent, London 1977. (Useful lists of names popular at different historical periods.)

Smith, E. C. *The Story of Our Names,* Harper and Row, New York, 1950. (Contains a superbly readable and informative survey of Christian names.)

Treasury of Name and Lore, Harper and Row, 1967.

Naming dictionaries

Browder, S. *The New Age Baby Name Book,* Warner Books, 1974, rev. 1987.

Cresswell, J. *Dictionary of First Names,* Bloomsbury 1990. (Useful for anecdotes and legends not found elsewhere.)

Dunkling, L. A. and Gosling, W. *Everyman's Dictionary of First Names,* 3rd ed. 1991.

Glennon, J. *4001 Babies Names and Their Meanings,* Robert Hale, 1989.

Gordon, Kate. *A Practical Guide to Alternative Baptism and Baby-Naming,* Constable, 1998.

Hale Instant Book, *2001 Unusual Babies' Names,* 1973, reprint 1979.

Hanks, P. and Hodges, F. *A Dictionary of First Names,* Oxford University Press, 1990. (Includes many European names and excellent sections on Indian and Arabic names.)

Hilarion, *Childlight,* Marcus Books, Ontario, 1987.

Loughead, F. H. *Dictionary of Given Names,* Arthur H. Clarke, Glendale, California, 1934. (Many unusual names.)

Moody, S. *What Is Your Name?* London, 1863. (Names listed under nationality and significance.)

Nicholson, L. *The Baby Name Book,* Thorsons, 1985. (Over 3000 names, easy to read, good illustrations and interesting additional information, astrological section.)

Norman, T. *A World of Baby Names,* Perigree, NY, 1996. (A rich compendium of over 30,000 names from all over the world.)

Nown, S. *Babies' Names and Star Signs,* Ward Lock, 1989. (Relates names to qualities of star-sign, planet and element.)

Parker, D. and J. *Compleat Zodiac Name Book,* William Luscombe 1976. (Suits names to birth signs and explains why. Also gives qualities to be expected of the child.)

Withycombe, E. G. *Oxford Dictionary of English Christian Names,* OUP, 1949. (Includes supplement of phrases and sayings derived from personal names.)

Yonge, C. M. *History of Christian Names,* 1884. (Very interesting reading. Names grouped in categories, and detailed histories given. Also charts giving European variations.)

Other Books from Hawthorn Press

Sing Me the Creation
Paul Matthews

This is an inspirational workbook of creative writing exercises for poets and teachers, and for all who wish to develop the life of the imagination. There are over 300 exercises for improving writing skills. Though intended for group work with adults, teachers will find these exercises easily adaptable to the classroom. Paul Matthews, a poet himself, taught creative writing at Emerson College, Sussex.

224pp; 238 x 135mm; 1 869 890 60 4; paperback.

Between Form and Freedom
A practical Guide to the Teenage Years
Betty Staley

Betty Staley offers a wealth of insights about teenagers, providing a compassionate, intelligent and intuitive look into the minds of children and adolescents. She explores the nature of adolescence and looks at teenagers' needs in relation to family, friends, schools, love and the arts. Issues concerning stress, depression, drug and alcohol abuse and eating disorders are included.

288pp; 210 x 135mm; illustrations; 1 869 890 08 6; paperback.

Told by the Peat Fire
Sibylle Alexander

The voice behind these much loved Celtic tales is the passionate voice of a true storyteller – it crackles with humour and ancient wisdom as it lifts the veil between us and the spiritual world. Sibylle Alexander is a midwife to the imagination; bringing ancient and timeless tales to ears and eyes alike. This collection of stories is for storytellers, teachers, parents, people of all ages – listeners and readers alike.

128pp; 216 x 138 mm; 1 869 890 23 X; paperback.

Birthday Book
Ann Druitt, Christine Fynes-Clinton and Marije Rowling

Everything you need for celebrating birthdays in enjoyable ways. There are suggestions for 'oldies', for teenagers, 18th and 21st parties as well as children's parties. You will find unusual celebrations for those on holiday, ill in bed, at Christmas or for rainy days.

192pp; 246 x 189mm; paperback; Autumn 2000 publication.

Manhood
An action plan for changing men's lives
Steve Biddulph

Most men don't have a life. So begins the most powerful, practical and honest book ever to be written about men and boys. Not about our problems – but about how we can find the joy and energy of being in a male body with a man's mind and spirit – about men's liberation.
Steve Biddulph, author of *Raising Boys* and the million-seller *The Secret of Happy Children,* writes about the turning point that men have reached and gives practical personal answers to how things can be different from the bedroom to the workplace.
272pp; 216 x 138mm; 12 black and white photographs;
1 869 890 99 X; paperback.

70 Years A-Growing
Jean Westlake

This book is the story of a magical life committed to organic and biodynamic gardening, and has been 70 years in the making. Packed with practical gardening information, it is also an enticing autobiography. It follows the twists and turns of the Westlake family from developing the famous New Forest holiday centre at Sandy Balls, Fordingbridge to the accolade of having their produce recognised by The Soil Association.
272pp; 246 x 189mm; 1 869 890 37 X; paperback; Spring 2000 publication.

Games Children Play
How Games and Sport Help Children Develop
Kim Brooking-Payne

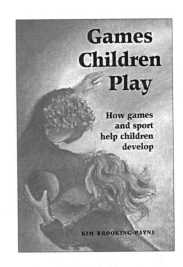

Illustrated by Marije Rowling. *Games Children Play* offers an accessible guide to games with children of age 3 upwards. These games are all tried and tested, and are the basis for the author's extensive teacher training work. The book explores children's personal development and how this is expressed in movement, play, songs and games.
Each game is clearly and simply described, with diagrams or drawings, and accompanied by an explanation of why this game is helpful at a particular age. The equipment that may be needed is basic, cheap and easily available.
192 pp; 297 x 210mm; 1 869 890 78 7; paperback.

All Year Round

Ann Druitt, Christine Fynes-Clinton, Marije Rowling

All Year Round is brimming with things to make; activities, stories, poems and songs to share with your family. Observing the round of festivals is an enjoyable way to bring rhythm into children's lives and provide a series of meaningful landmarks to look forward to. Each festival has a special character of its own: participation can deepen our understanding and love of nature and bring a gift to the whole family. *All Year Round* invites you to start celebrating now! 288pp; 250 x 200mm; 1 869 890 47 7; paperback.

The Children's Year

Crafts and Clothes for Children and Parents to make

Stephanie Cooper, Christine Fynes-Clinton, Marije Rowling

You needn't be an experienced craftsperson to create beautiful things! This step by step, well illustrated book with clear instructions shows you how to get started. Children and parents are encouraged to try all sorts of handwork, with different projects relating to the seasons of the year. 192pp; 250 x 200mm; 1 869 890 00 0; paperback.

Festivals, Family and Food

Diana Carey and Judy Large

This family favourite is a unique, well loved source of stories, recipes, things to make, activities, poems, songs and festivals. Each festival such as Christmas, Candlemas and Martinmas has its own, well illustrated chapter. There are also sections on Birthdays, Rainy Days, Convalescence and a birthday Calendar. The perfect present for a family, it explores the numerous festivals that children love celebrating. 216pp; 250 x 200mm; illustrations; 0 950 706 23 X; paperback.

Festivals Together

A Guide to Multicultural Celebration

Sue Fitzjohn, Minda Weston, Judy Large

This special book for families and teachers helps you celebrate festivals from cultures from all over the world. You will be able to share in the adventures of Anancy the spider trickster, how Ganesh got his elephant head and share in Eid, Holi, Wesak, Advent, Divali, Chinese New Year and more. 224pp; 250 x 200mm; 1 869 890 46 9; paperback.

Beyond the Forest

Kelvin Hall

The Grail Quest is an archetypal story of the journey of humanity and of each person. Parzival's search for wholeness – passed down by generations of storytellers – is re-told vividly here by Kelvin Hall. There is a Parzival in every one of us as we move from the innocence and naivety of forgetting, through courage and surrender, to love and redemption.

96pp; 216 x 138mm; 1 869 890 73 6; paperback.

Kinder Dolls

Maricristin Sealey

This well illustrated beginners' guide to doll making offers a step by step approach that even fathers can follow! Arising from many years of doll making classes, this book will help you get started when your children are in their early years. Maricristin Sealey's approach embraces what is known in North America as 'Waldorf doll making' and also draws on English traditions.

128pp; 246 x 189mm; paperback; Summer 2000 publication.

Storytelling for Parents

Nancy Mellon

Deep within us we sense that everyone of us is a storyteller by birthright, born with an endless supply of personal and universal themes which honour life. As storytellers, we can discover ourselves in each other. In this book you will discover how and why to become a storyteller yourself.

128pp; paperback; Spring 2000 publication.

String Games and Stories Book One

Michael Taylor

Stories and simple instructions for making string games with children – includes your own special string. Everything you need to create a string game craze!

128pp; paperback; Spring 2000 publication.

Ordering books

If you have difficulty ordering Hawthorn Press books from a bookshop, you can order direct from:

Scottish Book Source, 137 Dundee Street, Edinburgh, EH11 1BG
Tel: (0131) 229 6800   Fax: (0131) 229 9070   E-mail: scotbook@globalnet.co.uk

Anthroposophic Press, 3390 Route 9, Hudson, NY 12534
Tel: (518) 851 2054   Fax: (518) 851 2047   E-mail: anthropres@aol.com
www.anthropress.org